THE BOMBS OF ORSINI

By the same author

FIRST AIRBORNE

1948

THE LIFE OF JOHN STUART MILL

1954

Felice Orsini
From a portrait in the Museo del Risorgimento, Milan

THE BOMBS OF ORSINI

By

MICHAEL ST. JOHN PACKE

Yet, freedom! yet thy banner, torn, but flying,
Streams like the thunder-storm *against* the wind.
Byron, *Childe Harold*, IV, 98

London
SECKER AND WARBURG
1957

Printed in England by
William Clowes and Sons Limited, London and Beccles
and
first published 1957
by
Martin Secker and Warburg Ltd
7 John Street, London, W.C.1

TO
MARY COLEMAN WHARTON
WITH LOVE

Contents

List of Illustrations

Maps

To the best of the author's belief, the events recounted in this book are true in every detail. A list of the authorities from which they have been taken is given at the end.

The author's thanks are due to his wife, who has once again assisted him throughout the book: to Mr. T. H. White, and to Mr. P. W. Radice, of Alderney, Channel Islands: and in a special sense to Signor Cesare Milano, of Savona, the great-grandson of Orsini.

CHAPTER ONE

The Making of a Patriot

I

ACCORDING to the prosecution at his trial, Felice Orsini was born a conspirator. Whether that can be believed or not, quite certainly his mother had no notion of it. She was a gentle, cultivated girl of twenty; Florentine, graceful, kind and true. She suckled him and crooned at him in the normal manner. She treated him as, a year or so before, she had treated his elder sister Rosina; as she would likewise treat, in three years' time, his younger brother Leonidas, all with the best results. She did not realize that his infant thoughts were of a repressed and furtive trend: that when he waved his wooden spoon and gurgled, he was marshalling secret armies in craggy places: or that his wondering unfathomable eyes, jet black and shining, screened from her view a world of incipient revolution, wherein already he was blowing up Emperors and dethroning Popes. Yet such, maintained the prosecution, was the case.

He was born at Meldola, nine miles from Forli, in the Romagna. His parents occupied a fine brick mansion at the foot of the village square,* where his father Andrea Orsini was bailiff to the owner, Count Borghese-Aldobrandini. Forli is one of several inconsiderable towns between Rimini and Bologna, strung out along the flat straight Via Emilia wherever mountain torrents from the mass of the Apennines cross it in their passage through the plain of Lombardy towards the sparkling Adriatic. Meldola is a satellite of Forli, set amongst the foothills to the south, in the valley of the River Ronco. The boy was baptized there on the day of his birth, 18 December 1819,

* Now the barracks of the *Carabinieri*.

by the Reverend Canon Giovanni Grammatica; a proxy for his father's brother Orso Orsini, and his mother's sister Lucrezia Ricci standing sponsors for him while he was given the names Theobaldus Ursus Felix. His nurse, Caterina Poggi, came from a modest Meldolese family, who, until quite recently, still treasured the cradle in which she used to rock him. Some two years afterwards his parents left the Romagna and moved their home to Florence.

Nothing remarkable happened in the next six years at Florence, until Felice, at the age of eight, fell from a third-floor balcony into the courtyard of their house. He regained consciousness to find his arms and legs pinioned in splints and bandages, and the beloved figure of his mother bending over him, her dark hair trailing on his face, and warm tears flooding in her eyes. He soon recovered. And, strangely enough, this one dramatic incident of his childhood was also the only one not wrapped about with innuendoes ominous and sinister for the future. For, as must be expected in the life of a conspirator, none of the simple trivialities of his early existence were as harmless as they sound. They were all straws in a wind, undeviating and relentless, which would carry him to shame and glory.

There was, for instance, no reproach in having Meldola for a birthplace. But to be born Romagnuol was another matter. The men of the Romagna, and in particular the middle classes, artisans or professional gentry, were of a special calibre. Turbulent, fiery, resolute, they were of the toughest fibre in the whole of Italy: and his own father was an exemplar of the breed. Again, Forli was an inconspicuous province. Yet to the neighbourhood of Forli in the next few years would come, as if drawn to a magnet, men whose fates were to be inseparably linked with that of the young Felice: men who were to be Pope and Emperor, arbiters of Europe.

Next take the christening. The original intention of his closest relatives was that the boy should be known by his first name, Theobald. Theobald sounds, if nothing else, straightforward. In fact, it was nothing of the kind. Later it was dropped in favour of Felice, and for that too there was a special reason. As for the move to Florence, surely, one might suppose, his mother's citizenship would be sufficient explanation. But no.

Once more there were ulterior motives. The files of the Tuscan police reveal that they took the deepest interest in the movements of his father:

> "Andrea Orsini of Imola, clerk, agent for property: one of the leaders and first founders of the Carbonari society in Florence."[1]

Felice's father came from Lugo, on the other side of the Via Emilia from Meldola. When the forces of Bonaparte, in the first flush of conquest, overran his native land, he, with many thousands of his compatriots, had been swept off into the army of the invader. Under their so-called King, Eugène Beauharnais, stepson of the Emperor, they later crossed the Alps to join the vast concourse of the Grand Army massed along the Niemen for the assault on Russia.

Of the twenty-seven thousand Italians who had started out, fewer than four hundred came home safely. Andrea Orsini, who had gained the rank of captain, fell prisoner somewhere along the way. At the peace he returned to the Romagna, and found respectable employment at Meldola, where he met Francesca Ricci. Francesca, then little more than a child, had come to Meldola to stay with her married sister, and her brother-in-law Felice Grammatica, who kept house for their relative Canon Grammatica the incumbent. They married, and started a family, living quietly in the imposing residence of their noble patrons. Like many old soldiers, Andrea Orsini spoke freely of his military experiences, talking with animation and at length, professing that they had been the best times of his life. His son Felice, listening attentively, formed as any boy would do a prodigious admiration for his father.

But Andrea Orsini, aged now about thirty, found the trammels of domestic life too tame. He had many grievances against the world. He pursued secret appointments of his own. He would go out suddenly at night, and when his son showed curiosity, would put him off glibly, or even angrily. Sometimes, men with an air of haste and urgency would come to the house. Although they treated Felice with indulgence, he never could discover who they were or whither they went. Felice was deeply hurt. To him, his father was the source of power and good, a bulwark against evil. His father's friends were heroes;

[1] Luzio, *Biografico*, 8 n.

his father's enemies were knaves and tyrants. And yet it seemed as if his father did not trust him.

When Felice had recovered from his fall, it was resolved that they should make a family visit to the Florence Opera. The day arrived, and they set out, accompanied by one of his father's passing friends, a man from Modena. Felice was nine years old. To sit in a plush seat in the darkened house, to see the flaring of the limelights, to hear the anticipatory violins, to watch the ponderous billowing of the curtain, was expectancy indeed, the verge of wonderland. But the overture had scarcely ended before there was a commotion in the theatre. People in front turned round, shushing indignantly. Felice, lost in the music, took no notice until the uproar drew quite close to him, scuffling and the clattering of chains. Then he looked, and saw his father and his father's friend with fetters hanging from their wrists. He saw his father's face, defiant and afraid, upraised towards the gruff officials in three-cornered hats who were dragging him away. His mother rose, tight-lipped, white of face, hustling her children out. To their frightened questions and their tears she gave a single bitter answer. It was for political reasons, they must understand.

II

Thus early, at the age of nine, political reasons struck deep into the life of Felice Orsini. Henceforth he was to be their slave.

Italy, fallen from her ancient splendour, had become in the Middle Ages a chequer-board of petty dynasties.* To repel barbarian invasions, to resolve internal feuds, neighbouring armies had been called in from across the Alps. These forces took possession of the land. For three centuries the Italians had no history of their own. The rich and pleasant territories changed hands, new dukedoms were created, as a reward for alien services or to flatter foreign nuptials.

The process of division was arrested by three factors. The

* For the following description of the state of Italy, readers are invited to consult the map in the end covers of the book.

first was the sturdy independence of the Kingdom of Piedmont (or Sardinia), which for eight centuries had been ruled by the House of Savoy. The second was the long existence of the Papal States. The lost territories surrounding Rome, wrested from the Lombards by the Frankish kings, had been proudly presented by them to the Heirs of St. Peter. The Popes set great store by their Patrimony, all that was left of their extravagant temporal claims. And, since Papal Authority was the one infrangible rule of Europe, towering above princely annexation and intrigue, the Patrimony had remained inviolate, a solid wedge across the centre of the peninsula.

Thirdly, the cities, to protect their welfare in the time of chaos, had walled themselves in and become autonomous merchant empires. By an iron law of competition the greater devoured the less, until the wealth of Italy was centred in eight or nine municipalities. In the eighteenth century the Austrian Empress Maria Theresa, that matrimonial genius, successfully collected them all into her own hand. For the first time there was a kind of unity. By mere ubiquity, the Hapsburg princes brought a loosening of provincial barriers, a stimulus to trade and enterprise. The poor, as hitherto, hacked at their scanty vineyards and their olive groves on rugged mountain slopes: they paddled after livestock in the marshy plains: they clung to the resignation ordered by the parish priests, to the uncomplaining altars of their fathers. The rich basked in security. Lapped round by art treasures of the past, softened by music and by wine, they spent their days in languorous amours and sunny enervation.

Into their world of enviable lassitude stormed Napoleon with his confounding energy. He wanted many things from Italy: quick military fame, and plunder to swell his popularity in Paris; men and money for his army; thrones for his relatives, his reluctant dynasty. Especially he wanted use of "this convenient peninsula"[1] as a bulwark in the traditional feud with Austria, standing out into the sea like a giant dock, opening the way for traffic or conquest to Cairo and Constantinople, closing the ring of his blockade of England.

He scattered the dukelings and their feudalism: he carried off the Pope without ceremony, not once but twice, to France:

[1] Fisher, *Bonapartism*, 56.

he broke up the Patrimony of St. Peter. At Milan he crowned himself King with the iron crown of Lombardy. He rearranged the country into three large protectorates. He introduced the *Code Napoléon*, and a common administration over the whole peninsula: in the interest of economy, he insisted that the Italians should manage it themselves. He destroyed all local privileges in the way of centralization: he suppressed monasteries, and redistributed their estates: he trampled on the municipal franchises, especially those of the old republic of Genoa which without delicacy he incorporated with Piedmont. For reasons of strategy, he undertook many public works. Roads were constructed, especially in the direction of the Alpine passes. At Venice, the lagoon was dredged and refortified as a naval base. He introduced schools on a standard pattern, not through any belief in enlightenment, but simply as a means of instilling the Napoleonic dogma. Under his rule of order, science flourished in the great universities of Pavia and Bologna.

Many Italians were not at all sorry when finally he disappeared. Sixty thousand of them had died in Spain and Russia. Their art galleries were stripped. War taxation had been crippling, apart from the cost of quartering the military in transit. Their produce had been commandeered for France, and yet at the frontiers they were compelled to pay a heavy impost on it. In particular, the poor had nothing to thank him for: except as cannon fodder he had scarcely noticed them.

Still, not being on the main land routes to Austria or Russia, Italy had come off lightly in comparison with Germany or Poland. Her experience, although severe, had been in a way exhilarating. Many ideas, long forgotten in an extinguished nation, had been reborn. The three obstacles to national unity, the Papal States, the plethora of foreign princes, and the spirit of provincialism, had been for a time removed. There had been the beginnings of home-rule. The cities had felt the benefit of free internal traffic, of overall government, as aids to commerce. For the first time in centuries an army of Italians, led by Italian officers trained in France, had fought with distinction on the battlefields of Europe. When Napoleon escaped from Elba, his brother-in-law Joachim Murat, whom he had made King of Naples in place of the exiled Bourbons, marched north, albeit unsuccessfully, against the Austrians, under the standard of Italian independence.

The defeat of Napoleon struck the governments concerned as a dizzying achievement. The Powers assembling to discuss the terms met in a mood of brotherly chaff and gay duplicity. Anything went at the Congress of Vienna. They would waltz the whole night through; and as they danced, they danced the hours away, back to the time at which their clocks had stopped before the Revolution.

All over Italy, Germany, France and Spain, the rulers so roughly beggared by Napoleon were sympathetically restored. In Italy, they were old hands in every case but one. Marie-Louise, wife of the now disregarded Emperor, recalled that she was also an Austrian princess, and an attractive one at that: she appeared at Vienna, and was awarded the Duchy of Parma by general consent. The Czar Alexander and Castlereagh, full of good will, had nice ideas of political and personal rights for the liberated peoples. But with France prostrated, Austria was master of the Congress, and Metternich had no illusions. It was just such fancy schemes that had set Europe aflame: they must be prevented. One by one the hopeful lights went out beneath that "dull extinguisher".[1] "Constitutions are expensive experiments,"[2] Castlereagh sadly told the Lombard deputies. Said the Czar to the Genoese, "Republics are no longer the fashion."[3]

Very soon the Allies had to look to their own security in the face of Austrian gains. The whole of northern Italy as far as Rome was to come under Hapsburg rule; Lombardy and Venetia by direct control, the rest by family influence. The only exception was the Kingdom of Piedmont (or Sardinia) in the extreme north-west; as a mark of friendly confidence the Allies strengthened Piedmont with the return of Savoy and Nice at the expense of France. They also managed to resist Metternich's claim to the Romagna. It was, they pointed out, to be a holy peace. It would never do to begin by pilfering from the Pope.

So, unfettered by conditions, the exiled potentates re-entered their domains, escorted by Austrian soldiers in gorgeous

[1] Simpson, *The Rise of Louis Napoleon*, 11.

[2] Bolton King, *History of Italian Unity*, I, 9.

[3] *Ibid.*, 10.

uniforms and peaked *shakos*, and amid the plaudits of their people. The returning princes desired no further trouble. Although they were under Austrian protection, they knew that her armies once invited might not be easy to dislodge. In their anxiety to maintain the peace, they resolved to suppress anything that smacked of progress. They felt strongly that the French attack upon the Church, and the latitude allowed in family affairs, had struck at the very roots of social order. They proceeded to restore all that Napoleon had destroyed, and to destroy all he had created. Only two of his innovations seemed worth retaining. In breaking down the old urban privileges he had weakened the most active sections of the community, the centres of corrosive theories of commercial liberalism: they agreed that there should be no more Civic Guards, or other forms of municipal pretension. Secondly, they found his weapons of police surveillance, of espionage and censorship, most convenient, and enlarged upon them. There was no great difference in the government of the various provinces; each had its own peculiarity, its own degree of harshness, depending upon the temper of its people, the character of its rulers, and the amount of opposition they encountered. All were essentially reactionary.

The Austrian occupation of Lombardy and Venetia was, at first, orderly and just. For the Lombards it was a return to a familiar despotism, and they gave little trouble, except in Milan, where dreams of metropolitan aggrandizement had to be diverted by the encouragement of operas and carnivals, and the subtle fostering of vice. The Venetians, softly decadent, vastly preferred the Austrians to Napoleon. The Austrian law was sound and comprehensive; the clergy, though much respected, were kept in check; the educational system, compulsory for children of either sex from six to twelve, was one of the most advanced in Europe. The one great drawback was the Austrian passion for centralization. Authority shuffled between the myriad offices of a cumbersome, obtuse bureaucracy, from which all Italians were categorically excluded. Everything had to be referred to the Austrian capital; the soldiers' boots were sent to Vienna for repair; the permits necessary for the most trivial activities got lost in the files, sometimes for upwards of five years. The enormous cost of the secretariat, increased by the quantity of military, police, and civil informers required to subdue the resulting discontent, sent taxes up until Lombardy and Venetia were paying more than a quarter of the annual revenue of the whole sprawling Empire.

Adjoining Lombardy to the west was the Kingdom of Piedmont, where an ancient, crafty, coarse and ruthless royal house ruled over a crass, aggressive people. As the only Italian sovereign in Italy, Victor Emmanuel I on his return was wildly popular. He was not in any way more liberal than the others. Jews were penalized. The police were second to none in zeal and cunning. Agriculture was old fashioned and neglected. Heavy tariffs induced smuggling on a massive scale. The commerce of Genoa was ruined, adding to the constant grievance of that dignified republic at its union with this barbarous kingdom. His government was a complete military despotism, three-quarters of the revenue being spent upon the army. Nation and ruler suited each other like horse and rider. To be a general was the badge of aristocracy. Learning and culture were thought unvirile, and probably disloyal (as Cavour later remarked, "Piedmont is an intellectual hell"[1]). Breeding like ferrets, on an improvident economy, the population glared in unison across their frontiers, especially towards Austrian Lombardy, "the goodly artichoke".[2]

South of Lombardy lay the Duchies of Modena and Parma. Francis IV of Modena was an excellent family man and a conscientious ruler. Generous to a fault, he was a gracious patron of the arts, and open-handed with his loans to peasants in the time of famine. He also interested himself in the cause of reclaiming courtesans. He wanted good laws and efficient justice. But he was a true son of an Austrian archduke. His piety was practically morbid. He enriched the Church and re-endowed the monasteries. He gave the Jesuits proscriptive rights in education. He stifled literature; he censored love letters in the post. The least whisper of liberalism terrified him. Liberals were sinners: it was, he said, a false philanthropy to punish lightly.

Marie-Louise enjoyed her life-interest in Parma, and treated herself to frivolous sexualities. All the same, she had gained,

[1] Bolton King, I, 163.
[2] *Ibid.*, 50.

involuntarily, a knowledge of statecraft during her marriage to the great Emperor. She retained the *Code Napoléon*, and added to it. She encouraged education for both boys and girls. Her attitude to the Church was correct but firm. Alone among the states of Italy, Jews were admitted to the Civil Service, to the great benefit of the community. During her enlightened rule, Parma remained prosperous and peaceful. The same could be said of the neighbouring small Duchy of Lucca, under another Marie-Louise, of Bourbon Parma, where the industries—olives, silk, cotton and wool—flourished under her quiet administration. By the Vienna treaties, she had been given Lucca in recompense for Parma. On the death of the Austrian Marie-Louise, Parma would revert to her, and Lucca would be absorbed by the large adjacent state of Tuscany.

The mood of Tuscany was mild. The people were comfortable, easy-going, sensuous and cultured; the feuds of opera singers and ornate religious ceremonies provided all the excitement they desired. Duke Ferdinand III of Hapsburg-Lorraine, another archduke's son, was a liberal and something of a freak. In 1824 he was succeeded by Leopold II. Leopold, benign and doctrinaire, liked to bumble informally about his acres wearing gaiters and the traditional straw hat of Tuscany. He would inspect the model farms, and the Maremma, the pestilential swamp which he was gradually draining; he would descend the copper mines at Massa, or climb the marble mountains at Carrara. He was so firmly wedded to the theory of free trade that he would not allow the cabs of Florence to carry tariff cards. He had at his disposal all the machinery of oppression but permitted it to sink into disuse. His army was kept up largely for the sake of its military bands. The secret police suffered from the general lethargy, drawing upon themselves a reprimand from Metternich. The frontiers offered shelter to the fugitives from more intolerant states. The censorship was ostentatious rather than effective: when, for example, Giotto's portrait of Dante was discovered, it had to be retinted, since the original tones were felt to be suggestive of the revolutionary tricolour. In Florence, distinguished visitors from constitutional countries thronged the *Piazza della Signoria* and the Uffizi Gallery, or chatted in Viesseux's library, the only reading room in Italy where foreign journals could be studied with impunity.

There was, however, an adverse side to it. Except where the fancy of the Duke was stirred the government was negligent: petty dishonesty was taken for granted in the administration.

The whole area south of Rome comprised the Kingdom of Naples, or Kingdom of the Two Sicilies. Ferdinand I, a bigoted, vindictive Bourbon prince, a veteran of two revolutions, was determined not to undergo a third.* The reforms achieved by Murat in his absence had gone too deep to be overthrown by direct reaction—it was said that the country had advanced four centuries in nine years. Instead, he specialized in cunning and corruption. "The man who pays for a post is loyal, and wants to keep it"[1] was his axiom of government. He made use of the Sicilians' hatred for the hegemony of Naples to destroy the separatism of the one and the liberalism of the other. He abrogated the Constitution extorted from him in 1812 during his schismatic rule in Sicily. He restored his Bourbon courtiers, his fellow exiles, to their feudal dominions: he favoured the clergy and the monastic orders who numbered, all told, a thirteenth of the population. Beneath the cloak of respectable institutions, the conditions of his kingdom were chaotic. The capital swarmed with forty thousand beggars, the proverbial *Lazzaroni* of Naples: at the Foundling Hospital nine out of every ten children died: the jails were filthy and always overflowing. In the crags and gullies of Calabria brigands roved unchecked. In the towns, murder was used as an instrument of politics, and assassinations in broad daylight went unpunished.

His grandson, Ferdinand II, who acceded in 1830, was in some ways more straightforward. He aimed to make Naples an efficient, fear-inspiring despotism like Piedmont. He was never happier than when reviewing his troops, or designing some extra gewgaw for their uniforms, although they were beaten wherever they fought, and became known all over Europe as the

* Ferdinand IV of Naples, evicted by the French in 1798, was restored under Nelson's patronage in 1799. In 1805 he was exiled by Napoleon, and Joseph Bonaparte was appointed King of Naples. In 1808 Joseph, on his promotion to the throne of Spain, was succeeded by Joachim Murat. Ferdinand, however, had continued his rule in Sicily, and in 1815 the Austrians restored him to his capital with the title Ferdinand I of the Two Sicilies.

[1] Bolton King, I, 89.

Maccaronis. He was not dissolute; on the contrary, his devoutness took the form of prudery. He draped the Venus of Praxiteles. He spent hours regulating the length of ballerinas' skirts. When he was eventually persuaded that railways were not by nature impious, he took every precaution against impropriety: he allowed no tunnels, or trains that ran by night, and a chapel was attached to every station. Moody and capricious, his private blamelessness was marred by a taste for practical joking. Once, while assisting his Queen to her seat, he whipped away the chair from under her: she, scrambling to her feet, spat furiously at him that he was the King of the *Lazzaroni*. His unamiable sense of humour assumed more sinister proportions when allied to political activities, and many were to suffer under his malignant fun.

Later in his reign, his pitiless reduction of the city of Messina earned him the nickname Bomba. In the heyday of King Bomba's power, Mr. Gladstone, visiting Naples for his daughter's health, felt it his duty to make private inquiries about the rule of that "pious and ever-celebrated monarch", as a Catholic admirer called him. What Mr. Gladstone discovered moved him to moral indignation. "It is not mere imperfection, not corruption in low quarters, not occasional severity that I am about to describe; it is incessant, systematic violation of the law by the power appointed to watch over and maintain it. . . . It is the awful profanation of public religion. . . . It is the perfect prostitution of the judicial office. . . . This is the negation of God erected into a system of Government."[1]

The rest of Italy, the central belt stretching from Rome north-eastwards to Ferrara and Ravenna, came under the aegis of the Papal States, where a government of priests, adding the material to their spiritual function, administered a system fussy, incompetent and venal. It was "not militarism, or the rule of men with like passions to the governed, but the supremacy of that strange third sex which the Roman Church creates by training men up from boyhood in a world that is not the world of men". They interfered in the minutest details of domestic life. They forbade enamoured youths to call more than three times at the homes of their beloved. As Trevelyan has it, "it was as though some indefinable horror, at once monstrous and

[1] Trevelyan, *Garibaldi and the Thousand*, 52–3.

despised, at once eerie and most material, were in one's house and lord of it".[1]

Political authority was vested in the Secretary of State, who was also leader of the ascendant party. His task became more difficult as the distance from Rome increased. In the immediate environs of the historic city the people were quiescent. They looked on the Holy Father with pride and affection as their own exclusive property, the heart of their urban tradition. Besides, he was, for most of them, their source of livelihood. Apart from those holding direct positions in the hierarchy, apart from the military and the attendants, and the lackeys to the attendants, there were the candlemakers and embroiderers, the importers of incense, the manufacturers of relics, and a whole host of other artisans; while the housing, carrying, feeding, guiding of the endless visitors attracted by the yellowing monuments, by the glorious pontifical displays, was an industry in itself. For the rest, the shepherds of the Agro Romano, for the Trasteverines, dwellers in the riverside slums beneath the Vatican, there were horse races, carnivals, boating, fireworks, balloon ascents and the wanton festivities of *Ottobrate*, accompanied by a regular stream of largesse distributed by cardinals and convents.

Further north, the impoverished peasants of the mountains of Umbria were docile and superstitious. But beyond the Apennines, and as far as the Adriatic shore, lay the towns of the Romagna and the Marches. Truculent, disorderly, disturbed by murderous factions since the Middle Ages, they were much in need of government. Remote and inaccessible, they were difficult to govern, the more so since Napoleon had grouped them with the Lombards, their natural cousins, and they much resented going back to Rome. "Better the Turks than the Pope,"[2] said the Romagnuols. They looked to Bologna as their capital. Bologna, city of arcades, was the largest industrial centre in the Roman States. In her cathedral, the rich stained glass had shattered at the salute of cannon as Clement VII crowned the Emperor Charles V. Her old university had a fine scientific record. Here the human body was first publicly dissected. Here Galvani first electrified a frog.*

* Here too, a century later, Marconi would evolve the radio.

[1] Trevelyan, *Garibaldi's Defence of the Roman Republic*, 61–2.

[2] Bolton King, I, 83.

Bologna was contemptuous of Rome, and of Roman obscurantism.

The Vatican looked on its Romagnuol subjects rather as English politicians of the period looked on the Irish. Vice-regal power was confided to four Cardinal Legates, later increased to seven, who ruled like independent princes, as sovereign in earthly matters as the neighbouring bishops were in the eternal. Below them came a semi-clerical army of officials, Prelates and Monsignori, often no more than mere adventurers enriching themselves slyly all the while.

Their jobbery was made easier by the confusion of the law. Until the Bernetti Code of 1831 there were fifteen separate jurisdictions in Rome alone. The Pope's Auditor could quash the findings of any court. Criminal cases were heard in secret. There was no bail, or habeas corpus.

Behind the clericalism of the courts loomed the shadow of the Inquisition, unknown and terrible. They were the men who preyed on ignorance, who drove the people to confession and passed the secrets so obtained to the police. They confirmed miracles, canonized saints, investigated heresy. They kept their eyes on censorship: of English newspapers, *The Times*, to its honour, was graded suspect; the *Examiner* and the *Morning Chronicle* were banned. By them the Jews, confined in ghettoes, were forced to wear badges of their race, although at the same time the whole edifice of Papal Government floated on a Rothschild loan.

The powers of the police had no clear limits. They could order a curfew, open letters, close shops and cafés, levy fines. Without reference to anyone, they could imprison, banish or eject from office any person they suspected. Merely to wear a beard would draw an insulting warning; a hint from a priest was sufficient warrant for arrest. Their spies were everywhere, in homes, in jails, at lectures and at theatres, where they were placed to ensure there was no departure from the licensed script. Though they came from the dregs, their word was accepted as sound evidence, unless so obviously loaded with spite that it was quite incredible.

For all the exceptional methods they employed, the police were impotent. In the winter of 1820 Byron recorded forty murders in three months in the Romagna, and one night found the Commandant of Ravenna mortally wounded at his door. In such times of emergency the Pope would set up Special Commissions to restore order by ferocious summary assizes. If these measures did not suffice, the next recourse was to the Pope's Army of Swiss mercenaries, and after that to the white-coated *Tedeschi* up in Lombardy.

As the science of Political Economy was on the Index, the administration was more emotional than wise. Free trade, vaccination, railways, gas power and light, the telegraph, all were in turn forbidden. The charterless towns tried to do business with their neighbours across unconnected distances, across customs barriers, across different scales of weights and measures. Ancona was the only port with any measurable traffic. Smuggling abounded. The state finances were a matter of faith. For all these hindrances and abuses there was no constitutional redress.

In education at least the policy was plain. "Ignorant people are easier to govern,"[1] remarked a Monsignor. Only two per cent of the population were literate. The Jesuits had almost complete control of secondary education. Dante was banned, so were some verses mentioning the movement of the earth. The only provision for girls was in the convents, where the discipline seems to have been severe, and on occasion mordant. In one seminary the older students, rebuked by the nuns for buying handkerchiefs that were too luxurious, made impenitent replies. The archbishop's agent was summoned. The girls scattered in haste; some took sanctuary in the chapel; the ringleaders went to their dormitory and started calling through the windows, imploring rescue from the passers-by. Heedless of their cries, the agent seized hold of them one by one, bent them over a bench, and caned them soundly.[2]

"The States of the Pope are, I suppose, the worst governed in the civilized world,"[3] observed Macaulay, travelling there in 1838. His words have been re-echoed by Bolton King, who says, the administration of the Papal States "was one long

[1] Bolton King, I, 81.

[2] This incident occurred under the auspices of Cardinal Pallotta, whose "strange excesses" are remarked upon by Farini, *The Roman State, 1815–1850*, I, 21. See Orsini, *Memoirs and Adventures*, 254.

[3] Thompson, *Louis Napoleon*, 105.

misgovernment".[1] Having regard to the million small abuses, to the subaltern insolence that major insolence breeds, theirs would appear no overstatement. Supreme over all, approachable through seven stately corridors, through lines of Swiss Guards, through avenues of scarlet-cassocked cardinals, of purple-stockinged bishops, the Pope brooded, alone in his throne room. The system he maintained so resolutely in his own dominions was a pattern, a concentration of the system he advised and encouraged all over Italy, indeed, all over Europe. He governed, in prayer and anxiety, in the name of Christ Crucified.

III

Such was the Italy in which Felice Orsini grew to manhood; split into fragmentary tyrannies; ignorant and superstitious: all civic virtue systematically dispraised; all literature and learning stifled; narcotic pleasures, torpid vice deliberately promoted. The trade of a fruitful country was arrested at the domestic method of production, halted at an annual figure of eighteen million pounds, scarcely more than a pound per head of the fever-stricken population. Power and fortune went to reward the pliable or the corrupt. The whole was preserved by permission of a brutal foreign army.—Yet, worst of all, when all is said, was that hallmark of intolerable misgovernment, the secret police, the *sbirri*, universal, overweening.

This state of things could not long continue unopposed. In consequence of the Vienna settlement there was a frenzy of revolutionary unrest throughout the whole of Europe, and nowhere more so than in Italy. As early as 1812 the dashing Murat, King of Naples, had decided to cheat both Napoleon and the Austrians, and to make himself King of a united Italy. To that end he had rallied a secret society called the Carbonari (Charcoal Burners).

As was becoming to a secret society, the origins of the Carbonari were veiled in legend. They claimed descent from the Kohlen-Brenners of Germany, acknowledging as their patron

[1] Bolton King, I, 74.

St. Theobald de Brie, who died in the year 1066. Their meetings, known as *venditas*, or auction sales, were held in white-washed rooms, empty save for rush chairs for the officers and benches for the members along the walls—conditions menacing in their simplicity, as though everything were ready to vanish in an instant. In front of the Grand Master stood a block of unhewn wood, bearing amongst other things a crucifix: to his right was an axe for his use as a gavel: above his head, in glass transparency, hung the five symbols of the Order: at his back was a portrait of a venerable St. Theobald, sitting on a tree stump outside a log cabin in the woods. At the close of the proceedings, the Grand Master was informed that "the sun no longer lights the forest".[1] Rising, he ordered the Good Cousins (all members were Good Cousins, all outsiders Pagans) to rest from their labours, to "retire in peace to your huts in the great forest". Then, gathering their dark cloaks close about them, covering their tricoloured scarves of red for fire, blue for smoke, black for charcoal, the Good Cousins faded into the moonless night, silent save for the distant guiding notes of a guitar.

The Carbonari were traduced by Murat, and they turned their loyalty to the exiled Bourbons. But Ferdinand I on his return to Naples, instead of courting their goodwill, armed a rival society, the Braziers of the Counterpoise, from the worst cutthroats in the kingdom, with the express purpose of exterminating them. Thenceforth, tired of the perfidy of kings, the Carbonari resisted authority in every form. They warmed their creed with a dash of Rousseau and the Rights of Man, with loose demands for a Constitution. They added whatever local grievances happened to be foremost in their various districts. They devised their own religion to defy the Catholic Church. They swore secrecy and obedience on pain of death. They held their own trials and executions; at the Grand Lodge in Naples, the Black Book lay beside the Golden Book of Regulations. They grew into a vast conspiracy of irridentists, pledged to murder and rebellion, an avenging flame.

To all who felt themselves downtrodden or affronted by the Restoration; to officers of the Grand Army, restless after their travels, contemptuous of ostentation, returning to find themselves outranked by Bourbon popinjays; to displaced civil servants, to

[1] Frost, *The Secret Societies of the European Revolution*, I, 219.

impoverished priests making do on stipends of thirty-two pounds a year, to proprietors struggling in the brandy, oil and cotton trades, their mummery offered consolation. The Carbonari flared through the Kingdom of Naples like a spark in a tinder-box. The entire male population of Calabria and Abruzzi joined them almost overnight. They spread to other provinces: soon there were the Adelfi of Parma, the Federali of Lombardy, the Guelf Knights of Piedmont: in the Romagna, the American Hunters drilled in Dante's forest at Ravenna, assembled a secret arsenal in Byron's house, and carried the word across the Po into the Polesine territory of Venetia. They reached out beyond the confines of Italy. They had affiliations with the Spanish *Anilleros*, the Society of the Ring. They had lodges at Belfort, at La Rochelle and in the Jura mountains. In Paris, Lafayette and Louis Philippe became *Amis de la Vérité*. They had contacts in Vienna itself; for a time Metternich's private secretary was a Carbonaro, until he disappeared abruptly during a hunting expedition.

At Naples, in July 1820, the militia of 50,000 men raised to subdue the brigands in Calabria declared for "God, the King and the Constitution", under their Carbonarist leader, Guglielmo Pepe, a former subaltern of Napoleon. King Ferdinand had no choice. With his hand on the altar, he swore to the Constitution, professing himself a happy man to have lived to see the day. But when a separatist rebellion broke out in Sicily, he went off to Laibach and borrowed an Austrian army, which shortly afterwards defeated Pepe at Rieti. A few months later, a hot-headed group of nobles in Piedmont rose demanding a Constitution and war against Austria. They forced Victor Emmanuel to abdicate in favour of his son, but on marching into Lombardy were roundly beaten by a combined force of Austrians and Piedmontese regulars at the first battle of Novara. Everywhere the ill-concerted risings failed. After 1820 the Grand Lodge of the Carbonari moved to Paris, where they worked quietly towards the July revolution of 1830. Theirs had been an aristocratic, never a truly popular movement. Their entrance fees denied admittance to the peasantry, who were in any case slow and unresponsive. Their aims were political, not social; and of politics the poor knew nothing.

In Italy, the revenge was savage, but the martyrdom was not in vain. Public whippings, reddening the stones of Naples, made Europe gasp; even the Austrians urged moderation. In Genoa, the young Mazzini pensively watched his mother drop her *lira* into the purse of an officer of the National Guard who, with proud and burning eyes, was begging for "the proscripts of Italy". Exiles streamed everywhere. Panizzi, domiciled in London, started his unique library in the British Museum. Silvio Pellico's romance about his gloomy Moravian dungeon, the Spielburg, brought to the citizens of constitutional countries an uncomfortable pricking of their consciences. Liberal romanticism was in the air, a harking away from eighteenth-century scientism. To Italians in their misery it was inseparably bound up with a yearning after the forgotten glories of their country. So far, the fight for freedom had been on a sectarian or urban footing. Forces were at hand to weld it into unity.

IV

France, like Italy, had suffered a dictated peace. The restored monarchy, supposedly popular, had retained all the evil qualities of Napoleon's government without any of the good. Moreover, the new rulers were definitely not romantic. Louis XVIII showed tact and skill. Charles X showed skill and less tact. "*La France s'ennuie,*" yawned Lamartine.[1] Louis Philippe, who was to displace them in 1830 by a sort of constitutional legerdemain, had so much tact that there was no room for skill at all. Strolling through Paris alone with his umbrella, uxurious head of a large and happy family, incessantly dabbling with his investments, he was too blatantly bourgeois to be liked. Soon after his accession he received John Bowring. "*Asseyez-vous! Asseyez-vous!*" he cried. Still talking volubly he flung himself down in a heavy gilded chair which split in fragments, depositing him on his back.[2] The French groaned. Worn out by war, disgruntled by Metternich's repressive German domination, they began to think that after all the Emperor had promised less and given more.

[1] Fisher, 78.
[2] Bowring, *Autobiographical Recollections*, 258–9.

At Longwood, St. Helena, Napoleon meditated in querulous valetudinary wisdom. All over Europe statuettes were being made of him, forlorn on his Atlantic rock, gazing with bleared eagle's eyes towards France. In an age grown stale, he only was majestic. His sins had mellowed; the younger generation mourned the passing of those "great, seven-league-boot thoughts". "Our situation here may even have its attractions," he told Las Cases; "the universe is looking at us, we remain the martyrs of an immortal cause. . . . Adversity was wanting to my career."[1]

He had been misrepresented. In dignified retirement he would restate his case. Recorded by the faithful pens of his lieutenants, the portentous utterances rolled landwards on the breakers. "I did not usurp the crown; I found it in the gutter, and the French people put in on my head." He had desired for France no more than her natural frontiers, the Rhine, the Alps, the Pyrenees. He had proposed a mighty European order, greater than that of Charlemagne; a federation of free nations, prosperous and progressive, wherein religion, once divested of its temporal pretensions, was to have been respected in its proper sphere. In particular, he had reduced Italy into three well-conducted kingdoms. He had only been awaiting the birth of a second son to reduce it further, into one.

His mantle fell about the willing shoulders of his extraordinary nephew, Louis Napoleon. Louis Napoleon was the son of the Emperor's brother Louis, for a time a conscientious King of Holland, a sulky, rheumaticky, disapproving man; and of Hortense, daughter of the Empress Josephine by her first marriage. Hortense was a beautiful, spirited, gifted creature, a composer of lyrical songs. That she called her sons, successively, Napoleon Charles, Napoleon Louis and Charles Louis Napoleon, indicates the current of her mind. Her eldest son died young: her husband, from whom she separated, gained custody of the second: the youngest, Louis Napoleon, she kept always with her.

He was not a prepossessing youth. A later associate unkindly called him "the depressed parrot".[2] He was so unnapoleonic that it has been said he was not a Bonaparte at all—a suggestion not

1 Fisher, 70.
2 Thompson, 111.

Ferdinand II ("Bomba"), King of Naples
From a portrait in the Museo Mazziniano, Genoa

without plausibility since the fascinating Hortense was far from chaste. His love of her was in large part responsible for the astonishing medley of his qualities. "Unfortunately," says Simpson, "a highly impressionable boy in whose eyes his mother could do no wrong, was brought up . . . accustomed to the belief that the possession of an artistic temperament excused its owner from the exact observance of conventional morality."[1] He was docile, sensual, vain, confused and shy. Hortense herself admitted he was obstinate and soft. Mme Gordon, afterwards his secret agent, said he reminded her of a woman. Secretive, selfish, unoriginal, inconsistent, halting in speech, introspective, with a raffish taste for the company of the footman class and of *femmes galantes*, De Tocqueville said he had "the writer's habit", and hinted at "a little vein of madness".[2]

But Louis Napoleon also had his better side. He was as physically brave as he was morally uncertain, as active in body as he seemed to be passive in mind—a fine horseman, good shot, adequate fencer and an excellent swimmer. He was humane and kind; in Bismarck's words, essentially good-natured. There was a poetic strain in him, an idealism which was never quite defeated. When he was eight, he came home through the snow without his coat and shoes, having given them away to needy children. At fourteen, he dived fully clothed into the River Neckar to retrieve a flower dropped by a princess, his cousin. Equally capable of warm affection and of sullen anger, it was always a toss-up whether he would be treacherous or quixotic.

The rest was determined by his early environment. Napoleon, then childless, was his godfather. As a child he had lisped farewell to the Emperor as he set forth for Waterloo. Thereafter he had wandered with his mother, unwanted in any land, until at last they found the Castle of Arenenburg secluded in the mountains round Lake Constance. His first tutor, an elderly Abbé, smiled on his laziness, and called him by his nursery name of Oui-Oui. His second, a prim and scholarly young man whose immediate question on entering any town was "where is the library?",[3]

[1] Simpson, 140–2.

[2] De Tocqueville, *Recollections*, 226–7.

[3] Thompson, 13.

encouraged liberal principles. Louis Napoleon grew interested in military affairs, attended a Swiss artillery camp and lived a soldier's life, carrying his own pack and eating the black bread of the country.

He devoured the gospel as it came from St. Helena. It never occurred to him that he would not be Emperor. That two others stood between him and the succession, Marie Louise's son, the weakly Duke of Reichstadt, and his own remaining elder brother, Napoleon Louis, to whom he was devoted, did not trouble him. It was his fate, his destiny. He would dispense with meddling assemblies, and demand direct expression of the people's will. He would advance from a system of order to one of liberty. Although it bore no relation to his uncle's actual government, the Legend as revised in his *Idées Napoléoniennes* was a charter of grand and visionary statesmanship. Inconstant in so much else, he was unswerving about this. He flaunted his claim brazenly, cleverly, with a persistence utterly devoid of humour; and if he was sometimes forced by the pressure of events to deviate from his course, he always returned to his original programme as compulsively as an addict to his drugs.

Much of his youth was spent in Italy. Italy was a fixed star in his romantic universe. The traditional rivalry of France and Austria, his respect for his mother's brother Eugène Beauharnais the soldier-king of northern Italy, the obsession of the old Emperor, all made his duty plain. In the end, Italy's freedom was to be his most noble, his most chivalrous foible, spelling in the moment of its attainment his folly and his ruin. In the beginning, on his way with his mother to meet his father and brother in Italy he paused, a dreamy sixteen, and filled a flask with water from the Rubicon.

There were flocks of Bonapartes in Italy, living incognito in costly villas, headed by the matriarch, Madame Mère. It was natural that the Carbonari, with their large proportion of Napoleonic officers, should have great hopes of them. The Bonapartes were closely watched by both the Austrians and the French, and generally they steered clear. Hortense's lovely house at Rome was a hive of nationalist intrigue, but her plots and ambitions were of a strictly family kind. None the less, during one of Louis Napoleon's many visits to his father in Florence in the twenties, his brother's tutor secretly enrolled both the young princes in the Carbonari. Almost certainly they must have met that enthusiastic doyen of the movement, Andrea Orsini, who had so recently gone there with his family.

Since the purge of 1820 all Carbonarist hopes had been centred on the Papal States, where they had not yet shown their hand. So, when Pope Pius VIII died at the end of 1830, two separate groups, the Bonapartes and the Carbonari, were waiting to exploit the interregnum. The brothers were deeply involved in the designs of both.

The Bonapartes struck first. Hortense and Louis Napoleon having once more arrived in Rome, a family conference was held. It was decided, on funds produced by Madame Mère, to bribe the Papal Dragoons, to seize the Arsenal, to scatter gold in the poor quarter of the Trastevere, and proclaim Louis Napoleon as regent for the Duke of Reichstadt, King of Rome. The plan miscarried. Young Louis had one memorable moment riding through Rome in a tricolour (the French red-white-blue, be it noted, not the red-blue-black of the Carbonari). He was then frog-marched to the border, and thrust ignominiously into Tuscany, whereon he returned to his brother's house in Florence.

Meanwhile the Carbonari had grown confident of French support now that Louis Philippe had snatched the throne in Paris. In February 1831 their plot exploded in Bologna. With surprising ease the Papal Legate was overthrown. Within three weeks the whole of the Romagna and the Marches, Umbria, Modena and Parma were under the revolutionary Provisional Government. The temporal power of the Pope was declared abolished, and elections were called for the United Italian Provinces.

Loyal to their Carbonarist pledges, the two brothers joined the insurrectionary forces in the field, which by the time they arrived were threatening Rome. As commanding officers, they acquitted themselves well. Napoleon Louis repulsed attempts by the Papal troops to recover Terni and Spoleto. Louis Napoleon launched an attack on Civita Castellana, preparatory to marching on the capital.

Then came a change in the fortunes of war. As a last step, while he prepared for flight, the new Pope, Gregory XVI, called in the Austrians. The French failed in their promise to march in the Patriots' cause. With the Austrians now bearing down upon them in Bologna, and their army away in front of Rome, the Provisional Government was in a desperate situation. Thinking that the prominence of the Bonaparte princes was an affront to Louis Philippe, the government recalled them to the neighbourhood of Forli. There they were joined by a force of Romagnuols, who had been persuaded by the pacificatory Archbishop of Spoleto, the future Pio Nono, to lay down their arms and go home quietly. Andrea Orsini, after his arrest in the opera at Florence a year or so before, had been sent back to the Romagna whence he came, and may be assumed to have been among their number. So it came about that the Bonapartes and the Orsinis mingled in the ranks of the defeated at inconspicuous Forli.

The older Bonapartes were far from pleased when they heard of the sensational part their scions were playing in the rebellion. Hortense, who had believed them to be living quietly with their father, hurried from Rome to Florence, where she was horrified at what she learned. Return to Tuscany was barred to them; their lives were to be excluded from the amnesty. She also heard they had caught measles. Without hesitation she set out to look for them. At Pesaro she was met by a distracted Louis Napoleon, who told her how his brother had died in his arms, and how the whole of Forli had, the night before the Austrians marched in, followed him in silent procession to the grave. Louis himself was in high fever. For a week Hortense kept him hidden in Ancona, until at last they got away, with Louis disguised as a footman standing behind her on her post-chaise. At Spoleto they called upon the same obliging archbishop, who gave them a carriage emblazoned with his episcopal arms to carry them safely to the borders of Piedmont.

After the collapse of the rebellion, Louis Philippe of France, stirred by a tardy conscience, set up a conference of ambassadors in Rome to demand from the Pope an improvement in his government. The Austrians in due course withdrew. Forli, Ravenna and Bologna promptly rose again, only to be defeated by the Papal troops at Cesena south-east of Forli in January 1832. The Austrians returned; this time they were welcomed at Bologna as the alternative to Papal outrages. On that the French, jealous of Austrian predominance, despatched a fleet to occupy Ancona. They came in the name of Italian liberty, taking down the Papal coat of arms and singing the *Marseillaise*, but at a growl from Austria they quickly changed their tune. Nothing more was done about reform.

This second failure was the end of the Carbonari. There had, however, been some solid gains. Henceforth the Papal States and the question of the temporal power became a continental issue, inseparable from the major struggle between the liberal recovery of France and the iron despotism of Austria. Furthermore, he who by his brother's death, and that of the Duke of Reichstadt shortly following, rightly now could see himself as the Napoleonic heir, had good cause to remember Italy. He would be more than ever mindful of the Rubicon.

V

When Andrea Orsini was expelled from Tuscany in 1829, and sent back to the Papal States, he went to Bologna, where he required that his elder son be sent to join him. So young Felice, after a tearful parting from his mother, sister and brother, set out across the mountains in the care of friends. His father soon regretted his decision. Andrea Orsini was a conspirator, and in Bologna things were getting serious. The constant presence of a bright-eyed, inquisitive, serious-minded boy of nine was a distinct embarrassment. After a week or two he consulted his brother Orso on the subject.

Orso did not share Andrea's violent views on politics. An upright merchant who had gained a moderate fortune in the local hemp trade, by marriage he had become, according to local standards, very rich. He had everything to lose by gaining the ill-will of the Papal government; he therefore felt inclined not to run his head against a wall, but to make the best of the system as he found it. He pointed out that his brother's way of life was not fair to the boy, and would only get him a bad name. Much better to put him out of harm's way, in a respectable household where he would have some chance of finding a career. It was soon decided that Felice should go to live with his uncle Orso at Imola.

It was a tall, rambling, three-storied house occupying an

important corner on the main thoroughfare of the town. Its severe flat front of brick broke at street level into rounded arches, decorated with fine terracotta friezes. From the side, an impressive carriage gateway led into an open courtyard. Felice found it very strange. As his uncle was childless, he was for the first time lonely, except for the servants with whom he was not supposed to associate. His aunt, who came from a highly conservative Imolese family, was an ungainly woman, excessively religious. She was in her way kindly and well-meaning, but after his slender, loving mother, she seemed old and taut. His uncle, now in the middle forties, was handsome, brisk and well set-up. An educated man, he was charitable and very well respected, *persona grata* with the clerical dignitaries. He was fearfully strict. "I will not suffer fools at my table," he would roar. He had a profound contempt for women, so that Felice's upbringing "was not only masculine but somewhat *rude*".[1] He was extremely hard on vice of any kind, dishonesty, gambling, drinking, smoking—an attitude which Felice quickly came to share, and adhered to all his life.

Felice's mornings began early, since his uncle always rose at five o'clock. His education was confided to three priests, the chief of whom, his Latin tutor, he thoroughly disliked. Another taught him drawing, and for this he showed greater aptitude; there still exists a *Madonna Addolorata*, beatifically sanctimonious, designed by the young pupil and dedicated to his master. He was also passionately fond of music. But the best part of the routine was the short time left for walks with the third priest, a jollier man, who sometimes conspired to let him dodge one of the several sets of prayers taking up in all three hours of the day.

Still, there were compensations. Every week-end in summer Orso took his family in the carriage out to their country villa, where, away from the censorious atmosphere of Imola, appearances could be relaxed, and Felice raced as free as a young colt. He much revered his uncle, and liked to hear him talk; the good man, seeking to impart his own modest pride of country, unwittingly started lines of thought very different from those intended. "My uncle conversed on the ancient glories of Rome and Greece, upon the Latin authors, and our famous poet

[1] Orsini, *Memoirs and Adventures*, 9.

Dante, but he affirmed that those glorious times were gone for ever, that the present epoch was one of effeminacy, deceit, cowardice and lying. . . . This part of his education was useful to me."[1]

The question next came up, what was the boy to be? Though he showed signs of obstinacy, he was, when he liked, alert and active; his memory was good. Orso had hopes of a junior partner in the hemp business; his fashionable friends, however, poured scorn on the idea of a life of commerce for the boy. In the Church he should go far, become a Cardinal, or perhaps, who knew, a Pope. Or, if he preferred the laity, they saw him in the profitable business of the clerical law, a Monsignor, a Nuncio. The first step at least was obvious; he was sent to the public school in Imola where, in view of his uncle's standing, he should have got on famously.

These benign and pious plans for his settled future were upset during the troubles of 1831. For, though he had no knowledge of the part his father was playing in the rising at Bologna, though the name of Prince Louis Napoleon meant little to him, Felice encountered obnoxious influences among the other boys. When the authority of the Cardinal Legate was overthrown, the classes of philosophy and rhetoric, cheering and chanting forbidden Romagnuol airs, produced a tricolour. The uproar grew so great that the school had to be closed. Felice, his blood tingling wildly, went out into an Imola transformed, an Imola that had become, in an instant, a gay garden of cockades. On his way home he procured one for himself, only to have it snatched away hastily by his uncle. When the Austrians arrived, the general rejoicing gave place to leaden gloom, a gloom not at first shared by young Felice, who for his part was captivated by the smart white uniforms of the invading army, and by the thrilling thumping of their bands. He missed his dinner, following the soldiers through the town, to the fury of his uncle, who muttered, very much beneath his breath, about "vagabonds and rascals".[2] Felice learnt better later, when the priestly visitors came hurrying round, rubbing their hands at the Liberal defeat, vaunting the praises of the Austrians. His uncle said little; Felice said less, glowering at them from a corner.

[1] Orsini, *Memoirs and Adventures*, 8.

[2] *Ibid.*, 3.

While the Provisional Government was in office, Felice's mother and her other two children left Florence to join his father in Bologna. Soon after their arrival she decided to pay a visit to her sister in Meldola, his godmother Lucrezia, wife of Felice Grammatica whose christian name he now bore in place of the question-begging Theobald. On her way she proposed to stop at Imola to see him, bringing his sister Rosina with her. For days before they came Felice was in transports of excitement and delight; for days after their departure he wandered miserably through the dreary, barn-like rooms feeling outcast and deserted. Then came disastrous news, another of those sudden horrors as stark and unexpected as the arrest of his father in the Opera at Florence. On returning to Bologna Rosina developed cholera contracted on the journey. His mother nursed her, tireless and devoted, but in vain: worse, his mother herself was stricken down, and in a few days she too was dead. Felice was dumbfounded. It seemed impossible. His mother, dead? Now truly he was loveless and unprotected, finally and bitterly alone. His brother Leonidas was sent to join him at his uncle's. In less than a year his father, with what seemed to Felice a shocking callousness, was married again to an unforgivable woman called Mathilde Fabbri, and started a new family which eventually numbered three.

There followed the second rising of the Romagna, the rout of the Liberals by the Papal troops at Cesena, the return of the Austrians, and the reaction of Gregory XVI, who for fifteen years subjected the Papal territories to a crippling repression. He closed the universities from time to time, he dissolved town councils, he forbade scientific congresses, he discountenanced railways. He denied opportunity to all who had taken part in the insurrection: all honourable professions—the army, civil service, law, journalism, teaching and commerce—were closed to them.

His Secretary of State, Bernetti, perceived that if the Austrians were to be kept out of the Romagna, he must succeed in keeping order. To support the Papal Army and the *sbirri*, he raised a force of volunteers called Centurions, or Sanfedists, who were given the utmost licence. Centurion peasants could refuse their rents; Centurion artisans could threaten their employers. Recruitment was brisk, and soon they numbered fifty thousand, a large part of them unmistakable ruffians. The result was anarchy and assassination. Everyone took sides between the Brigands and the Liberals: the common question was "are you a two or a three?",[1] meaning a follower of the Papal yellow-and-white or of the Liberal red-white-green. Felice proclaimed himself a Liberal, despite the disapproval of his uncle's friends and the active hostility of his teachers.

At school the persecution grew so bad that a number of the boys decided to run away. Their plan was to go to join the French at Ancona, who still enjoyed an unmerited name for liberalism; they reckoned that, although they were under age, they would be welcomed by the garrison and taken on as drummer boys. For one reason or another, they all thought better of it in the end except Felice, whose patriotic ardour was further inflamed at being confined by his uncle, for some domestic misdemeanour quite apart from politics, in a tiny room at the very top of the house, for a week, on a diet of bread and water. By means of a rope he had smuggled in, he lowered himself perilously from the high window of his first prison into the courtyard, pawned his watch, and set out alone for Ancona, reckless and twelve years old. He got only five miles down the Via Emilia before the horsemen sent after him overtook him. When they brought him home his uncle lectured him, before handing him over to his Latin master for a condign thrashing, endured by the truant in rebellious silence.

Thinking it over afterwards, his uncle reached the conclusion that the boy was incorrigible. Part of his intransigeance no doubt sprang from the natural high spirits appropriate to his age. Equally plainly, a larger part derived from the stormy, headstrong, Romagnuol pride so ruinous to his father. To leave him at school under the eyes of the priests would be to damn him finally. So Felice was taken away, and sent with young Leonidas to a smaller private school in the parish of Valverde.

The change was not at first propitious. In his old age Leonidas remembered as clearly as on the day it happened the time that his brother, in whom all systems of coercion or oppression produced a resentment that was almost suicidal, determined to challenge their antique pedagogue who, devoid of other authority, resorted too freely to the whip. For some weeks past

[1] Orsini, *Memoirs and Adventures*, 6.

Felice had been lazy and contumacious. One morning, on being asked to recite the lesson for the day, he answered coolly that he had not learnt it, persisting in his mutinous defiance even when the master reached for the cruel-looking crop on the wall behind his desk. With superb indifference he received fifteen resounding cuts, after which he faced his mentor, rattled off the lesson perfectly without a flaw, made a tight little bow, and resumed his place.[1]

Though a terror to his teachers, Felice was not by nature mean. With other boys he was kindly, generous, full of fun; he was inquiring and unvindictive. Having thus gained his Pyrrhic victory he voluntarily applied himself to work. To be taught by a layman, even an incompetent layman, was like a breath of air; and his uncle gave him money which he was actually allowed to spend on books of his own choosing. He made rapid and substantial progress. As a reward, knowing how much he loved the country, his uncle gave him a pony, and he galloped joyfully away. Regrettably, he soon abused his freedom. He used his pony to assemble with his friends in the plains where, contrary to all rules, they practised pistol shooting.

His pistol was a source of great illicit pleasure to him. It was an old-fashioned weapon, with a rusty barrel of unwieldy length, but it was fitted with brass hammers and boasted a stock of dark, ornamented, ruby-coloured rosewood. He had bought it secretly from his uncle's cook and general handyman. This man, Domenico Spada, who combined his domestic duties with a part-time tailoring business in the town, was his chief ally in the lonely house. Orso Orsini did not discourage their association, thinking that the friendship of a sensible man of forty-two ought to keep the rash deeds of youth in check; while Spada, as his most trusted servant, would surely give him warning if his nephew's exploits threatened to go too far.

One summer evening after dinner (the exact date was 5 July 1836), Felice's aunt and uncle announced that they were going to the country, and sent Spada to harness the horse and bring out the carriage. Seeing them getting ready to depart, Felice slipped up to his room, got out his pistol, and started to load it for one of his private expeditions. While he was thus engaged, Spada, who had been sent back with some message for him from

[1] Orsini (Luigi), *Il mio Sentiero*, 59–66.

his uncle, came silently into the room: Felice whipped round, the pistol went off, and the man sank heavily to the floor. In terror Felice dashed downstairs, straight into the arms of his uncle and his brother who had heard the shot. A lad, a hemp-dresser in Orso's employment, was in the courtyard drawing water when he too heard a shot, and screams. Running to the scene he found his mistress with her hands to her head crying out "Oh God!", and poor Spada sitting on the floor in a pool of blood, clasping his stomach, rocking rhythmically back and forth, moaning again and again, "Oh God, mistress: oh God!" In uproar and lamentation the whole household assembled round the dying man. Felice, crying passionately, flung himself down, kissed him, and held him in his arms. Spada in return was able to gasp out a statement he later repeated to the magistrate before he died, "I know that it was an accident which has befallen me and him; I pardon him, and make peace."[1]

In the midst of his grief, Orso Orsini suddenly recalled that Spada, while having been an excellent and faithful servant, had dangerous connections. Felice had been brought up once already before the Centurions for the illegal possession of arms, and had been discharged only because of his uncle's good reputation. The situation was very bad: the police would arrive at any minute. As one man, the family hustled Felice down to the courtyard, propped a tall ladder against the wall, and sent him shinning up it. He climbed across the adjoining roofs, and in at one of the windows of the house of Count Faella, a friend whom they could trust. Here he was concealed during the hue and cry which immediately followed.

After a few days, when the first excitement had died down, Felice was carried in a sedan chair, with the blinds drawn, to the palace of the brother of Count Faella, Count Hercules Faella. A coupé was waiting in the court. The two young Marchionesses Alessandretti, wives of the two counts, pushed him inside and covered him with a rug. They then climbed in themselves, and went for a drive in the country. Ten miles outside the town, two mules were waiting in the charge of a muleteer. Felice got out, and swung into his saddle. His slim, supple, sixteen-year-old figure, his black tumbling hair, his dark and flashing eyes cut a

[1] Luzio, *Biografico*, 22.

striking picture as he ambled off to his first exile. The Marchionesses craned after him from their carriage windows till he was out of sight. Then they sank back amongst the cushions, looked at each other and sighed deeply.

The guide led Felice through valleys and passes of the Apennines to the house of a Signor Allai, a countryman friend of his uncle, who lived up in the mountains at Borgo San Lorenzo in Tuscany, not far from Florence. Signor Allai did not know the reason for the visit, but he had his orders and he asked no questions. Nor did Felice in the least know how long he was to stay. He supposed it would be until his uncle had had time to buy indulgences, and make the other necessary appeasements.

As a matter of fact his uncle was finding the affair more thorny than he had anticipated. Matthia Spada, brother of the deceased, was a keen Centurion. Not only had he many scores to settle with Felice, but in his edgy, discontented way he welcomed the chance to ruin a wealthy patron of the hemp trade. In a shrill accusation to the Governor of Imola he complained that when the rich committed crimes it was always the same, the matter was glossed over. In this case he demanded the most earnest prosecution; it was no question of mere accident, it was a question of premeditated murder. One of his brother's tasks, he said, had been to report to his employer on the conduct of his nephew; something he had said had made Felice angry, and many times in the presence of witnesses the young aristocrat had threatened to shoot the informer with a blunderbus. Domenico Spada had made many grim allusions to his fate. On going to be shaved he had told a startled barber that he did not wish to leave it to be done for him by the gravediggers; and in a low, melancholy frame of mind he had told a fellow tailor he would gladly make him heir to his scissors, as he was going to another world. On the afternoon of his death, so far from being already in the Orsinis' house, he had gone home without intention of returning; on the contrary, he was showing his fiancée how to make a pair of trousers, when Felice, after seeking high and low, sent a message impatiently to summon him. Finally, between the shooting and the arrival of the magistrate, a certain pork-butcher would aver that he had gained access to the wounded man, and had urged him to exculpate the criminal, seeing that his family would receive a heavy compensation, and that Orso Orsini would do the funeral handsomely.

The worst of it was, thought Orso, that of the many charges against his nephew there was not one he could positively deny. It was said Felice had already wounded two of his enemies with his pistol, one of them a monk, who had preferred to hush it up out of regard for the influence of the Orsinis. It might be true. On 8 June Felice had been seen to deride and insult a priest in full panoply during a service in San Giovanni; that sounded very like Felice. As for the immediate cause of the alleged quarrel with the cook, their neighbour, Signora Gottarelli, had two pretty daughters. Spada, apparently, had found out something; prudence prevented Orso from inquiring what.[1]

Intervention came from an unlooked-for quarter. At the end of 1832, Gregory XVI, alarmed at the continual trouble in the Romagna, had moved Mastai Ferretti, the urbane and soothing Archbishop of Spoleto, to Imola. It was a wise appointment. Mastai was a Romagnuol himself, and to some extent he shared their aspirations. Now forty years of age, he came from an old family at Sinigallia, well known for national sentiment "down to their cats". He had become a priest from necessity rather than from choice, when his first intention of joining the exclusive Papal Guard of Nobles at Rome had been frustrated by youthful attacks of epilepsy. He had travelled; for two years he had held efficiently an administrative post in Chile. Though far from intellectual, he was well informed. He knew something of free trade, he was alive to the more glaring shortcomings of the government, and took a genuine interest in education. Both as a patriot and as a loyal churchman, he was determined to oppose the Austrian designs on the Romagna. Fortunately, for he was not unambitious, Imola, though only a bishopric, was no demotion from Spoleto, on account of its peculiar difficulty.

He was a gentleman. His dress, his habits, were the acme of quiet good taste. Abstemious for his own part, his hospitality was generous, and his spectacular charity sometimes brought him to the edge of poverty. Never strident, he yet possessed a certain shrewdness, a certain obstinacy. He was much liked for his kindly, self-deprecatory humour; he was noted for his unaffected piety. He was very handsome and intoned beautifully

[1] Luzio, *Biografico*, 23–31.

in a soft sonorous voice. If he had his failings—he was inclined to lazy optimism, to a feeble shrinking from unpleasant issues, to a longing for applause—they were of a graceful kind, not likely to prove invidious in his present station.

Mastai Ferretti was always alive to quality. He liked the rugged virtue of his new flock. He thought more could be obtained from them by sympathetic coaxing than by curt severity, especially from "the enlightened propertied classes".[1] He knew Orso Orsini as one of the most respected pillars of the church. He was interested in Felice; the boy was well-bred, proud, sincere; he must be played like a fish, not bludgeoned like an ox. It was a matter admirably suited to the methods of the Jesuits, who had recently been readmitted to the Romagna. They had already made some overtures, but so far the boy had disdainfully rejected them. Now, in view of this silly accident, the case was rather different; they had some kind of hold on him. Mastai talked the thing over with Orso Orsini in that sense, and they quickly reached agreement.

Felice, it suddenly transpired, was, after all, a plaster saint. His clerical teachers who had suffered so much at his hands vied with each other to extol his praises. He was "an angel in flesh and blood", "a chosen vessel", "always quiet and gentle and respectful, never in a temper, a future luminary of our Holy Church". He was devoted to his uncle, like whom "he held in abomination the impious enemies of the altar and the throne". He was full of a miraculous determination to forego his future wealth and become a Jesuit, and Domenico Spada, his trusted friend, had been a party to his secret. It mattered not that many had their doubts: that Felice's own father, on hearing of his change of heart, said "I should split my sides if he became a priest": or that the bereaved fiancée of Domenico Spada, sniffing coarsely, remarked "he would make a pretty monk, with those two sly eyes of his". By the end of the year Orso had somehow managed to extract Acts of Desistance from all of Spada's relatives, and sent them off in the same folder as the priests' certificates of character, antedated to before the accident, to the Governor of Imola.[2]

Away in the country at Borgo San Lorenzo the subject of

[1] Hales, *Pio Nono*, xiii.
[2] Luzio, *Biografico*, 32–5.

their deliberations spent the first month of his banishment galloping about on horseback, a riotous young pagan, quite unchecked. Inevitably, the day came when he tried to master an unmanageable steed; inevitably, he had a heavy fall. His recovery was lingering and dull: for weeks—much longer, he suspected, than was necessary—he was on his back; and when he was up and about again, all further field sports were forbidden him. He was not encouraged to do anything. After a time, out of sheer boredom, he began to notice the visitors who seemed to drop in with surprising frequency. They were, he observed, religious, and to his eyes bigoted; but they were very different from the bland, superior worthies who made free in his uncle's house. They were mentally alert; they talked to him frankly, man-to-man; despite himself, he found he looked forward to his discussions with them.

Another thing he slowly came to notice during his convalescence was that the daughter of the Allai family with whom he was staying, a girl of about his own age, besides being very pretty, took a sweet, shy interest in his welfare. It was pleasant to walk beside her, whiling away the tedious summer evenings. She was so light, so delicate, so warm, so fragrant; in her company he felt an exhilaration, a light-headedness he had not known before. They exchanged deep secrets; though she was never reproachful, he could see that his bitterness, his lack of religious feeling, made her sad; while for his part, though he knew he could not aspire to it himself, he was deeply moved by her decent, simple faith. For her sake, he started going to confession.

Early in the new year 1837, much softened in his outlook, he had to leave her and enter an Augustinian convent in Ravenna, pending the formal clearing of his name on which his uncle had insisted. The trial came on in February, ending in April, when he was declared innocent of murder but guilty of unintentional homicide, and was sentenced to six months' detention in the convent.

As a sign of his contrition, it was suggested that he should seek from the Pope a final dispensation of his crime so that he could enter a religious order. He complied with due humility, and while waiting for the Pope's decision was accorded a great deal of attention. Archbishop Falconieri, spiritual head of the northern provinces, spared a flattering amount of time to walk and talk with him. The envied banquets of the Contessa Caterina Rasponi, a small lady of prodigious wealth, were never complete without him. "Come here my little Jesuit," she would shriek as he appeared, and mincing across her drawing-room she fawned hideously upon him.[1] Yet, despite these blandishments, when left to himself he wandered in the pinewoods of Ravenna, or mused by Dante's tomb, not lost in the wonders of theology, but pondering problems of ballistics or of military manœuvres, dreaming of Italy united and free.

In December he was summoned to the Jesuit college at Forli to receive his absolution. The Jesuits knew exactly how to make their order sound attractive to him. They were forthright, matter-of-fact. They spoke like soldiers of the dangers of their calling; the hardships, the adventures of their work in India. They were, they said, fighters, thinkers, a free and equal brotherhood; and though purposely unobtrusive, they wielded more real power than the Pope himself.

Felice's uncle wrote to say that all was ready for him to enter the Society of Jesus at Chieri near Turin. He seemed so happy at the successful outcome of his negotiations that Felice felt he could not disobey without being churlish. During the long journey he was accompanied at intervals by young princes, and was welcomed everywhere by dukes and countesses. On arrival he was required to sign a book, giving in Latin his family, his politics, his reasons for joining, and his chosen field of labour. To the last question he put "India", trying to resign himself to a life of militant evangelism. It was no use. On receiving absolution his sense of vocation had unaccountably disappeared. Throughout his eighteen months of indoctrination, the only time he had experienced an emotion that might have been religious was with the girl at Borgo San Lorenzo; and even then, he felt, looking back on it, his motives had probably not been very sacred. After a week or two he said his leg was troubling him again, from his fall, and went to see a doctor. The doctor obligingly said the best cure would be for him to go to take cold plunges at a certain spa in the Romagna. That was good enough for Felice; at the beginning of 1838 he reappeared in Imola, to the rage of his uncle, to the pain of Bishop Mastai.

[1] Orsini, *Memoirs and Adventures*, 16.

The situation was most unsatisfactory. He was now eighteen, and as his guardian never tired of pointing out, the last few years spent in resistance to his wishes had been an utter waste of time. The atmosphere became so strained that Felice left his uncle's house and went to live with his father in Bologna, though remaining strictly under his uncle's tutelage. This arrangement was worse than ever. His father and his stepmother ignored him, whereas his uncle was no longer able to keep an eye on him. Felice wrote letters virtuously describing his professors and his books, so that the worthy man believed him to be studying philosophy and rhetoric. In fact he was doing nothing of the sort. Any form of study, he discovered, produced in him an unconquerable drowsiness. For a year he lived a life of listless dandyism, sauntering about the Bolognese picture galleries, lolling about in cafés with his friends. Fortunately he was not prone to vice, and his natural energy kept breaking through. He spent much time in counterfeit gymnasia improving his illegal sword and pistol play. Every morning he was up at dawn to see the Swiss troops on parade. He got to know some of the officers, who promised to find a place for him as a cadet in their military academy; but when he put the project to his uncle, it provoked a storm of wrath and indignation.

Felice finally began to realize that the right place for him was the University of Bologna. There, beneath the surface of its harmless erudition, pounded the great heart of liberalism; every strand of intrigue in the turbulent Romagna could be traced to that celebrated seat of learning. How, in his present state of idleness, could he ever make himself acceptable? Listening to his friends as they nonchalantly tossed their philosophic theories to and fro, his ignorance shamed him. He returned to Imola, and started studying in earnest: he was, he said, resolved upon the law as his career. Perceiving the change for the better, his uncle and the Bishop tried to send him to the College of Ecclesiastical Law at Rome, a proposal which he skilfully avoided.

A close observer would have seen that side by side with his intellectual pursuits he was continuing to train himself in the occult arts of a more desperate calling. His student pranks were exercises in impersonation and disguise. One of his uncle's friends, the old Canon of Bergullo, a passionate antiquarian, had collected with the greatest care a museum of worthless curios dug up in the neighbourhood of his parish, a foible fostered with glee by the youths of the district, who were not above burying old bits of crockery for him to find. Soon after the Canon had unearthed an especially fruitful cache, Felice, whom he had known since childhood, drove out from Imola in a carriage, dressed as a typical English *milord,* wearing enormous whiskers of the kind then recognized as the badge of irreproachable conservatism, with green spectacles, top hat, and a flowing traveller's cloak. He asked to see the collection, emitting startled foreign cries at the sight of each new specimen, and finally shot out an offer for the lot. The Canon, in whom mild avarice conflicted with the pride of ownership, stammered a far higher figure. They bargained for some time before Felice drove regretfully away, leaving the Canon to console himself for the lost deal with the thought of how much treasure he had saved for Italy.

Felice began the course of jurisprudence at the University of Bologna in 1840. In the intervals of his legal seminar he made full use of the opportunity to instruct himself in other useful fields. He acquired on his own account an excellent background in all the military sciences, mechanics, chemistry, physics, topography, mathematics, "without which nothing can be done especially in the matter of fortifications". He read Livy and Tacitus; Macchiavelli; Thiers' *French Revolution* and Napoleon's *Commentaries.* His mind became a whirlpool of excitement; the lays of Rome, the right of tyrannicide, the soldierly ideal, tears for those who had died in the cause of freedom, all combined to conjure fiery, extravagant schemes for the liberation of his country. "I saw in every youth a conspirator, in every man a hero." His fits of exaltation alternated with moods of loneliness and gloom, when he was torn between obedience to his family and the hard, almost impossible course he believed to be his duty. At one of these times he was gravely shocked by the unexpected death of his cousin, Cesare Salvigni, a popular, well-favoured young man who blew out his brains for no discoverable reason. Was not that also his way out? Felice wondered. Night after night he pored over Rousseau's novels, meditating suicide. It was the crisis of his life. Instead, at the age of twenty-two, he joined Young Italy.[1]

[1] Orsini, *Memoirs and Adventures,* 24.

CHAPTER TWO

Young Italy

I

YOUNG ITALY was the brain-child of Giuseppe Mazzini. Fourteen years older than Orsini, Mazzini was born in 1805 the son of a doctor and professor of anatomy at the University of Genoa. Until the restoration, Dr. Mazzini had been something of a liberal; but later, numbering the father of Queen Victoria among his patients, he gnarled into respectability, as professional men so often do. Mazzini's mother was a Jansenist, the furthest degree to the left permitted by the Catholic Church. One day, trotting beside her in the street, the boy ran off and flung his arms about the knees of a hairy and repulsive-looking tramp. "Love him well, ma'am," growled the beggar, leering vaguely at her; "he is one who will love the people."[1]

He was a weakly child with a tendency to spinal trouble, clever, silent and emotional. By the time he entered the University of Genoa at an unusually precocious age, he had already jettisoned the conservative tenets appropriate to his class. Already he was a sceptic, a republican, though of a mystical, not of a scientific bent. In 1821 he saw the defeated Carbonari trailing through Genoa on their way to exile, and fell into a dark depression. Needing something to worship, he began to worship sorrow. He commenced his lifelong custom of wearing black—in which he looked particularly well—in mourning for his country.

While at the University, Mazzini was as a model of the eternal student. Able, eager, inordinate, somewhat missish and opinionated, careless with his money, he was fond of late

[1] Rudman, *Italian Nationalism and English Letters*, 33.

hours, and coffee, and cigars, although in other ways he was abstemious. When he was not talking, or reading, he enjoyed a game of chess, a turn with the foils, an hour's strumming at his guitar, and falling mildly in love. He was especially given to solitary nocturnal rambles, a habit which caused the Governor of Genoa to warn his father that "the Government does not like young men of talent, the subject of whose musing is not known to them".[1] Nor was the Governor mistaken. Mazzini had founded a literary society for smuggling books into the city in defiance of the censorship.

In 1827 he graduated brilliantly as Doctor of Law, and devoted himself to conducting poor men's cases, without fee. With his friend Jacopo Ruffini he joined the Carbonari, but not finding their organization altogether to his liking, he soon made enemies, as much by his implacable integrity as by his serene, unhearkening assurance. He was betrayed to the Governor, and in November 1830 he was carried off to prison at Savona, a kindly jail on the Italian Riviera. He was not uncomfortable at Savona. He was lodged high up in a cell of which the grating gave a view of sea and sky, without contact with the earth. A greenfinch came to share his solitude. He was allowed books, and had ample opportunity for reflection.

The Carbonari, he decided, were not adequate to their task. Obscure, exclusive, and bound in by ritual, they had no message for the people as a whole. What was wanted was "an association simple in organization, positive in faith, direct in aim, open in purpose, to be recruited from the youth of the country". What, then, was the end in view? "Republican Italy, one and independent, with Rome for its capital." Unfortunately, deplorably, such an end envisaged bloodshed. Behind the despotisms that divided Italy stood Austria, and "you cannot *pray* Austria out of Italy".[2]

Mazzini's programme, though disarmingly concise, was very comprehensive. It confused the ideal with the politic, and tried to do too much at once. Italian unity, for instance, was still a distant dream. So great an historian as Sismondi thought it absurd to pretend that Italy had any special aptitude for being a nation. All the evidence supported the sensible protest of Maz-

[1] Gangulee (ed.), *Mazzini: Selected Writings*, 13.
[2] Griffith, *Mazzini: Prophet of Modern Europe*, 67–8.

zini's father: "There *are* no Italians; there are Genoese, Lombards, Tuscans, Neapolitans, etcetera."[1] Certainly, divided interests were an obvious drag on any concerted effort against Austria: but why could they not be overcome by some form of federation between the various states? Mazzini was adamant. Eventually a national war against Austria was a necessity, and until that time insurrections in the name of united Italy must be continuous. He went further: risings must be made by Italians only, without reliance on any foreign power. There was a world of moral earnestness in this; sacrifice was the supreme regenerative virtue; it would be good for the Italians to prove themselves a nation, and good for them to suffer in the process.

Again, if the main purpose was to oust the Austrians, why insist on republicanism, seeing that all the existing states of Italy were monarchies? From the point of view of Italy's resurgence there was much to be said for a working agreement with one or more of the less vicious princes, who would provide standing armies, ample treasuries, and ever-ready diplomatic corps. But Mazzini was a Genoese, and Genoa hated the Piedmontese monarchy which had usurped her proud republican tradition. For him, kings were the evil forces keeping Italy divided and enthralled. Even if constitutions were extorted from them, the fabric of the social order would remain unchanged. No final compromise was possible with monarchies; and least of all with the one best able to assist, the Kingdom of Piedmont.

More presumptuous still was Mazzini's claim to Rome. Rome to him was more than a city, she was a magic symbol. ROMA—AMOR—the very name was capable of magic anagram. Rome of the Caesars, Rome of the Popes: now dawned the spiritual, the conjoining, the Mazzinian era. "Why should not arise from a third Rome, the Rome of the Italian people, of which I seem to see the indications, a third and yet vaster unity, which, harmonizing earth and Heaven, Right and Duty, should speak, not to individuals, but to peoples, a word of Association, teaching to the free and equal their mission here below?"[2]

The difficulty was that another religion had presided from Rome for the best part of two millennia. The people of Italy

[1] Griffith, 47.
[2] *Ibid*, 65.

were not, by instinct or tradition, either united or republican; they were, on the other hand, Catholic. Credos apart, Catholicism was their way of life; such liberal opposition as the Church had hitherto encountered had recognized the Catholic climate, abided by its absolutes, argued within its terms of reference. Young Italy did not. It was no mere heresy, or disgust with Papal government; it was worse than atheism. It was a rival church, demanding to reign in the same capital; it was a direct invasion not only of the temporal but of the spiritual power. The odds were all in favour of the Papacy. In his struggle for republican unity Mazzini already had to overcome, apart from the natural Latin lethargy, all the forces of the existing civil order, and the commercial rivalries of the city states. Why additionally offend the only factor common to all Italians? Why, when for all practical purposes Florence would have made as good a seat of government as Rome?

In order to justify his antagonism to the Church, Mazzini had to rest his dogma upon a broad basis of philosophic principles. "We are not merely conspirators: we are believers,"[1] he proclaimed. He discerned in history a steady progress of mankind, an unfolding of a divine purpose, moving through individuals to nations, and from nations to humanity at large. Christianity had provided the ideal of individuality, an epoch which had found fulfilment in the Revolution and had since become outmoded. The second phase was now beginning, the phase of national association, wherein the exercise by each people of its own special genius would serve as a prologue to one great perfect brotherhood of man. The culminating sign would be an Italy reborn to lead mankind across its artificial boundaries; then, with all attendant scaffolding removed, the finished edifice of sovereignty would stand upon its primal foundations, God and the People.

The social tendencies of this creed may be described as those of the St. Simonians, from whom it had borrowed much, confounded with Mazzinian ethics. The march of the divine purpose conceded no rights, it only imposed a duty. It followed that all theories of natural rights, in particular communism and socialism, looked in the wrong direction, back to the sterile beginning instead of up to the fulgent end. Economics as a whole were

[1] Griffith, 80.

distastefully materialistic, putting well-being and self-interest before moral obligation. Nevertheless Democracy figured largely in the canon, though defined in a covert, authoritarian sense as "the progress of all through all under the leading of the best and wisest".[1] The aim of government must be the levelling of class distinctions, the merging of all divisions into one organic entity, the People.

When at the age of twenty-five Mazzini left the fortress of Savona, the doctrine of Young Italy was complete. If its parts did not exactly fit together, its slogans were compelling. It had been designed not as a scholarly exposition but as an invocation to a predetermined course of action. Explicit and yet vague, simple and yet pretentious, disciplined, abandoned, atavistic and progessive all at once, as a revolutionary manifesto it was sublime. All it now lacked were its martyrs and apostles, and the hagiolatry of a religion. He went to Marseilles, where he found a number of fellow-exiles in hiding after the affair of 1831. As though from force of habit they had formed a Carbonarist lodge, a regular chip of the old block. Mazzini would have none of it; very soon they all had joined Young Italy.

The organization of Young Italy avoided the errors of its predecessors. There was a single oath of fealty. Its flag was a tricolour of red, white and green, the old masonic colours conspicuous since the struggle against Napoleon in 1796. The ritual was reduced to the minimum required for recognition—a special handclasp, a paper cut-out of peculiar shape, which were altered every three months. The entrance fee was small; members contributed according to their means, the only general levy being a businesslike one, a musket and fifty rounds. Mazzini, and the Central Committee at Marseilles, communicated with local committees in the Italian cities, who in turn were in touch with the members, divided into Initiators and Initiated. Of these, the Initiators, experienced prudent men, were entrusted with the vital responsibility of recruitment. Within six months, Young Italy, working through the Ruffini brothers at Genoa, riddled Piedmont. In a year it pervaded the entire peninsula, the mountain lakes, the pine woods, the olive groves and vineyards, the marshy lowlands, the shimmering seaboard, the towns, the lonely hostelries on white dusty roads, the villages perched high

[1] Griffith, 177.

between the rocks: in the cathedrals, uncelestial murmurings rose from the confessionals.

Mazzini was a journalist of considerable power, and in 1832 the organ of the party, *La Giovine Italia*, began to appear, two-thirds of which he wrote himself. Italian vessels sailing from Marseilles carried the word to every port in Italy. Unpacked in wharfside warehouses, copied in clandestine printing presses, the tracts were distributed in crates of fish or barrels of pumice stone, and were bought in markets by Initiators who had been warned to watch for containers bearing certain figures. Nothing could stop its progress. Before long, Louis Napoleon was offering contributions; and Metternich, into whose hands a copy fell, thoughtfully ordered the back numbers.

Beside Mazzini stood his muse and mistress, Giuditta Sidoli, the young widow of an exiled Carbonaro. She it was who had first unfurled the tricolour in the central provinces; according to her police record she was "beautiful and extremely dangerous".[1] A raven-haired, rather strapping Milanese, she made short work of Mazzini's black depressions and kept him to the point. Their baby died, and soon she had to leave him to return to her other children in Italy, but she lingered in his memory as Italia incarnate, a brave and lovely woman with a melancholy smile. Her place as his support was taken by a god-like creature, drawn to Mazzini by the scent of battle. Known as "Borel" (for they all had *noms de guerre*) he was a youthful, foursquare figure with a seafarer's gait, who spoke in a calm low voice. He had a leonine head, a flowing mane of chestnut-gold, and fiery dark blue eyes. In the presence of such beauty, who noticed, or who cared, if those heroic features carried a touch of petulant vanity, if in those eyes a glaze of stupidity could sometimes be detected; if, as d'Azeglio said, "Garibaldi had a heart of gold but the brains of an ox"?[2]

The first blow struck by Young Italy was directed not against the foreign enemy, but against the Kingdom of Piedmont, where the accession of Charles Albert seemed to threaten Mazzini's control of the Italian cause. Without doubt, Charles Albert had some liberal elements; as a young prince, he had sided with the

[1] Griffith, 81. See also Hales, *Mazzini and the Secret Societies*, 72, 89–95, 218–20.

[2] Bolton King, II, 31.

Carbonari in 1821. It might be that he would decide to grant a constitution, and lead a national crusade against the Austrians; in that case, what would become of the republican nature of the movement? Without hesitation, Mazzini published a strong appeal to him to do so. Charles Albert was enraged. Certainly, like all the Piedmontese, he was a soldier, and wanted war with Austria in his own good time, but only for the greater glory of Piedmont. Meanwhile, he was a pious Catholic, the respected head of a despotic royal house; he had no use for the schemes of a fractious Genoese. He replied by a sentence of banishment for life.

Mazzini was very much relieved, since his appeal had really been an ultimatum. He had arranged for a rising, leading to a general war, to start at Genoa in April 1833. But Charles Albert was prepared; there were mass arrests, and flight. Jacopo Ruffini, confronted with a forged list of his confederates, tore his throat open with a strip of metal from the door of his cell, and scrawled on the wall with his dying blood, "Behold my answer. To my brothers the vendetta."[1] Mazzini was sentenced to death, *in absentia.*

He moved to Geneva, whence, in February, he led an invasion of Savoy. It failed. Mazzini, succumbing to the wintry humours of the Alps, was brought back to the neighbourhood of Geneva on a stretcher. Bitterness and recrimination started, but he would not give up. Cheated of Italy for the moment, he lectured to Poles, Hungarians and Germans about Young Europe. Finding the Swiss disgracefully backward in their nasty little Cantons, he founded a Young Switzerland. For this he was at last expelled from Switzerland, and went to London in January 1837.

He took lodgings at 24 Goodge Street, Tottenham Court Road, an uninspiring neighbourhood. He was almost penniless. English cooking, English ways, depressed and worried him. He fell out with his friends. It was all Mazzini's fault, they said: his dogmatism, his arrogance, his elaboration of irrelevant detail caused him invariably to miss the wood for the trees. He grew very disconsolate, and there was nothing about the state of Italy to comfort him. The Austrians were once more ascendant; the old tyrannies were more secure than ever; in Modena Duke Francis was saying: "God has made Hell, and the godliest prince is he who makes the hangman his prime

[1] Griffith, 87.

minister."[1] Young Italy was for the time being dead. Perhaps his friends were right. "Perhaps I had been led, not by an Idea, but by *my* idea; by the pride of my *own* conception—an intellectual egoism. . . . I felt a criminal. . . . How many mothers had I caused to weep!"[2]

Despair refined Mazzini's mettle. Poet, and puritan, penitent and autocrat, schemer and idealist, he reconciled within himself all the normally conflicting symptoms of fanaticism. Though his philosophy was leaky, his conspiracies inept, he acquired the supreme power of infecting others with his own enthusiasm. According to William Roscoe Thayer, he became "the greatest individual moral force in Europe during the nineteenth century".[3]

His fortunes improved. His mother came to his rescue with money and supplies in bulk—barrels of oil, casks of vinegar, whole cheeses, macaroni and mortadella; he was able to afford Cuban cigars at ten for a shilling. He began to earn money by his writings. Panizzi, at the British Museum, found work for him. John Stuart Mill listened gravely to him, searching for his own measure of agreement, and then suggested that Mazzini might care to write some articles for his *London and Westminster Review*. Mazzini also met Carlyle with whom, in spite of many differences, he was at one about duty, and not happiness, being the end of life. "Happiness! Happiness!" roared Carlyle, pacing up and down the room, shaking his grey locks in disapproval. "The fools ought to be chained up! Man is born to work, not to enjoy . . ." When at last he paused for breath he fixed his visitor with a furious eye. "You! You have not succeeded yet because you talk too much!"[4]

Mazzini's charm, animated and naïf, was irresistible. Jane Carlyle was fascinated by the quaintness of his speech, and equally dismayed by the childish intensity with which he pursued his plots and principles. "I never saw a mortal man who so completely makes himself into minced meat for the universe,"[5] she cried. She mothered him. She showed him round

[1] Griffith, 115.
[2] Gangulee, 59.
[3] Rudman, 31.
[4] *Ibid.*, 50.
[5] Bliss (ed.), *Jane Welsh Carlyle*, 119.

London, took him up to the dome of St. Paul's and into Madame Tussaud's; she moved his lodgings nearer to her home, in Chelsea; through her husband she arranged for Mazzini to give Italian lessons to the hated Lady Harriet Baring. Yet the more he had, the more he gave away. Beggars were always at his door, and he had his Causes—in 1840 he started an Italian Working Men's Association, and a year later an Italian Ragged School. Above all, there was always the Fund, for private revolutions are expensive.

In Italy the movement he had founded managed somehow to get along without him: his influence was indefinable, but ever growing. From time to time word came of Ugo Bassi, a saintly Barnabite friar, whose migrant sermons in the open air were drawing audiences larger than could be explained by pure doctrinal fervour. In the summer of 1843 Mazzini was ready to liberate the whole of Europe at a single blow. Action would start in Sicily, where perpetual discontent was aggravated by the loss of 40,000 lives from cholera in Palermo alone. Nicholas Fabrizi, one of his right-hand men, was in Malta preparing to descend on Naples, whereupon a supporting movement in the Romagna under Count Livy Zambeccari would spread to Lombardy, Tuscany and Piedmont. Exiled volunteers would come from Corsica and Spain. Garibaldi, at present in South America, would land at Genoa with his Montevidean redshirts. There would be a rising in Poland, another at Barcelona. Hungary would revolt. The disaffected Slavs in the Imperial Army would mutiny. Switzerland would dissolve her cantons. Russia would be embroiled with Turkey. French liberals would prevent their government from interfering. Britain would be sympathetic. America would send mailbags full of Protestant goodwill and money.

The event was disappointing. The patriots, unwilling to compromise themselves, each waited for the next move. The signal from Naples never came. In the Romagna, Zambeccari's rising paled away. Colonel Ribotti, arriving from Spain with a handful of exiles, persuaded some two hundred Bolognese to follow him in an attempt to seize Amat the Cardinal Legate, Archbishop Falconieri of Ravenna, and Bishop Mastai Ferretti, all assembled in a house near Imola. Cardinal Lambruschini, who had succeeded the milder Bernetti as Papal Secretary of State, reacted with the utmost violence. Roving military commissions were set up. Twenty-one death sentences were passed, and over fifty life sentences to the galleys were imposed. Centurions and Sanfedists did as they pleased: the activities of the *sbirri* reached their zenith. To escape the Papal wrath, one Muratori led a band of desperadoes up into the mountains. Chaos and terror reigned throughout that year, and on through 1844.

There was an epilogue of sad futility. Attilio and Emilio Bandiera, young Venetian officers in the Austrian navy, resolved under Mazzinian influence to make a private invasion of southern Italy. Deserting their ships, they fled to Corfu, where they recruited other desperate spirits, and in June 1844 the party sailed for Calabria in a fishing boat. Landing at dusk, they flung themselves down to kiss the sunbaked earth, crying ecstatically, "This is our fatherland! Thou hast given us life. We spend it for thee!" Their letters to Mazzini had been opened by the Home Office in London. Next morning they were rounded up by King Bomba's troops, and soon afterwards nine of them were shot.

II

In the name of God and of Italy—
In the name of all the martyrs of the holy Italian cause who have fallen beneath foreign and domestic tyranny—
By the duties which bind me to the land wherein God has placed me, and to the brothers whom God has given me. . . .
By the memory of our former greatness, and the sense of our present degradation
I, Felice Orsini,
Believing in the mission entrusted by God to Italy . . . give my name to Young Italy, and swear:—
To dedicate myself wholly and for ever to endeavour with them to constitute Italy
ONE, FREE, INDEPENDENT, REPUBLICAN NATION
To promote by every means in my power the education of my Italian brothers towards the aim of Young Italy. . . .
To assist my brothers of the association both by action and by counsel—
NOW AND FOR EVER[1]

[1] Frost, *Secret Societies*, II, 147–8. Gangulee, 132–3.

The Jesuits had been quite right about Orsini. He was cut out to be a soldier. As a child he had listened enthralled to his father's stories of the Moscow expedition. As a boy, he had run away to join the French in Ancona. As a student, he had tried to join the Papal Swiss. All his games, his exercise, had been in military affairs. A servant of his Aunt Lucrezia at Meldola remembered in her old age how he used to sit at table deploying armies with his forks and spoons. Even his detestation of the Austrian oppressors melted easily into admiration for the trim and glitter of their ceremonial. He had a soldierly mistrust of politics. He had a soldier's rigid and aggressive honour. All he needed, to be capable of fierce unswerving loyalty, was a soldier's forthright creed. In Young Italy he found what he required.

During the preparations for Zambeccari's rising at Bologna, he was still living in his father's house there, and his new activities did not escape his father's expert eye. Apart from doubts about the soundness of Mazzini's plans, Andrea Orsini felt that his days as a conspirator were over; he wanted to spend his later years in the bosom of his second family. But the police still had a hold on him. He knew very well that the good conduct of his son was the chief condition of his own liberty. He therefore joined forces with his brother Orso in the attempt to keep the lad in check.

His son found the consequent restrictions on his liberty extremely irksome. He was allowed no money; he was forced to account for every second of his day; he was confined to the house under the hostile supervision of his stepmother. In December 1842, unable to stand it any longer, he once again set off to seek his fortune as a simple soldier on a foreign field, in the rebellion about to break out at Barcelona: but his father warned the Cardinal Legate, with the result that he was stopped at Florence, shortly before Barcelona was pounded into submission.

Begging pardon for his "over-sensitive and irascible nature",[1] he returned to his uncle at Imola, where it was decided that he should go back to Bologna to sit for his law degree. At dawn on the day of his departure, his uncle from his sickbed grasped his hand and pronounced a homily. "Felice! Study, but

[1] Ghisalberti, *Lettere di Felice Orsini*, 7.

remain quiet. . . . Love your country, but after a proper fashion; love her to do her good and not to cause her sorrow,—where there is great cry there is little wool. . . . You are used by the Liberal chiefs for their own ends; they will get the honour, you the blows. Have the fear of God before your eyes. . . . For the future try to render my existence more tranquil. I know every step you take." Orsini, his heart full of the dark mischief brewing in Bologna, managed to answer, "Do not doubt me." The old man studied him intently; then with a sigh, turning his face to the wall, he said, "I fear those eyes of yours."[1]

During the next few months Orsini worked hard and in June 1843 emerged from his baccalaureate as a Doctor of Law with three university diplomas to his credit. His professor, the distinguished Dr. Vecchietti, later gave the opinion that had he persisted at the bar he would have become one of the foremost advocates in Italy—a technical judgment, not invalidated by the fact that Dr. Vecchietti himself had been deeply involved in the insurrection of 1831, and that his entire class was a hotbed of sedition.

Dr. Vecchietti's most brilliant student, Cesare Baccarini, and Eusebio Barbetti an accountant engaged to Baccarini's sister; Ulisse Bandera, Dr. Felice Orsini—these and others called each other Cousin, wrote letters with mysterious hidden meanings, met privately in churches, or over spaghetti in the *Locanda della Posta* away at Lugo, or in the piazzas of hill-top villages on market days. Felice had come into his own. On holidays, he warned his family, instructing them about the hours for meals, he might be out till eleven or twelve o'clock at night: in any case he would use the secret stairway, and carried his own keys. His father, unable to resist the infectious lure despite himself, became mixed up in it as well. That summer of 1843 they saw, at Imola, Ribotti come and go; at Bologna they watched the cannon drawn up outside the palace of the Papal Legate to turn back Count Livy Zambeccari. They heard rumours of Muratori in the mountains. When all was over, having recently made the acquaintance of the Fabrizis of Modena, the young Orsini made bold to write his scathing criticisms, together with sweeping, bloody proposals for the future, in the form of a long essay addressed to their fabulous

[1] Orsini, *Memoirs and Adventures*, 25.

brother at Malta, Nicholas Fabrizi, the intimate of the Chief, Mazzini.

In the midst of the general excitement Orsini fell, rather offhandedly, in love. It was not an easy courtship. From the point of view of the girl's parents, conspiracy was not a settled calling, while his obvious preoccupation made him an unconvincing suitor. The crash came quickly. On the last day of April 1844, going to supper at the house of his intended, he felt a "sad presentiment"—as well he might. His friend Eusebio Barbetti had been arrested during the previous October, and in Barbetti's lodgings there were certain portions of his letter to Fabrizi, which there had been no time to burn. These, he now had reason to suspect, had been discovered; though fortunately, he tried to reassure himself, they were unsigned. He had no heart that evening for tender glances or for family chat; the most exquisite *polenta* stuck like sawdust in his throat. He excused himself and went home early; his girl and her parents thought his manner very odd.

At three o'clock the following morning his father's door echoed to peremptory thuds. Colonel Freddi of the Papal gendarmes entered importantly with a platoon of men who immediately started to ransack the house. After they had searched for eight hours without finding anything, at a nod, the inevitable chains came out. To a chorus of convulsive sobs, to the imprecations of his stepmother and her children, Orsini and his father were led away to the local jail of San Giovanni in Monte, where they were separated, and where Orsini first became distastefully aware of the peculiar rancid smell of prisons.

Two days later he was taken, after dark, to the jailor's room, where he found himself in the presence of two persons. One of them he recognized by his lean pale face as the Prosecutor to the Military Commission; the other, fussing with some papers, was the secretary. The Prosecutor stared at Orsini for some time in silence, his beady eyes glittering in the light of a single candle. The questioning began. Orsini's answers were unsatisfactory.

"You deny all, then," said the Prosecutor, setting his finger tips together. "You wish to be your own ruin; poor young man, I pity you. You are in the flower of youth; twenty-one of your companions have been condemned to death; you will be the twenty-second. But let us go forward." Orsini was asked about the Fabrizi letter found in Barbetti's rooms; he acknowledged his handwriting, but said he had found the paper in the street, and copied it. The Prosecutor gave a snort. "You will ruin yourself," he said again.[1]

After a few days Orsini was taken away in a closed carriage to an unknown destination, handcuffed to another prisoner. Peeping through the crack of the blind, he saw that they passed through Imola; beneath the bellies of the horses of the escort, he watched as they passed the school, and his uncle's house; he began to wish that he had heeded his uncle's warning. At Pesaro, locked in a stifling solitary cell, he heard a great uproar and a clattering of chains. By judicious rapping on the wall he found out that it concerned the twenty-one: seven had been shot in the back; the rest were on their way to the galleys *a chiodo*—to be chained to the wall for life. In the habit of his countrymen he sang to keep his spirits up; but suddenly his strength would leave him, and he would fall upon his pallet.

In July 1844 he was brought, with his father, to the Papal fortress of San Leo. San Leo was a tenth-century castle, perched on top of a mountain opposite the ancient city-republic of San Marino. The infamous Count Cagliostro had been imprisoned there in the eighteenth century; it was now used for the worst political offenders, or for important prisoners awaiting trial. In company with twenty-four young men from nearby Rimini they were housed in the main dungeon called the *Spico*. Families were allowed to visit, and to while away the tedium of captivity, Orsini gave rein to his artistic impulses, depicting in an excellent pencil sketch the wife and children of one of his cellmates, Andrea Borzatti, imploring Providence to set him free.

At San Leo, the view was marvellous and the air like wine, but with winter approaching the cold became intense. Orsini's father succumbed to a severe attack of ague combined with chronic constipation, and had to be moved to a private cell to undergo a course of purges. Having obtained permission to correspond with his brother Orso, Andrea Orsini, requested that warm clothes should be sent for both of them, and made financial arrangements to cover their confinement. Felice also

[1] Orsini, *Memorie politiche*, 40–1.

wrote, apologizing for the trouble he had brought upon his aunt and uncle, and asking for his law books, since "the romances and other empty stories which the Governor offers me are useless".[1]

The Governor was very correct, and disposed to lenience. He was another ex-Napoleonic officer, and there was some suspicion that he had been given the fortress of San Leo because of its remoteness and impregnability, to keep him out of mischief. There were tears in his eyes when he broke the news of the execution of the Bandieras. Orsini concluded that most of their enemies were like the Governor. It was imperative to strike a lofty note, to show no sign of cringing, to scorn them through their better consciences. He wrote a letter to the Military Commission at Bologna, demanding the immediate hearing of his case, and proclaiming that he had done nothing which either he or they should look upon as shameful: he had only done his duty as a patriot and citizen.

His companions had urged him that his attitude was foolish. They proved to have been right. The Governor's geniality disappeared when he unearthed a plan to escape by bribing the soldiers of the garrison, and he clapped Orsini into solitary detention. At the end of November when the prisoners were removed to Rome for trial, Orsini was again separated from his father who, because of his poor health, was kept at San Leo for another month.

For seventeen days they travelled in an open cart, shackled together in sixes, verminous and half-frozen. Once an hour the guards came up and tugged at the chains, ostensibly to make sure that they had not been tampered with, but in reality because they thus produced an excruciating wrench upon the wrist of each man in turn. At night they were lodged in local jails. At one place Orsini found himself in a cell with two condemned murderers, coarse, red-haired, and horribly depraved. They boasted lustfully of how they had broken into a peasant's cottage, killed the peasant, dragged his young daughter from her bed, raped and then slain her on her father's body. Orsini could not sleep: "for the first and last time in my life," he admits, "I felt something akin to fear."[2] Similar

[1] Paolo Mastri, *Felice Orsini nel Forte di San Leo.*
[2] Orsini, *Memoirs and Adventures*, 34.

experiences began to tell upon the minds of his companions. At the next halt, where a crowd had gathered to watch them come clanking out of prison and stumble into their waggon, they moved with downcast eyes as though in disgrace and shame. It would not do. Orsini cried out boldly, "What are you afraid of? Are we thieves?" The heads came up; the line went forward with a firm defiant gaze.

They came in sight of the seven hills of Rome, and Orsini gained his first view of the eternal city crowned by the great dome of St. Peter's. Approaching from the north, they were not, as political prisoners, allowed to enter by the People's Gate. They made a detour to the west, through the Porta Angelica, arriving in the Piazza of St. Peter's beneath the windows of the Vatican. Orsini was lodged in the secret dungeons of St. Matthew on the banks of the Tiber, where he joined several of his friends, pale and haggard, some of them already wearing the two-coloured uniform of the galleys. A few days after his arrival it was Christmas, and the congregation of the Holy Heart of Jesus came to dispense their annual charity; Orsini had to stand in the passage, cap in hand, and thank them for their penitential coins. His cell was deep and damp; no gleam of sunlight ever reached it. It was immediately below the *Conforteria*, or room where the condemned received the final sacrament before their execution. One night he heard a restless pacing up and down above his head. At dawn the pacing stopped, and later a bloody guillotine was carried away outside his window. He learnt that two men had been beheaded. Although it was not for political offences, it was a far from reassuring spectacle.

Meanwhile his uncle Orso, once he got over his dismay at finding that Felice was not, as he had hoped, diligently pursuing his studies at Bologna, had exerted every influence in his behalf. He had managed to get the case transferred from the Military Commission to the Sacra Consulta at Rome, a clerical court which was supposed to be less savage. He had also retained the services of the advocate Dionisi, one of the most expensive counsel in the Papal *curia*. Dionisi said it would be best to be quite frank. "Your case is a bad one, a very bad one; it is better that you confess everything."[1] Orsini denied that he had

[1] Orsini, *Memorie politiche*, 51.

anything to confess, whereupon the great advocate threw up his hands in consternation: "Well, if you will go to destruction, you may go your own way." Orsini was able none the less to find out much about his fate from Dionisi. The sentences, he gathered, were already settled: the object of the trials was merely to collect sufficient evidence to give them an appearance of legality. He was relieved to hear that his father was to be released as a much-needed example of Papal clemency. He himself would go to the galleys for life—to be fastened by a chain a yard long to the foetid dungeon walls of Civitavecchia. On the day of the trial Eusebio Barbetti whispered to him that it was senseless for them both to suffer for his, Barbetti's, carelessness. As he was the more deeply compromised, and as Orsini was the younger man, he would take all upon himself. It made no difference. One by one they were thrust into the presence of half a dozen Monsignori. Orsini was faced with a most damaging general charge of "conspiracy against all the governments of Italy", and his counsel Dionisi made it plain that he was stubborn and uncooperative. They all received the expected sentence, all save one, who, having been used to some extent in evidence, was let off with three years.

Escape was now more necessary than ever. As the gratings of the cells were at ground level, it did not appear impossible. The patrolling sentries were bought over; saws for the bars were obtained from the Committee of Young Italy in Rome; a rescue ship was sent from Leghorn. Unfortunately the bars took longer than had been expected, and before they were ready the guards were changed. After being forced to attend the observances appropriate to Easter, the prisoners were hurried away to Civita Castellana, there to wait until death created sufficient vacancies in the galleys of Civitavecchia.

Civita Castellana was a mediaeval fortress, whose towering parapets and rocky ledges had rendered it a perfect summer villa for the horrifying Borgia Pope Alexander VI. Its audience chamber, now the prison hospital, was still adorned with priceless frescoes, all more or less obscene. The main building consisted of an open courtyard surrounded by two arcaded cloisters one above the other, leading to the cells. The hundred and twenty inmates, long-term convicts, were demoralized and mean; the Commandant seemed to encourage their dissensions.

Orsini organized a prisoners' committee to resolve disputes, to criticize the food, and to provide instruction for the ignorant. It was no sinecure. Intervening in a quarrel, he was set upon by six contestants, armed with jagged weapons made in the prison workshop, and was wounded many times, though not before he had grabbed the chief aggressor by the throat and almost strangled him. His wounds were dressed by a fellow prisoner, a doctor, who told him that he owed his life to his stout leather belt which had been cut in two. Next morning Eusebio Barbetti had a violent altercation with the assailants, resulting in their removal to another prison, after they had pleaded forgiveness from Orsini at his bedside.

When they had been a year at Civita Castellana, the Commandant received instructions to begin sending his charges in batches to the galleys, but he dared not do it openly. Two by two he called them out for medical examination, and those so called were seen no more. His tactics became known; there was a prison riot, subdued under threat of cannon trained upon the courtyard. Orsini, as head of the committee, went forward to parley through the railings with the Commandant; uselessly, for he was compelled to yield on every point. Next day, sixty of his companions were chained and taken off to Civitavecchia; three weeks later it was learned that ten of them had died. There now seemed to be no further hope of avoiding the same living death.*

Desperate plans for escape were once more in the air, when redemption came quite unexpectedly. One day, prison rumour spread the news that Gregory XVI was dead. From cell to cell all round the courtyard, a plaintive chant was taken up, a mocking dirge to speed the spirit of the Pope from this world to Eternity. The warders, rattling their keys in the locks, entered demanding the cause of the disturbance. They were received in silence, with obsequious bows.

Every day the guns on the battlements were heard firing salutes to Cardinals passing on their way to the electoral conclave. The wildest stories went about, until at last the Commandant appeared in the upper cloister and scattered copies of a leaflet to the captives assembled down below, who scrabbled for them

* Eusebio Barbetti died two years later, in 1848, his health having been undermined by his imprisonment.

incredulously, too stunned to make a sound. The most impossible report of all was true. They were to be released. The new Pope was Mastai Ferretti, Bishop of Imola; and his first act was to pardon all political offenders. The Commandant's features bore a smile of grim contempt. "Cry Hurrah!" he ordered them.

They were required to sign a paper, acknowledging their former guilt, and promising never again to resist the Pope, "never in any manner to abuse this act of his Sovereign mercy". They did not hesitate to sign. Conspire against good Pio Nono? What an idea! That evening they were allowed to hold a banquet at their own expense. The cells were opened, the fortress was festooned with lamps; they dragged their beds and chairs and tables out into the middle of the courtyard, where they kindled an enormous bonfire which blazed all through the night. There was singing of arias from the operas, there was dancing to accordions and guitars. Soldiers and prisoners wept and embraced each other. And, as the sparks soared up into the summer sky, cheer upon cheer rang out: "*Viva l'Italia!*"

III

On 15 June 1846, a twist of smoke mounting from the Quirinal announced to the expectant multitude that the Cardinals had failed to agree upon the election of a Pope. There were groans and execrations. To the Cardinals it was evident that the people, after fifteen years of forcible misrule by Gregory XVI and his terrible counsellor Lambruschini, were in a dangerous mood. The instinct of the Cardinals was to keep the rate of concession as low as possible. After hasty compromise it was announced that the finger of God had lighted upon Mastai Ferretti, Bishop of Imola.

No one was more amazed than Mastai, who had been acting as a teller of the votes. In truth, his amazement was excessive. During his time at Imola his moderation and good sense had averted many clashes. Moreover he had made friends with the aristocratic, up-to-date Count Giuseppe Pasolini and his charming wife Antonietta. It had become his habit to visit their sunny villa, and to listen to her melodious voice reading aloud the recent important works of the *avant-garde*. Among these was Gioberti's *Primacy*. Frankly admitting dissatisfaction with the present state of things, and yet rejecting the extravagant pretensions of Young Italy, Gioberti pictured a regenerate Italy safely built upon the historical traditions of the old. He looked towards a federation of the existing states under the presidency of an enlightened Pope. The Austrians were to be expelled. All the princes were to undergo a change of heart, and constitutions were to be freely granted. Although Gioberti did not say exactly how these wonders were to come about, he did depict the sort of Italy which all respectable Italians wished to see. "It was," says Bolton King, "a safe book; the timid, the devotees, the priests found in it palatable doctrine, that reconciled patriotism and prejudice. The clergy were won by its Catholic tone; the nationalist statesmen by its praise of the Savoy princes."[1]

Mastai entered on his high office as Pius IX with shrinking and reluctance, but there was no hesitation in his course of action. Much of the Gregorian repression vanished almost overnight. A month to the day after his election he granted his amnesty to all political prisoners in the Papal States. Soon afterwards the streets of Rome began to fizz and flare triumphantly in recently forbidden gaslight. A commission on railways was set up, and a gold medal offered for the best projected line across the Apennines. The Customs were standardized; Scientific Congresses were allowed freedom of meeting and debate. Habeas Corpus was introduced, and the Pope in person visited the prisons. A new Press Law was passed, and within a year nearly a hundred newspapers had sprung up in Rome alone. In October 1847 these practical advances were consecrated to liberalism by the creation of a Consulta, an elective assembly of the laity with limited powers to advise the clerical executive.

Pio Nono's popularity soared beyond formal adulation to a level of truly filial trust and love. "Applauding thousands followed him through the streets: . . . torchlight processions would march to the Quirinal in the warm summer nights, and the Pope from his balcony would bless the kneeling multitude. Hymns were written to him. . . . All men bowed before the

[1] Bolton King, I, 155.

conception of a reforming Pope; and when the amnestied exiles crowded to receive the sacraments, it seemed a symbol of the dawning time, when liberty and social redemption would go hand in hand with religion and moral reform."[1]

Yet below the surface it was not so sunny. In the first place, the conciliatory measures angered the old protectors of the Papacy. Metternich made no secret of his displeasure: the accession of Pio Nono was "the greatest misfortune of the age".[2] "The spectre has assumed a body in the visible Head of the Church. . . . Warm of heart and weak of intellect . . . he will be driven out of Rome. . . . A *liberal* Pope is not a possibility."[3] Worse, many of the Cardinals shared the Austrian view. Jesuits, Sanfedists, Centurions, and the entire civil administration, enlisted and trained in reaction, refused to carry out a policy which to them seemed suicidal; they sulkily enhanced their habitual inefficiency so as to hinder the progress of reform.

In consequence the new Pope, for all his personal favour, could not keep up with popular expectations. Each concession, instead of being welcomed as a single blessing, was engineered by stump orators into a demand for more. Conspicuous among the agitators was a fat, voluble horse-dealer and wine-carter known as Ciceruacchio, a vulgar fellow but jovial and good-natured, well-liked by the slum dwellers in the Trastevere, whom he filled with tales of Jesuit plots and Curial intransigeance. On the Pope's birthday in December 1847 the attentions of the crowd were so boisterous and pressing, and the greetings of Ciceruacchio, who had just presented a demand for thirty-five additional reforms, so blatant, that the good man, sensing the menace underlying the enthusiasm, fainted in his carriage.

During the summer things had been taken a stage further. Reacting strongly to the creation of Civic Guards, and determined to teach the reforming Pope a lesson, the Austrians had come south across the Po and occupied the Papal city of Ferrara. It was a mistaken move. The Pope's Romagnuol temper blazed as hot as that of any of his subjects. He sought, and readily obtained, a promise of protection from Charles Albert, the most powerful

[1] Bolton King, I, 173.
[2] *Ibid.*, 182.
[3] Hales, *Pio Nono*, 67–8.

prince in Italy, with his aggressive little kingdom of Piedmont and its convenient army. As was required of him, Charles Albert had become a valiant and able soldier; but off parade he was a morose, undecided, conscience-stricken individual living principally on spinach and potatoes. Under the guidance of his local philosophers, Cesare Balbo and d'Azeglio, his policy looked forward to one thing only, a military expansion by Piedmont at the expense of Austrian Lombardy. The Pope's appeal encouraged him: he struck a medal showing the lion of Piedmont standing over a prostrate Austrian eagle, above the words, "I await my destiny".[1]

Mazzini also was awaiting his destiny. The Ferrara episode gave him an opportunity to challenge the Pope, as once before he had challenged Charles Albert his other rival, to set himself at the head of the Italian national forces for the liberation of the country. This highfalutin document, flung into Pio Nono's carriage, was received with characteristic pleasantry: "My God, they want to make a Napoleon out of me, who am only a poor country parson."[2]

All the same, the incident caused Pio Nono to take stock of his position. His well-intended efforts to make necessary reforms within his own dominions had set the whole peninsula alight. Everything was topsy-turvy. Liberalism, hitherto the enemy of the temporal power, was now its champion; Austria, its natural supporter, had turned into its aggressor. The Pope, so long the stern exponent of submission, had become a revolutionary Pied Piper, drawing together all brands of patriotic feeling, forgetful of their differences at the magic of his call. It was inevitably now his lot to lead, as an Italian potentate, a crusade against a foe which was, in his pontifical capacity, his faithful Austrian flock. Miserable in the midst of adoration, too late he pondered Metternich's warning: "He will be driven out of Rome. . . . A *liberal* Pope is not a possibility."

[1] Bolton King, I, 166.
[2] *Ibid.*, 171.

IV

Orsini was a loyal member of Young Italy. Although he concerned himself no more with the higher flights of Mazzinian theory than a soldier bothers about the General Intention of his superiors, he understood his daily orders well enough. He knew that the Pope's Indulgence was not to be permitted to become the source of any sense of obligation beyond the strict terms of his promise. Accordingly, on his release from Civita Castellana in July 1846 he did not, like many others, hasten to make peace with the Church and spread the fame of his deliverer. Instead, he went limping home to Imola. He found there no shining eyes of love waiting to make the jailbird feel a martyr. It is true that the girls of Imola flung wide their windows or came running to their doors to see Felice Orsini, who had long been given up for lost, but he could not help thinking that the flutter was largely due to ghoulish curiosity. They could not in any case make up for his faithless young lady of Bologna, who had apparently decided to seek a less exacting marriage.

It was a melancholy fatted calf with which his uncle greeted him. An old man now, Orso still had not recovered from the shock of learning that his nephew was serving a life sentence in a Papal dungeon, and his showers of tears and gales of laughter were punctuated with reproaches. To Orsini the old house seemed to reek of emptiness and superannuation. His brother Leonidas was ill with worry. A dust sheet wrapped about a familiar bust informed him silently that his former protector Count Hercules Faella was now dead. And his aunt? His aunt, too, was dead. Shortly after his arrest his Doctorate of Law had been rescinded, and the shame of it all had been too much for her. From the flaccid clerics who surrounded her during her long illness she had heard that Felice, as a galley slave, would not be entitled to receive what she had intended to bequeath him; she had therefore disinherited him in favour of his brother.

The repining in his uncle's house accentuated his existing mood of languor and dejection, which proved to be the onset of a sharp attack of jail fever. Though hardly well enough to move, he left Imola for the safe green hills of his native Meldola, where he struggled through a desperate crisis and entered, lonely and emaciated, upon a bleak convalescence. The big house at the bottom of the square was no longer open to him since the family disgrace, so he lived with an old friend of his father, Antonio Fusignani, a respectable pharmacist of moderate, orthodox views. In Meldola Orsini found that he was something of a hero. He rallied himself to make a graceful speech of thanks from his window to the applauding population, but it cost him a great effort. He was more commonly to be seen in the Farmacia Zavatti, belonging to two brothers, other friends of his boyhood, with his head sunk in his hands, the picture of depression.

Imprisonment had not improved him. He had emerged, to use the word he so frequently applied to people of religious disposition, profoundly bigoted. He was convinced he went in peril of his life. The Pope's reforms had not reduced the age-long chaos in the Romagna, and taking advantage of the sudden rise in Catholic popularity, Centurions and Sanfedists were harrying liberals more violently than ever. Shackled by his oath not to take arms against the Pope or against his officers, Orsini's only hope of safety lay in swelling the chorus of praise to Pio Nono. That he would not do; he was a disgusted witness of the pride the rabble took in the triumph of their local bishop; he was also aware of his duty to his Chief, Mazzini, to further the future of Young Italy. The only way was for him to quit the Pope's dominions. In September, on his recovery, he obtained his uncle's sanction to go to Florence for the pursuance of his legal practice.

It was his first return to his mother's birthplace since his father's banishment eighteen years before. Little had been changed. The Archduke Leopold was still pottering about in his gaiters and straw hat. Everyone still bathed in the soft radiance of the past. The youths of Florence still put ballet dancing before politics. Certainly each innovation in the Papal States produced a corresponding convulsion in Tuscany, but Orsini found the plotting there a kind of conspirator's holiday, it was on such a gentle scale; he revelled in deluding the authorities.

He took an apartment and consulting room at Via degli

Orci, no. 1117, on the second floor. He engaged with gusto in the struggle for the freedom of the press, the leading issue of the moment. In defiance of the censorship, illegal tracts were scattered everywhere, showered like confetti in the theatres, dropped into the archduke's carriage, even circulated through the post. Orsini thought such constitutional protests very tame. In April 1847 a customs officer was murdered at Terra del Sole, and a bomb exploded in the house of a royal commissioner at Rocca San Casciano. That was more like it; he wrote a warm defence of the two incidents, small beer to a Romagnuol, but hideous atrocities to the horrified Florentines. In May a new Press Law was granted, so incomplete and niggardly that fresh disturbances resulted.

The Chief of Police in Florence, determined to get rid of Orsini under any pretext, ordered him to Bologna to obtain a visa for his passport, intending meanwhile to take steps whereby he would never see the man again. For Orsini it was an inconvenient suggestion; apart from his plotting, and to some extent his legal practice, he had an extra reason for wishing to remain. On the look-out for a wife once more, he had met Assunta Laurenzi, a beautiful young Florentine. Assunta, the only child of a physician who had lately died, Dr. Ercole Laurenzi, lived with her widowed mother Luisa. She was easily attracted by the handsome stranger, and he for his part saw in her his ideal of womanhood, to be worshipped in the abstract, to be turned to for comfort, but in all practical matters to be ignored. On hearing that her lover had to leave her so suddenly and so soon Assunta was most dismayed. Orsini wrote her a few lines of blithe encouragement: "Rest assured, my Assuntina, that I shall be with you more quickly than you think. . . . Greet your mother and your friends for me, be good, console yourself that to be deprived for thirty days is not the death of anyone, and receive an affectionate kiss from your Felice."[1] He left Florence as ordered on 1 June, but instead of going to Bologna he sent his passport to one of his friends there, hiding in the Tuscan countryside until it was returned to him in perfect order. Before the promised thirty days were up he was back in Florence, the Chief of Police unable to prevent him.

[1] Ghisalberti, 39.

In August 1847 he published a *Discourse to the Youth of Italy*, an anonymous panegyric on the Bandieras, dedicated to Eusebio Barbetti and secretly printed at Leghorn. Again he was ordered to leave Tuscany; again he refused to go, forcing the government to arrest and physically deport him. He returned to Imola, where he discussed his engagement to Assunta with his uncle, and explained that as he was almost the last of his countrymen to be expelled from Florence he must have been behaving well. His uncle "very properly did not believe it".[1] Thinking nothing of his proscription, Orsini continued to enter Tuscany as and when he liked. On one occasion, heavily disguised, he approached the frontier in a gig with two companions, and showed the sentry a letter he had acquired from a captain of gendarmes in Bologna to allay suspicion at their lack of passports. The device was over-successful: it required the greatest tact to dissuade the guard commander from providing them with an armed escort to conduct them safely, straight to police headquarters at their destination.

In September the example of the Papal States and the fear of Austrian invasion following the occupation of Ferrara led to the authorization of Civic Guards in Tuscany. Agitation subsided, security measures were relaxed, and Orsini was shortly able to reappear openly in Florence. He immediately plunged into a new intrigue. On the death of Marie-Louise, Napoleon's widow, the Duke of Lucca succeeded to her Duchy of Parma in accordance with the Treaty of Vienna. Lucca was absorbed by Tuscany, and in compensation the outlying Tuscan district of Carrara-Massa in the Lunigiana was divided between Modena and Parma. The tough inhabitants much resented being forced to exchange the easy-going Tuscan rule for the tyranny of Austrian-ridden Modena. Egged on by Orsini and his friends, fighting started in the towns. TheDuke of Modena marched in to claim his own; Tuscany, sympathizing with the rebels, very nearly attacked Modena, which would have precipitated a general war with Austria. In the end, as Orsini had disgustedly predicted, the matter was patched up by diplomacy, and in December, as he had also expected, Metternich withdrew his forces from Ferrara. But feeling in the Carrara-Massa area remained permanently rebellious.

[1] Orsini, *Memoirs and Adventures*, 61.

The winter of 1847 was unusually hard in Tuscany; olive trees were damaged, and bread riots in Florence led to the newly-armed Civic Guard chasing the hated *sbirri* into hiding. In November Orsini made a new approach to Nicholas Fabrizi, who had left Malta for Italy and joined Colonel Ignazio Ribotti, the leader of the attempted coup at Imola in 1843. With the utmost respect, he asked for advice how best to exploit the situation in the central provinces, revealing as he did so the forthright, clear-headed honesty of his own motives:

> "I do not wish to assume the direction of anything: I wish only to do my duty as an Italian, and as one of those who look towards the unity of Italy, and who desire the redemption of the country for no ulterior designs: these principles, in which I shall remain firm till the end of my life, demand that each shall keep in his own place and not interfere in things to which his capabilities cannot aspire: that, therefore, is why I submit myself wholly to you, to Ribotti, to Giuseppe Mazzini . . . and to those who know better than I.—You others command me, and whatever the task may be that tends to the ransoming of my unhappy country, count on me with your eyes closed, and also on several others who, for love of country, and from a certain deference they have for me, without too much reason follow me wherever I may go."[1]

As a result, Fabrizi and Ribotti came to visit Orsini in Florence; there was ample discontent, and the three conspirators rode the whirlwind merrily enough. In January 1848 the Central Revolutionary Committee of Young Italy summoned them to Rome to undertake a mission in support of a Sicilian rising just then breaking out against the King of Naples.

It struck Orsini before he left that Assunta, quite naturally he told himself, for a girl so much in love, was growing very downhearted at their frequent separations; so he wrote to her mother concerning the arrangements for their wedding. As he was still bound by his monastic oath of celibacy, either he had to obtain formal release from it, or else the marriage must be in secret. He had inclined towards the latter course as the less troublesome, but his family would not hear of it. A public wedding would, of course, be more agreeable both for him and for Assunta; he would try to get his uncle to pursue the matter. In the meantime he had to go away, for how long he

[1] Ghisalberti, 44.

did not know; if Assunta's mother required some form of promissory note of his intentions, he would be willing to furnish it at any time.[1]

Fabrizi, Ribotti and Orsini went to Rome, whence Ribotti set out for Calabria, was captured at sea, and sent to imprisonment at Naples. Before the others could follow him, the revolt in Sicily was crowned with overwhelming victory, and King Bomba was compelled to grant a Constitution. During the next few magical weeks the shock spread through Europe like the tremors of an earthquake, Piedmont, Tuscany, Rome, Modena and Parma, France, Poland, Prussia, Bohemia, Hungary, even Austria securing the same transient liberties, until it died out in Chartist ripples on the English shore.

To Orsini, left lingering in Rome, the concessions extracted from the princes afforded little satisfaction. He feared they would prove harmful to the cause of republican unity; they would act as a soporific, increase dissensions, prolong the lives of moribund kingdoms; and then, when the moment was ripe, they would be withdrawn. The rain, incessant since before Christmas, continued to pour down from leaden skies. Restless and disheartened he trudged through the streets thick in yellow mud, past ruins gleaming tawny under the dark clouds, through galleries damp and cold as tombs, waiting for some assignment from the party. He was a marked man, and they dared give him none. In February outbreaks inspired by Ciceruacchio and wrongly laid to his account forced him to leave Rome; he made for Imola once more, but finding the vendetta worse than ever, he turned back hurriedly to Florence. In five years of action for the cause he had achieved exactly nothing, except to become a sick man, outlawed, homeless, nameless, and worst of all, a man without a mission.

V

While the other states of Italy were gaining constitutional liberties, the Austrian-occupied provinces of Lombardy and Venetia watched in envy and exasperation, well knowing that

[1] Ghisalberti, 46.

no such privileges could come to them. Their impatience was increased by signs of mobilization in Piedmont, and the knowledge that war, of which the first issue would be their independence, was drawing daily nearer.

Feeling in Milan ran very high. Small boys would strut along behind the foreign soldiers in daring mimicry. Down apparently deserted alleys snatches of the Hymn to Pio Nono would be hummed or whistled in startling proximity. In the theatres, actresses accepted bouquets of red, white and green, curtsied and blew kisses amid thundering applause. Early in the new year 1848 the Milanese decided to hit the Austrian finances through their most important source of revenue, the tobacco tax. With one accord they gave up smoking because "tobacco ill-mated the sweet odours of Italian flowers".[1] In retaliation, the Austrian commander made a special issue of cigars to all his troops, who flaunted them about the town and insolently puffed them in the faces of the passers-by. When scuffles ensued, a cavalry charge was ordered, with the result that many workmen returning innocently home were killed or injured.

The responsibility for keeping order in Lombardy and Venetia rested upon an Austrian army of 75,000 men. 20,000 of them were Italian conscripts of doubtful loyalty; many of the rest were Hungarians, Croats, Moravians, Kossuthite supporters doomed to military exile. The wonder is that they would fight at all. It was due in part, no doubt, to the habitual acquiescence which keeps all armies in a state of dull momentum. No doubt as well, the hatred and contempt surrounding them induced a sort of brutish comradeship. Then again, the officers, whatever their nationality, were all fanatical reactionaries devoted to the Emperor; despite linguistic difficulties they did not fail to make their orders clear by frequent use of the *cavaletto*, if not the firing squad.

The real cohesive force, however, was the personality of their commander, "Papa" Radetzky. "This astonishing old man",[2] as Trevelyan calls him, was the very model of a German field-marshal, feared and loved in equal parts by every officer and man. He had seen action in many theatres; he had been wounded by five bullets at Marengo; he had made his name as chief of

[1] Bolton King, I, 197.

[2] Trevelyan, *Manin and the Venetian Revolution*, 77–8.

staff at the battle of Leipzig, where he had been responsible for the costly manœuvres of the Austrian army. Brave, ruthless, coarse as a soldier, off-duty he was a hearty, jovial veteran, fond of carousing with his junior officers and expert in exploiting jealousies between his generals. At the age of eighty-two he had indignantly rejected all suggestions of retirement; he was still an excellent horseman and as much alive as ever, the last of his many bastards having been born at Milan only two years previously.

For seventeen years, ever since he was given the Italian command, Radetzky had been preparing for a day of reckoning he knew to be inevitable. Sensing that the situation in Milan was coming to a head at last, he did all he could to make it worse, lest death should rob him of his final victory. "Three days of blood will give us thirty years of peace," he said.[1] On 24 February 1848 he decreed martial law throughout Lombardy and Venetia.

The storm he reaped was more far-reaching than he had expected. On 17 March tremendous tidings reached Milan: Bohemia was blazing in revolt; Vienna had risen, Metternich was on his way to Brighton; Mazzini, after greeting Lamartine upon the barricades in Paris, was rumoured to be coming south. The Emperor had promised a Constitution, a free press, a Civic Guard throughout his realms; grimly across his proclamation the Milanese pasted the fateful words: "Too late."

The populace rose against 13,000 troops; barricades flung up pell-mell of furniture, carriages, pulpits, pianos, school benches and scenery from *La Scala* were desperately defended with a few old muskets snatched from armourers' shops or police repositories. Men, women and children, all joined in; those who had no other weapon pelted the Austrians with tiles, bricks, crockery, boiling oil or water, from the roofs and windows; a whole battalion was driven back by a shower of empty wine bottles. Astronomers with telescopes climbed church steeples to spy upon the enemy; chemists manufactured gunpowder; coopers constructed cannon out of wood and iron hoops. For five whole days the battle raged. In a military sense, Radetzky commanded only the castle and the city walls, apart from a few sharp-shooters concealed among the pinnacles of the

[1] Bolton King, I, 196.

cathedral. His troops, cut off from their supplies and their commanders, dumbfounded at the scarcely human hatred, bemused by pouring missiles, deafened by the joyous pealing of bells, drenched with rain, and put to panic, in the case of the superstitious Croats, by an eclipse, were fighting for survival. On the evening of the twenty-second an army of volunteers streaming towards Milan from Piedmont breached the western walls. Radetzky ordered a massacre of prisoners; then, after bombarding the city with the castle ordnance all night long, he marched his garrison, diminished by 5,000 men, out through the eastern gates into a grey and watery dawn.

Despite the violence of their onslaught and their lack of military training, the Milanese behaved throughout with great restraint. The doors of rich and poor were open to each other; prisoners were fed and sheltered, their wounds were scrupulously nursed. The cruelties of the enemy on the other hand are well-attested, and are revolting even to hardened twentieth-century consciences. Women were raped and bayoneted, or burnt alive, or buried alive in wells. A child spiked through with a bayonet was pinned to a tree and left to writhe just out of its mother's reach. In the pockets of a Croat were found two female hands, the fingers loaded with rings. Another chopped an infant clean in two; then, moved by a ghastly stirring of his dim humanity, and realizing that some parent would be looking for the pieces, he apologetically tied the two halves together with their own steaming entrails.[1]

On the same day, 17 March, a similar revolt broke out in Venice, contemporaneous although quite unrelated, and happily of a less grizzly character. The previous afternoon, the wife of the Austrian governor Count Palffy had been seen walking arm in arm with a certain Count Ragusa, an over-reticent Italian suspected of collaboration. They were hissed and booed; the mysterious Count Ragusa disappeared, while the giddy lady hurried back inside the palace. Next morning the packet steamer from Trieste arrived bearing a charred portrait of Metternich which was torn to pieces in the lagoon. The hunt was up. The mob released their heroes Manin and Tommaseo from their elegant prison overlooking the lagoon, connected to the Doge's Palace by the Bridge of Sighs, and carried them in triumph to the

[1] Pepe, *Narrative of Scenes and Events*, I, 76.

Piazza San Marco. The next few days were spent in icy negotiations between Manin and Palffy, interrupted at intervals by tearful intercessions from the latter's wife. Periodically the Croats would fire a volley at or over the mob in the Piazza, and were answered with a storm of paving stones, whereat one or other of the two antagonists inside the palace would appear at the spacious windows and harangue the crowd on the necessity for order.

On 22 March the dock-hands in the naval Arsenal turned on the Austrian adjutant, pursued him in gondolas round the basins, and murdered him in cold blood. All hope of negotiation was now ended, and it became essential to forestall Austrian reprisals. Manin marched to the Arsenal and captured it almost single-handed; he then led a roaring multitude to the Piazza, where he proclaimed the old Republic of St. Mark. The Venetians ran wild with excitement. The troops guarding the palace, remembering that they too were Italians, reversed the cannons trained on the Piazza so that they were pointed at the Governor's windows. Palffy and his wife were packed off in a steamer to Trieste. By 27 March the revolution was complete throughout the province of Venetia.

The simultaneous risings in Milan and Venice placed Marshal Radetzky in a very difficult situation. As his weary forces straggled eastward from Milan in streaming rain, he expected that the eager, compact army of Piedmont would be in full pursuit and might at any moment fall upon his rear. In front of him Venice stood athwart the sea and coastal routes connecting him with the Fatherland, the only routes available until the snows melted in the Alpine passes. Only one recourse was open to Radetzky. Between Lombardy and Venetia in the centre of the plain lay a position, about thirty miles square, of great natural strength, hinged at the corners by four powerful fortresses. Its western flank, from Peschiera south of Lake Garda down to Mantua, was guarded by the River Mincio; to the south it overlooked the swampy valley of the Po from Mantua to Legnago; in the east between Legnago and Verona it was bounded by the wide-flowing Adige; while its northern limit rested securely on the foothills of the Alps. If he could reach the safety of the Quadrilateral, Radetzky could hope to delay the army of Piedmont to the west, while assailing his less professional opponents to the east; at all events he would have hold of a lifeline which, come the spring, would give access to Austria either for reinforcement or escape.

By the second day of the Milan rising the road from Turin was crowded with volunteers; had they been accompanied by the regular army of Piedmont, quite possibly the Italians could have prevented the Austrians from reaching the Quadrilateral. As it happened, there was hesitation. Charles Albert had looked forward to a war of royalist expansion, not to a democratic revolution; the republican tone of the Milanese offended him, and his doubts were confirmed by Manin's proclamation of the Venetian Republic of St. Mark. It was not therefore until after the fighting in Milan was over that Charles Albert tardily assumed the tricolour, and led his troops across the Ticino.

The news of his advance was received in Rome with the utmost exaltation. Roman citizens embraced each other, crying out *Miracolo! Providenza!* "Men danced and women wept for joy along the street. The youths rushed to enrol themselves in regiments to go to the frontier. In the Colosseum their names were received."[1] The double-headed Austrian eagle was taken down from the great door of the Palazzo di Venezia, and replaced by the Papal colours, white and gold. Pio Nono, deeply regretting the heroic role he had brought upon himself, had no choice but to despatch his regular forces and to bless the Volunteers. As they streamed northward over the sodden Campagna the weather cleared at last; hundreds of larks rose up on every side, carolling ever more distantly till lost to sight in skies serene and blue. Below, the motley column wound along, the red cross of the crusaders pinned upon their breasts, singing as always, and glorified by the rays of the returning sun.

On hearing what was happening in Milan, Orsini came hastening back from Florence to Meldola, his head high, light of heart, his disillusionment forgotten; here was the end of murky midnight plotting, of evasion and disgrace; now at last he could set forth as a patriot soldier with an honest weapon in his hand. He enlisted in the 21st Section of the Civic Guard, and soon became a corporal in charge of a squad of eight, whom he

[1] Margaret Fuller, *Memoirs*, III, 170.

drilled in the cattle-market behind the big house where he was born. He made them wear tall stove-pipe hats, the nearest he

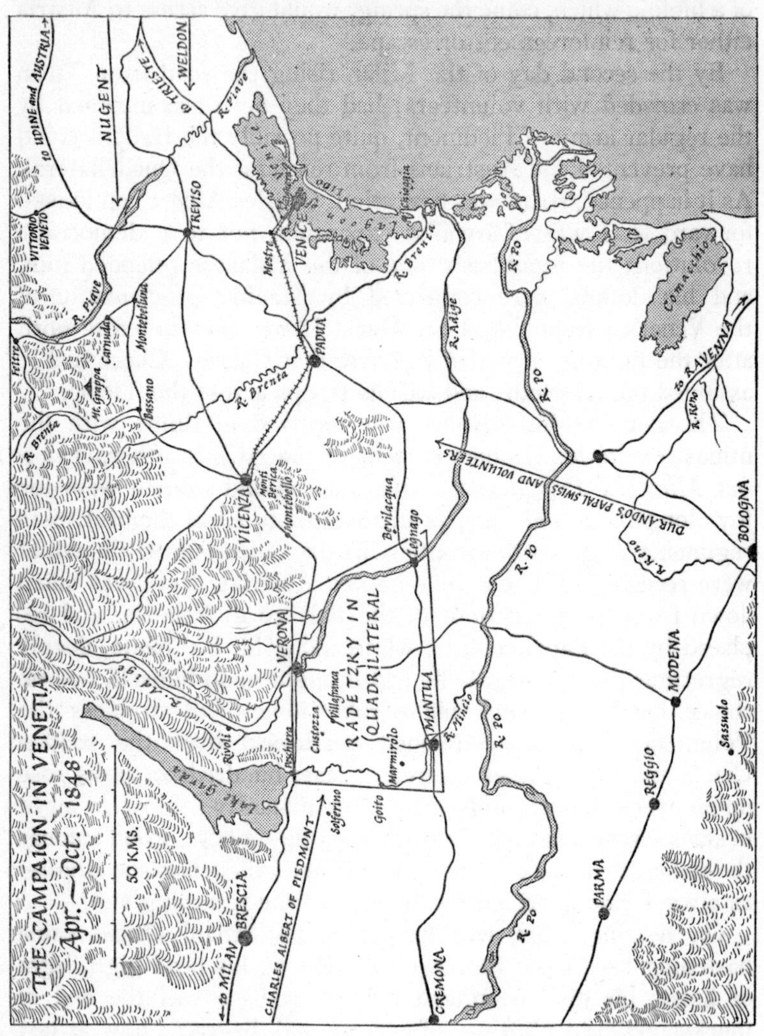

could get to helmets, and black overcoats buttoned tightly across the chest to accustom them to the constriction at the throat which was then the universal feature of all uniform.[1]

[1] Angelo Santi, *Il Pensiero Mazziniano*, July, Aug., 1951.

After a week or two he led them to Bologna, where they were incorporated in the newly-formed 4th Company of the light infantry battalion Alto Reno, the Reno being the river of Bologna, under Colonel Count Livy Zambeccari, who had directed the abortive rising at Bologna in 1843. In view of his keen military interests, Orsini was appointed lieutenant. He chose as his batman a fellow Meldolese, Giuseppe Mazzi, whom he called Fafita, and who served him loyally throughout the subsequent campaign.

He found Bologna transformed, excitable and gay: there was music, with singing and dancing, in all quarters of the town. From the wide steps of the Cathedral two Barnabite friars, Ugo Bassi and Gavazzi, in turn exhorted a delirious throng in the Piazza Maggiore; the one wild-eyed, prophetic; the other operatic and portentous, swirling his cloak or depressing the corners of his mouth to emphasize a point. Under their influence a spirit of radiant dedication spread about. Men set aside business, love and litigation to join the colours; women gave up their sons and lovers; all gave up the lottery. Boys ran away from school; novices drilled each other in the Catholic seminaries; romantically-minded university students affected a mediaeval costume evoking the defeat of Barbarossa. By way of arms, a few had muskets; the rest had pikes, or whatever they could lay their hands on, from old iron railings to swords and halberds from antique shops. In the Piazza, free gifts of jewellery, silver ornaments and household goods were piled in heaps; people cheered and wept as a girl gave all of gold she had to offer, her lovely head of hair.

By virtue of its situation south of the Po, Bologna was the concentration area for volunteers from all over Italy. Besides those from the Papal States, others came from sleepy Tuscany, from Modena and Parma, from Sicily, ravaged and far away. Last to arrive was a contingent of regulars from Naples, under the great-hearted midget General Pepe; for Bomba, much against his will, was compelled by his parliament to lend some of his treasured paladins to the national cause.

Early in April Orsini marched with the vanguard of the Volunteers through madly-shouting avenues of spectators out to the north towards Ferrara. They made a striking spectacle.

"Young men of education and sometimes of high birth, students and artisans, veterans who had fought at Borodino or at Waterloo, middle-aged gold-spectacled professors, Austrian deserters, smugglers, the flower and the dregs of society, . . . followed by peasants with folks and scythes, their priests with pistols at their head."[1] Going to fight an army of seasoned whitecoats there was only one thing in their favour; they were all free men, standing on ground which to them was hallowed, cheered in their common tongue by an adoring population, and liberally supplied with whatever comforts the country could provide.

Crossing the Po into Venetian territory, the 4th Company of the battalion Alto Reno joined their colonel, Zambeccari, and the rest of the regiment at Bevilacqua, some five miles north-eastward of Legnago. By this time Radetzky was beleaguered in the Quadrilateral. From the west Charles Albert of Piedmont was bearing down upon the Mincio. To the south General Durando had reached the Po with 7,000 Papal regulars of whom half were tough, taciturn Swiss mercenaries, a very tolerable fighting force in their white-and-gold cockades. From the east, on Durando's right, Zambeccari was operating towards Legnago from the Padua road. North of him the Venetians marched gallantly on Verona from Vicenza, only to retire precipitately when they encountered Austrian outposts at Montebello.

The situation was abruptly changed when, at a partial restoration of order within the Empire, a second Austrian army under General Nugent appeared on the eastern frontier of Venetia. Sweeping past Udine and other scattered strongholds, Nugent advanced a hundred miles to the River Piave almost without opposition. Venice was directly threatened, and Manin began to call for help. To meet this threat Zambeccari and his Venetian allies turned back from the Quadrilateral and hastened to secure Treviso, protecting Venice from the north and covering the crossings of the Piave. There they came under the command of General Ferrari who was called up from Bologna with the main body of the Volunteers, now fully mobilized. In addition, Durando and his Papal regulars left their position on the Po to reinforce the eastern theatre. So that early in May

[1] Bolton King, I, 230, 249.

some 45,000 Piedmontese were grappling with Radetzky's roughly equal force ensconced in the Quadrilateral; while on the Piave Nugent's army of 15,000 faced Durando, who had, strung out along the river line, about 8,000 Roman and Venetian Volunteers commanded by Ferrari, with 7,000 Papal regulars in reserve behind them.

Orsini, in camp on the high banks overlooking the wide and stony Piave, was happier than he had ever been before. For him, as it could never be for others, the sound of the morning bugle was an elixir; in skirmishes towards the enemy he was always fiercely in the lead; the duty officer's midnight round in rain or sleet was a time for proud contemplation of the sleeping host. In moments of leisure, he joined his fellows round the fire, and added his deep voice to the jocular martial airs or traditional melodies redolent of home.

His contentment was short-lived. The movement of the Papal troops so far across the Po caused Pio Nono an acute embarrassment in his relations with the Catholic powers, and on 29 April he published an Allocution clarifying his attitude towards the war. He said, first, that he had not intended his soldiers to do more than secure his legitimate possessions; second, that he could no longer countenance an internecine strife between his Italian and Austrian children. He later modified his statement so that no troops were actually withdrawn, but the damage done was past repair. Rightly or wrongly he had been regarded as the head of a crusade; thousands had taken up arms on that understanding. Coming at such a time, his pronouncement caused complete confusion in the army, increasing the already lively feeling between the Papal regulars and the largely republican Volunteers.

Before the excitement had subsided, Nugent struck. His intention was to link forces with Radetzky in Verona, and in so doing to reconquer the Venetian mainland and restore the normal Austrian communications. For this end, he had two courses open: either to make a frontal attack across the Piave, a matter of great difficulty; or to strike north into the mountains and debouch once more into the plain in the rear of the defenders of the river. In the event he employed a compromise. On 8 May he descended from the mountains by the valley of the Piave, and at

Cornuda fell upon the left flank of Ferrari's Volunteers guarding the river line. At the same time, by a clever feint round the *massif*, he prevented Durando from going to their assistance. Pouring imprecations on the long-suspected treachery of the Papalists, the Volunteers fell back to Montebelluna, and from thence, in a rabble, to Treviso. Meanwhile Zambeccari and the battalion Alto Reno, left patiently manning a splendid line of earthworks they had erected on the Piave against an attack which never came, found themselves being rolled up from the north. To avoid encirclement they had no choice but to make for Treviso too.

By the morning of 10 May all Volunteer forces in Venetia were boxed up in the little town: some battle-stained and truculent; the rest, like Orsini, much cast down at having been defeated without a chance to fire a shot. The word went round that Nugent was approaching, and panic spread. Three Italian travellers entering the town were instantly cut down as spies. The Venetians deserted by the score, and were to be seen a few days later in their capital city, the Queen of the Adriatic, pawning their weapons, thronging the cafés, and boasting of their prowess.

To scotch the rumours and induce a measure of self-respect, Ferrari next day ordered a strong reconnaissance towards the north. The idea was good, and as they marched his men regained some confidence. But at a bend in the road they came face to face with an enemy detachment, guns unlimbered, deployed on a bank across the line of their advance. Caught in a withering fire on a causeway road, the Volunteers jostled in confusion, and finally fled helter-skelter back to Treviso, to the dismay of the townsfolk who had proudly gathered at their principal monument, the Porta San Tommaso, a magnificent sixteenth-century arch of triumph, to welcome them home as victors.

Fear spread to the inhabitants; the Civic Guard refused to man the walls. To make things worse it happened that Durando ordered Ferrari to join him in his new position at Vicenza, covering the main line of the Austrian advance towards Verona. That evening most of the Volunteers left Treviso by the southern gate, at the opposite end of town from that which they had so hurriedly re-entered in the morning. The enraged Trevisans, mistaking the movement for a craven retreat and base betrayal of Venetia, hooted them out and fired a cannon after them.

Nugent, hearing of disaffection and thinking he might as well pick up the place in passing, did in fact attack Treviso the next day, but by that time passions had subsided as quickly as they had arisen. The Civic Guard were at their posts, and Orsini as part of the residual garrison accompanied his commander Zambeccari in a violent sortie through the same north gate, the scene of the previous day's disgrace. Finding the defence so magically stiffened, Nugent called off the attack and resumed his march towards Verona.

Then came another disappointment for the patriots. Bomba, King of Naples, seeing in the Pope's Allocution a way of getting out of the war, recalled his contingent from Bologna where they were belatedly preparing themselves for action. The Bolognese fell on them with sticks and stones, nevertheless they all departed, all save General Pepe who, defying his sovereign's orders, managed in the confusion to make off across the Po with a composite brigade of followers. Robbed of her expected Neapolitan reinforcements, Venice was once more dangerously exposed. At Manin's urgent request Durando changed places with Zambeccari, calling Orsini's regiment in to hold Vicenza while he himself returned to Treviso with the main part of the army.

No sooner had he gone than Nugent appeared before Vicenza, and on 20 May made a probing attack upon the northern suburbs. The battalion Alto Reno, left almost in sole command, put up a spirited resistance. For two days Orsini was engaged in bitter, constricted fighting in the long arcaded street leading to the gateway of San Lucia, during which his great friend and brother officer Antonio Liverani of Faenza fell at his side badly wounded in the leg and died in his arms from loss of blood before he could be got away. Laying him gently down, Orsini, huzzahing loudly, swept forward with his company in a wild bayonet charge which carried them through the gateway and brought them to close grips with the enemy outside the walls. As at Treviso, Nugent did not persist in his assault. Having successfully passed his army round Vicenza to the north he called off his diversion and went on his way unchallenged to Verona. The following day Durando, hastening back from

Treviso, could do no more than harry his fast-receding rear-guard, a futile operation watched with foolish pride by Manin who came out by train from Venice.

The Austrian armies thus achieved their junction; it remained for Radetzky, with his interior lines of communication and his strength increased to nearly 70,000 men, to exploit the dissensions of his enemies and attack them one by one. On 23 May he returned to launch a second assault on Vicenza with a powerful force liberally supported by artillery. In the interval Durando had taken sound measures for defence; the low-lying ground to the south by the railway had been flooded, denying access to the vital straggling ridge of the Berici heights overlooking the city, where the defenders' guns were mounted. Vicenza was in excellent heart; "the town was in an uproar of enthusiasm. The bells in every tower rang the tocsin, the streets were illuminated as for a *festa*, the ladies leaned out of the windows cheering the men as they hurried to the gates."[1] In a two-day battle the Austrians were severely repulsed, but Orsini, still guarding the San Lucia sector away to the north, saw nothing of it except for a solitary cannon ball which rolled along the street and petered to a halt within a yard of him. Its useless trundling seemed exactly to express his own frustration. A few days later he and his regiment were sent to fortify Treviso once again.

At the end of May, on the other front, Radetzky was defeated by Charles Albert at Goito, and recoiled in the direction of Verona, enabling the Piedmontese to take the fortress of Peschiera. With the Italians inside the Quadrilateral, and with further trouble breaking out at home, it seemed probable that Radetzky would quit Italy altogether by the Adige valley and the Brenner Pass, before that route too was cut. So certain was Charles Albert that this would be his course that instead of following up closely he made a triumphal entry into Peschiera and held a solemn Te Deum for his decisive victory. Radetzky however did no such thing. On the contrary, he marched straight through Verona and attacked Vicenza for the third time in overwhelming strength. On 10 June, after a bitter battle on the Monti Berici, and under the threat of Austrian cannon lowering from the heights, a white flag at last fluttered from the great belfry in Palladio's Piazza dei Signori. In return for a promise

[1] Trevelyan, *Manin*, 181.

not to fight again for a period of three months, the defenders were granted easy terms, being allowed to march out to Padua the following morning carrying their arms and accompanied by droves of refugees. When Charles Albert, having finished his devotions at Peschiera, made a desultory advance upon Verona he found the Austrians once more fully in possession. "*C'est trop tard, Sire,*" said one of his generals as they turned away.[1]

Meanwhile yet another Austrian army under Welden had entered Venetia from the east and proceeded to reduce the remaining outposts. On 12 June Padua fell, and Zambeccari taken by surprise was surrounded in Treviso. The battalion Alto Reno underwent a merciless bombardment for two days, spent mostly in the cellars since they were unable to retaliate once their few guns were silenced: at length Treviso too capitulated on the same terms as Vicenza.

Leading the 4th Company of his regiment home from Padua to Bologna (for he was now a captain), Orsini could not but feel crestfallen. For the second time in three years he owed his life and liberty to the indulgence of his adversaries, to whom he was bound by an undignified parole. The high hopes with which the Italians had set out had come to nothing; not only had they been out-generalled time and time again, but their own dissensions were as much as anything to blame. The best that could be said was that the false gods had been exposed: the Giobertian moderates who had looked for a federation under Pio Nono were discredited: Charles Albert had shown himself, like the other princes, inadequate as a commander and perfidious as an ally. The future of Italy must depend henceforth upon the true, the thorough Mazzinian regeneration.

When they reached Bologna, the gloom was partly lifted by the heart-warming reception given them by their fellow citizens. At least, it was said, they had returned with their weapons in their hands. Their failure was attributed to the Pope's apostasy, to the treachery of Naples, the cowardice of the Venetians, the errors of Charles Albert—never to any fault of theirs. Followed wherever he went by the admiring gaze of boys, by blushing glances from the girls, for the first time in his life Orsini felt the comfortable glow that comes from being acknowledged in the right. For once his uncle had no fault to find, and treated

[1] Trevelyan, *Manin*, 195–6.

him with some consideration. He took to preening his black beard, and to walking with the faintest swagger. His thoughts dwelt more and more fondly on Assunta.

Before he went away he had, he thought, occasionally discerned if not a restiveness, a certain hesitation in her manner towards him; due, he supposed, to his having been at that time, through force of circumstance, sudden, secretive and peremptory by turns. Now, he assured himself, all would be well; he was now an established officer in a famous regiment; neither her mother nor the girl herself could have any doubts about one so respectable. So long loveless, he expected love to bloom as his due reward for valour. In his knightly battles for his country Assunta should become his lady page; out of their shared vicissitudes and hazards would come fulfilment. His uncle, thankful for a sign of settling down, told him that the Pope, as a wartime measure, had been able to grant permission for him to be released from his oath of celibacy in whichever diocese appeared the most convenient. Orsini went to Florence, where he completed the required formalities; and on 28 June, at an evening ceremony, he was married to Assunta. It quickly became evident, however, that domestic ties were still to be subordinate to the claims of duty, for after an abbreviated honeymoon he left Assunta with her mother and rejoined his regiment in Bologna, having been away in all no more than eighteen days.

The situation there was very tense. Pio Nono's Allocution had so embittered the Bolognese that they had begun to consider seceding from the Papal States and seeking fusion with their Lombard blood-brothers in Charles Albert's North Italian League. After the fall of Vicenza, with the League shattered and Charles Albert in retreat, the Austrian general Welden sought to exploit this dissidence as a means of adding the Romagna to the Empire. Early in August on his own initiative he crossed the Po with a considerable force, passed through Ferrara, and appeared before Bologna.

Bologna was full of para-military units like Orsini's, armed and still spoiling for a fight though under Austrian parole. The clerical administration, indignant yet powerless at Welden's action, resolved to avoid all provocation that might give him an excuse for going further. Accordingly on 4 August the battalion Alto Reno took part in a general march of a hundred miles down the straight and dusty Via Emilia, through Imola, Forli and Rimini, to a rest camp in the pleasant seaside village of Cattolica. Their prudence was worse than useless. On the eighth Welden occupied the city so conveniently abandoned. The disgusted Bolognese found the *Tedeschi* once more in their midst, the officers in their white capes and plumed *shakos* more insolent than ever, puffing cigars and clattering into genteel cafés, calling sarcastically for tricoloured ices of red, white and green.

Welden had mistaken the Romagnuols' temperament. Whatever their feelings about the Papal government, their hatred of the Austrians came first. Next day the Civic Guard beat to arms; joined by two hundred police and *Carabinieri* they chased the astonished soldiers through the town, followed by customs officers and citizens with sticks and knives. The Austrians eventually rallied in the Montagnola, the public gardens on the northern outskirts. There, after a furious four-hour battle, the Bolognese stormed the central mound to the cry *Italia e Pio Nono*, and drove them out through the Porta Galliera. Meanwhile roving bands outside the town streamed from their crevices in hills and valleys to barricade the walls. Welden's army fled, leaving wounded and prisoners by hundreds.

Having no longer any reason to exercise restraint, the Papal government gave permission for the troops to return from Cattolica. Orsini, who had been chafing with impatience, rode hell-for-leather up the Via Emilia, reaching Bologna in time to add to the exuberant rejoicing. He was none too soon. Not all of those who had taken part against the Austrians were estimable in other ways. Bloodthirsty ruffians, having obtained arms from the Civic Guard, used them for rapine and intimidation: under the guise of punishing the *sbirri* they pursued their rivals through the arcades of Bologna, hacking them down like martyrs in a colosseum. They broke open prisons, looted villas, murdered a judge whose sentences were too exact; they cut the throat of a police official lying ill in bed before the eyes of his wife and children. The decent residents left in terror; Bologna was given over to "nomad tribes of motley garb and arms".[1]

[1] Farini, II, 331.

Hearing that things were just as bad at Imola, Orsini hurried off to see if his uncle were all right. He found the old man very nervous. Orso said that the town was in the grip of a gang called the *Squadraccia*; they had him on their list, he knew, because of his wealth and clerical opinions. Only that morning, on getting out of bed and going to his window to tell the time by the clock-tower over the road, he had seen a loiterer in an alleyway who he felt sure was keeping watch upon the house. That evening Orsini visited the *Squadraccia* in their headquarters, the "Café Plunderer", where they were making up their plans for the next day's work. Brushing aside the entreaties of the proprietor he flung wide the door and stood in full uniform upon the threshold.

"They tell me that you intend harm to my uncle. Be careful what you do. Whoever touches a hair of his head will have to look out for me."

His appearance produced an astonished silence in the grimy den, a dull silence hardening slowly into menace.

"Signor Orsini makes so bold because he has an officer's sabre," sneered one of them at last. In a flash Orsini had undone his belt and tossed the sabre in a corner. He threw back his black hair in an habitual gesture.

"Now let him who dares come forward."

The brigands stirred uncomfortably under his brilliant gaze. The tension broke. They got up and crowded round him; they pawed his braided epaulettes; they picked up his sword; they dashed him out a tot of acquavite, swearing with oaths that they bore not the least malice against Signor Orso Orsini.

"Be sure of it," said Orsini, striding to the door.[1]

Unable to control the terrorists, Cardinal Amat, the Papal Legate, was at his wit's end, and in September Pio Nono sent Luigi Carlo Farini, one of the most able of his new liberal counsellors, to assist his old friend in Bologna. Acting with firmness, Farini arrested Zambianchi, the most notorious of the brigand chiefs, and by judicious use of the Papal Swiss restored some kind of order. But in ordering the Volunteers to be disbanded he replaced one sort of trouble with another. The Volunteers were jealous of the Papal Swiss, nor did they consent to be disarmed. Thoroughly suspicious of the Pope's intentions, they

[1] Orsini (Luigi), 59–66.

also had their score to settle with the Austrians. Besides, Farini himself was most unpopular. From 1843 to 1845 he had been one of the most ardent of the liberal conspirators: it was suspected that a certain letter which, wrongly attributed to Orsini's father had led to his arrest, and later, again wrongly, was presumed to have been written by Orsini to Eusebio Barbetti, had in fact been meant for Farini. By his old confederates, Zambeccari, Nicholas Fabrizi and Orsini, whom at Bologna he now met again, he was considered a traitor for undertaking government employment.

Skirmishing led to pitched encounters. By an elaborate *coup de main* Farini's troops secured the gates and walls and made the city prisoner for the government: next night Orsini and his friend Angelo Masina, with a handful of men from Orsini's company, seized them all back and reversed the situation. Farini decided to bargain with Orsini. He declared that he respected, and shared, the patriotic fervour underlying the disturbance: at the same time they must both admit that Bologna was rapidly becoming uninhabitable, and the last thing either of them wanted was to give the Austrians an excuse for coming back. Why could Orsini not reserve his admirable dash and dare for the proper recipients, the *Tedeschi*?

Upon the fall of Vicenza there had followed Radetzky's defeat of the army of Piedmont at Custozza; Charles Albert's headlong flight; his failure to defend Milan, where Mazzini and Garibaldi with the inspired assistance of the Milanese had prepared for an heroic final stand; his inglorious return to his own kingdom; and on 9 August, his still more inglorious peace. All Italian patriots still in arms, such as General Pepe and his Neapolitan brigade, had fallen back on Venice, lonely and besieged, the only place in Italy where the tricolour still flew. It was resolved between Farini and Orsini that Colonel Zambeccari should enlist a Free Corps and embark for Venice too.

Easily agreed on principle, they fell to lively wrangling about the details. Orsini insisted that the Papal government should bear the whole cost of fitting out the expedition; it was the least they could do towards the national cause they had betrayed. Farini protested that the government was penniless, and that in any case he was already doing more than he should in allowing the rebels to go free. Eventually, under threat of a public rising headed by the battalion Alto Reno, Farini reluctantly gave way, and Orsini spent some happy days ordering new uniforms for his regiment; after all, as the Pope was going to pay the bill, he could afford to be extravagant. But though he visited all the textile factories in Bologna he could not find the right material for winter breeches; on embarkation day he was short by a hundred uniforms and as many bandoliers and knapsacks, and had to leave an officer behind to see that they were sent on afterwards. As soon as he was gone the last word rested with Farini; when the stuff reached the manufacturers Farini commandeered it for the Papal government, so that in the end, to Orsini's fury, the Venetians had to make up the deficiency.[1]

The voyage to Venice was a risky one, for in accordance with the articles of peace Piedmont had withdrawn her warships from the Adriatic, and the Austrian battle squadron from Trieste was once more in control. The Free Corps sailed from Ravenna in thirteen overcrowded fishing smacks. At once a violent equinoctial gale arose, perhaps fortunately, for the little sailing ships were scattered, and only one unlucky one was seen and caught by the Austrian steam-cruiser *Vulcan*. Orsini, with a hundred and twenty of his men groaning and copiously seasick, lay off Chioggia unable to navigate the mudbanks admitting to the lagoon until taken in tow by a Venetian steamer. Rippling over the smooth lagoon under an autumn sky now calm and golden, the patriots soon recovered, and even found a cause for laughter. In front, their sturdy-buttocked tug paddled purposefully ahead, her name displayed for all to see; she was the *Pio Nono*.

Venice was well placed to endure a lengthy siege. Secured by the Lido from the blockading Austrian fleet, to landward a single railway bridge two and a half miles long connected her to the mainland, where Welden's army sickened in thousands on the fever-infested flats. So long as they held the powerful redoubt of Fort Malghera at the further end, the Venetians were not only safe from attack but out of range of all bombardment—indeed they remained so, except for some much-derided efforts to bomb them from balloons, almost until the end, when the Austrians thought of dismantling their guns and burying them in the ground at a maximum elevation.

By general consent Manin had become dictator. About

[1] Ghisalberti, 96–7.

20,000 soldiers carried arms, under the shrewd and cheerful leadership of General Pepe. The Arsenal was stocked full of ammunition; the warehouses held plenty of provisions; gondolas plied to and fro in the lagoon bringing fish and vegetables from the islands. Appeals for money and material met with a magnificent response. Pepe gave up his salary, theatres combined their takings to fit out a ship, placards appeared asking for "silver from the churches, gold from the women, bronze from the bells, copper from the kitchens, iron from the enemy's balls: anything rather than Croats".[1]

On landing at the Riva degli Schiavoni, Zambeccari and his men were allowed to see the many wonders of what Orsini called "a strange and magic city":[2] then the people in their turn were introduced to their new protectors. Drawn up among the pigeons in the Piazza San Marco the troops were reviewed by General Pepe, his huge sword clanking along behind him on the marble paving, his whiskered face peering quizzically up into theirs beneath his enormous, old-fashioned Napoleonic hat. After three days they were sent across the bridge to defend the key fortress of Malghera.

Orsini was put in charge of *lunette* no. 12, one of three earthworks in advance of the main fortification. He had, he noticed, a good field of fire, and the surrounding marshes were floodable at will. It was damp and chilly; as he gazed through the narrow loopholes towards Mestre two miles to the north, it reminded him of prison. To his left the railway ran off from the bridge, bearing south of Mestre to Padua. To his right was the road to Mestre, and alongside it a canal. For an endless month in thickening autumn gloom he tried to keep up the spirits of his company. At last, on the evening of 26 October, he was ordered to hand over the *lunette* and report to Colonel Zambeccari in the fortress. He found the adjutant, Joseph Fontana of Modena, poring over plans and papers spread about in guttering candlelight.

To maintain battle trim, the Adjutant told him, General Pepe had decided on a sortie against Mestre, where there were about 2,000 Austrians with smaller detachments at La Rana south of the railway and at Fusina lower down the coast. The main

[1] Bolton King, I, 343.

[2] Orsini, *Memoirs and Adventures*, 65–73.

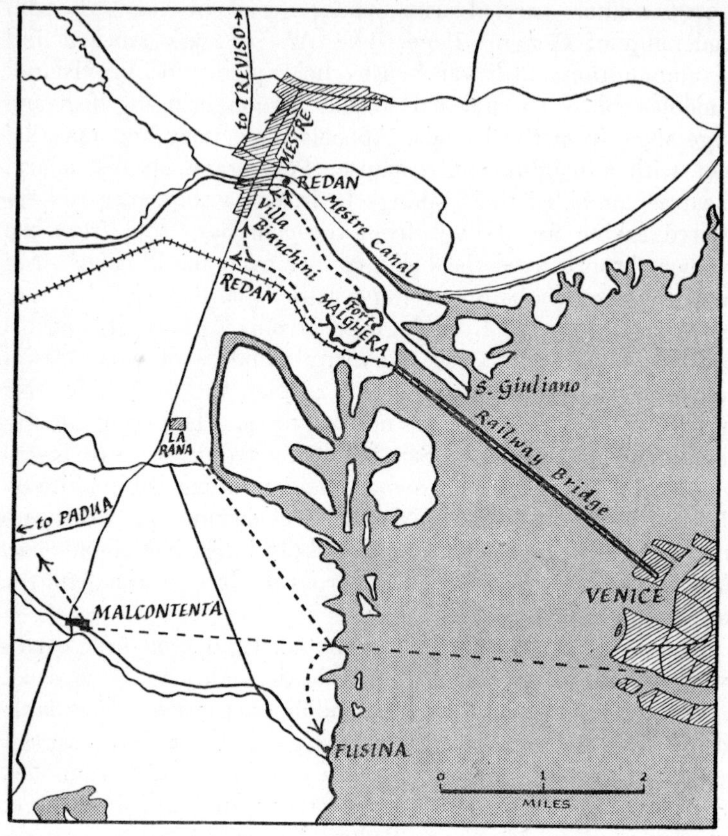

THE SORTIE OF MESTRE 27 OCTOBER 1848

reserves were at Padua, twenty miles away, and it was intended to complete the operation before they could intervene. A central column would follow the line of the railway into Mestre, entering by the Padua road. On their left a body of riflemen in gondolas from Venice would negotiate the shallow inlets south of the bridge,* and would engage the outposts at La Rana and Fusina; they would then get astride the Padua road at Malcontenta, whence they could cut off all retreat from Mestre and at the same time observe any movement towards Mestre from Padua. On the right, the Free Corps from Bologna would advance along the road by the canal, reduce a redan in the canal

* Now the new port of Marghera.

bank harbouring two cannons, and continue into Mestre.[1] It was intended that Orsini should lead the vanguard in this attack on the right flank. Almost apologetically the Adjutant added that he, Fontana, would be at Orsini's side. Orsini's dark eyes flashed; in silent understanding their right hands gripped each other until the knuckles showed livid in the candlelight.

The morning of 27 October dawned foggy. Orsini had his company paraded early by his Sergeant-Major, Etture Venturi, but the two field guns which were to have come by water from the Lido were delayed. At nine o'clock it was decided to proceed without them. Silently waving his men forward, Orsini advanced into the mist.

Slowly, with the utmost caution, turning their heads and straining their eyes into the swirling hallucinatory shroud, they progressed for a mile, a mile and a half, until they came close to where they knew the enemy advanced posts must be lying. Here they had to wait interminably, numb with cold and sickened by excitement, before the musical sound of firing on the left from the direction of the railway announced that the central battle had been joined.

Advancing again, they blundered upon the redan looming over them from the canal bank. Wheeling to the attack they stumbled into an unexpected flood, floundering waist deep, their weapons drenched and for the moment useless, while a cacophony of musket fire and close-range cannonade broke out on them. There was some wavering, until Orsini, perceiving that the flood proceeded from a moat surrounding the redan, so close to it as to be below the angle of depression of the defenders' guns, rushed forward crying "Long live Italy" and hurled himself headlong into it. In an instant Fontana rallied the men and followed him, not without loss, for he and fourteen others were struck down by grapeshot; but the violence of the charge was too much for the Austrians, who broke and fled, abandoning their smoking cannons. Orsini climbed out of the ditch, tended the wounded, and arranged for them to be picked up by the main column, together with the captured guns. He ordered his company to dry their muskets and reform their ranks. Then, borrowing Fontana's sword, since Fontana's right arm was shattered and he had no present use for it, he brandished

[1] Pepe, I, 341.

it towards Mestre. Entering the town he was held up by heavy firing from the Post Office; with fifteen men he attacked and captured it, taking forty-seven prisoners whom he sent under escort to the rear.

The final citadel in the Villa Bianchini was manned by a garrison two hundred strong, and here there was violent opposition. By this time the field guns had come up and were firing in support, on the orders of General Pepe who was personally directing the battle from *lunette* no. 12 in Malghera. After a long engagement the gun crews were all killed and the artillery fell silent; there was no option but for the infantry to take the place by storm. The villa was surrounded by a wall eighteen feet high, a formidable obstacle, the more so since every yard of it was covered by riflemen inside the house. Accompanied by another officer Orsini scrambled to the top, vaulted nimbly over and dropped into the garden, a rain of bullets smacking against the masonry behind him as he fell. The others followed, and soon the ornamental glades and shrubberies whispered and stirred with creeping movement, working nearer to the house on every side. Crouching, Orsini led his men in a dash across the lawns to the shelter of the terrace parapet, where on one knee they kept up a steady firing and reloading. The garden was filled with drifting smoke and the bitter smell of exploded powder; flash and flame spurted from the shutters covering the windows; bullets cracked the air above their heads, ricochets hissed and whined. With a rousing *Viva l'Italia* they swarmed across the terrace, up the steps to the stately portico, and started to hack at the barricaded door. The door splintered inwards and they went in with the bayonet.

As they entered from one side, the central column advancing from the railway poured in from another, and in the confusion, beneath the gilded pillars and ornately decorated ceilings, for a time Italian grappled with Italian in deathly combat. When finally they recognized each other they went from room to room, and shriek upon shriek was heard as they plunged their bayonets into the shrinking bodies of their victims or shot them point blank so that the powder scorched their faces. Shocked at the unmilitary savagery Orsini interposed himself, cursing and shouting at the other officers to come to help him, until the slaughter ceased and the survivors were permitted to surrender.

It was now past three o'clock, and on word being received of a large enemy force approaching Mestre by the road from Padua, the retreat was sounded. Supporting the wounded and herding the prisoners, the Volunteers returned victoriously to the fortress of Malghera. The action, though limited in scope and in duration, had been costly; Italian casualties were about four hundred, or roughly one in five, including the much-loved Alessandro Poerio, the soldier-poet from Calabria, who died in Manin's arms in Venice. But they had killed or wounded an equal number of their opponents, and brought six hundred of them back as prisoners—in all, nearly half the total force engaged. They had also captured seven fine bronze cannons which were dragged in triumph by the Venetians into the Piazza San Marco; many horses, large quantities of ammunition, and last but not least the enemy commander's *secretaire*, the papers of which disclosed that he had been fully warned of the attack the night before by some unknown spy at General Pepe's headquarters.

In the deepening dusk and drip of Malghera, Orsini and his companions refought the battle time and time again. It had been a victory, no doubt of that; yet their satisfaction was tinged with sorrow. Many of their comrades had been lost in the war now drawing to a dismal close in Venice; what exactly had they gained? Not an inch of soil had been wrested from the Austrians, and Italian unity was as far away as ever. Truly, the task they had set themselves seemed too ambitious. An epidemic fever sweeping through the fortress rendered the regiment unfit for action, and early in November they were withdrawn to Venice. At the end of the month dramatic news of the breakdown of the Papal government made it urgent for them to return to the Romagna; they were exchanged for a fresh battalion, and reached Ravenna at the beginning of December.

VI

A great deal had happened in Orsini's absence.

Pio Nono had grown so unpopular that he had been forced to dismiss his minister, Cardinal Antonelli, who was held responsible for his withdrawal from the war. The revolutionary Clubs organized by Ciceruacchio and Sterbini among the impoverished citizens of Rome had become all-powerful. Not willing to debase his office by alliance with them, and yet afraid for his personal safety if he offended them, Pio Nono appointed Pellegrino Rossi as his Secretary of State.

In many ways the choice was reasonable. Rossi was neither a Jacobin nor a bigot. A personal friend of Guizot, the apparently undislodgeable minister of the French King Louis Philippe, whose system of controlled democracy he much admired, Rossi was a nationalist, and a thinker so advanced that he had married a Protestant wife. He was a lover of order, and extraordinarily efficient. He went to work at once, cleaning out the cosy nests of idleness and self-enrichment thriving in the ancient clutter which was the administration of the Papal States. But like many men of facts and figures, Rossi offended everyone. He insulted the representatives of the people, he despised the Clubs, he dismayed the Cardinals by developing schools, railways and telegraphs at an unheard-of rate. He demanded work from the civil service, taxed the clergy, and interfered with the activities of brigands. He overhauled the Papal army, and tried to disarm the *reduci*, the patriotic irregulars returning from the war. As an ultimate indiscretion, hearing of threats against his life at the opening of the Constituent Assembly, he entrusted himself to the hated Swiss instead of to the outraged Civic Guard. He was jeered at and hooted in his progress. Had he reached the Chamber, he would have found the entire Assembly ranged against him on the opposition benches. But as he climbed the steps he was surrounded by a group of men, and stabbed in the neck.

His death was so universally welcomed that for some time no one knew, or cared, which of his many enemies had struck the blow. The Clubs took control. Shouting and brandishing, the mob advanced upon the Quirinal, pausing only to chant a mocking *Miserere* beneath the windows of Rossi's widow, and to chase Cardinal Lambruschini, caught like a cat in the middle of the street, up into the refuge of a hayloft. They then besieged the palace, their torches flaring angrily.

Inside the palace Pio Nono, alone save for his personal retinul and a handful of Swiss Guards, at first showed obstinacy, aspiring to a martyr's crown; later, he was persuaded to a less dramatic course. On the night of 24 November he divested himself of his pontifical robes: accompanied by Antonelli he slipped away to seek protection of King Bomba of Naples in the frontier fortress of Gaeta. His escape was not sensational. The carriage of the Bavarian Ambassador was waiting for him. During the journey he cheered his loyal companions by his whimsical philosophy, unpacking and showing them his travelling ciborium and chalice, the very same that Pius VI had taken with him when he was kidnapped by Napoleon. At Gaeta he was lodged at an hotel, where shortly afterwards the French Ambassador arrived, with all the luggage. King Bomba was delighted at the honour done him. He too had lost caste with the other states by giving up the war. He placed his palace in Gaeta at the disposal of his distinguished guest, and hastened to join him there in person.

Rome did not seem like Rome without the Pope, and applications were sent for his return. Piedmont, too, hoping still for leadership in a league of Italian princes, offered him a rival home in Nice. Bologna, jealous of Rome, suggested that Pio Nono should come back to the Romagna of his birth. To all their invitations the Pope remained quite deaf. The death of Rossi had convinced him that the federal ideal of the Moderates was impossible. Metternich had been right, liberalism was incompatible with his holy office. Henceforward he would humbly follow the strict path mapped out by ecclesiastical tradition. His new resolve won praise from Antonelli, to whom increasingly he left all decisions. Dark, suave and fascinating, Antonelli was for twenty years the *eminence grise* of the reaction.

His immediate attitude was that the Pope would return when he could do so unconditionally. In the meantime he discountenanced everything that was going on in Rome. The Moderates were disconcerted, the Republicans confirmed in their defiance. A provisional Junta was set up, and instructions were issued throughout the Papal States for a general election by universal suffrage. Partly because of intimidation by the priests, and partly from sheer ignorance, a good number of the new voters voted for St. Peter, and a proportion of blank ballot forms were cast. None the less the election went off smoothly in these areas so unaccustomed to the exercise of democratic rites.

The Romagna was excitedly republican. Orsini, invited to

stand for his native province of Forli, accepted with alacrity. On 21 January 1849 he was duly elected with 4,802 votes, and attended a banquet given in his honour in the village hall of Meldola, his birthplace, where he made a forthright and invigorating speech. He put off his handsome uniform, and donned the frock-coat of the politician "with the peculiar *chic* with which all military men wear civilian dress".[1] On his way to Rome he called on his uncle as he passed through Imola. His uncle fussed about, arranged a dinner party, and proudly addressed the assembled guests. "Deputy! A state matter, what think you? Ho, Ho, Ho! I find that I did not feed an ass after all!" He buried his face in his *lasagne* and his friends, Papalists to a man, did likewise. "But at Mestre he was nearly killed," the old man went on. "Providence saved him! We shall see what good will come of it. He is sure to get killed in some way or another." He paused and bowed his head. "Enough. May God keep His Holy Hand over him, and protect him."[2] He walked with his nephew to the coach, and there embraced him with a fond "Addio", as though in some strange way aware that they would meet no more.

Orsini went by way of Florence, in order to spend a few days with his wife. Assunta was living alone in his apartment in the Via Orci, and was petulant because this was but the second fleeting visit he had paid her since their rapid honeymoon six months before. He gave her some money, and her orders. All hinged upon what Tuscany would do. If, as he hoped, Tuscany threw out her archduke and joined the Republic, Assunta should stay in Florence, and he would come to visit her when the affairs of state permitted. If not, she must be ready to leave at a moment's notice; for if there should be an Austrian intervention in Tuscany she must come at once to Rome. Assunta sighed; and he went out. In the bitter whispering wind of February he stood for a moment outside the cathedral, gazing blankly at that vast chequer-board of marble. Returning, he stopped before Benvenuto's bronze of Perseus and Medusa, and nodded in approval. Next day he went on to Rome, and took lodgings at 11 Via Bocca di Leone, an address which pleased him.

On 9 February he took his seat with the other deputies, many

[1] Herzen, *My Past and Thoughts*, VI, xiii.
[2] Orsini, *Memoirs and Adventures*, 73–4.

of them well known to him, many marked out for an early death, but all of them exalted and inspired in that brief moment when the temporal power of the Pope was declared abolished, and the Roman Republic proclaimed. The same evening it was known that Leopold of Tuscany was on his way to join the other exiled potentates at Gaeta.

The decision of Tuscany to join the Republic was in part the work of Mazzini, who had stopped there on his way from Switzerland to Rome where he was eagerly awaited. The Assembly was composed for the most part of plain, blunt men little given to philosophizing. But they all knew Mazzini, and during the long years of waiting had devoutly read his works. If perhaps they did not fully understand his mystic nuances, they all knew about the third Rome, the Rome of the people, and the dawning Republic of Mankind. They trusted him implicitly; they were awed by the religious radiance which he shed about him; they responded as best they could to the impossible standards of purpose and devotion which he laid upon them. "While Garibaldi was being fashioned into a hero on the breezy uplands of Brazil, the more painful making of a saint had for eleven years been in process amid the squalid and fog-obscured surroundings of a London lodging-house. And now at last the finished product of so much pain and virtue shone before Europe in Italian sunlight, on the great stage of Rome."[1]

Mazzini was quickly elected one of a triumvirate in which he was the only active force. It was his Rome, and his Republic. He did not delude himself. He knew that it was insecurely founded on a chance combination of events, on a thin crust of enthusiasm concealing a number of unworthy elements; that it was hemmed in by powerful interests waiting for the first opportunity to destroy it. That did not disturb him. He was an aesthete. No one in that vastly serious age was more aware of his responsibility before history and the world—not even Lamartine or Abraham Lincoln. From the moment of his first deliberately leisured entrance he was determined so to conduct the Republic that it should stand out as an epic, flawless and superb.

"Here in Rome," he told the Assembly, "we may not be moral mediocrities."[2] He tramped round the echoing corridors

[1] Trevelyan, *Garibaldi's Defence of Rome*, 97.
[2] *Ibid.*

of the Quirinal until he found "a room small enough to feel at home in".[1] There he worked incessantly, and yet was constantly accessible with a quiet smile for all. Of danger he was utterly oblivious. He lived on two shillings a day, taking his meals at a small *trattoria*; his nominal monthly salary he always gave away. His luxury was a vase of flowers, daily renewed by an unknown hand. Alone at night he smoked his cigars and plucked at his guitar.[2]

Through week after week of unbroken sunshine in that marvellous winter the Assembly listened spellbound to the dark, spare man with the huge cadaverous eyes, as his quiet voice laid before them measures to capture and erect in Rome the pure forms of democracy, as if in glass cases in a museum. The great estates of the church were taken over and divided out as peasant holdings. The offices of the Inquisition were turned into tenement flats. The death penalty was abolished, the freedom of the press ensured, tariffs were lowered and unequal monopolies removed. Fees for religious duties were forbidden. The poor clergy were paid more, the richer less. Work was found for the unemployed. Mazzini thus defined his policy: "No war of classes, no hostility to existing wealth or unjust violation of the rights of property; but a constant disposition to ameliorate the material condition of the classes least favoured by fortune."[3]

Meanwhile, outside Rome, the storm clouds gathered. The response of Pio Nono, or rather of Cardinal Antonelli, to the proclamation of the Republic was an appeal to the Catholic powers. They all made warm promises, but nothing was done at first except that the Austrians once more occupied Ferrara. At the end of March 1849 the situation was clarified by the rash action of Charles Albert of Piedmont. Always looking forward to the day of his revenge on Austria, he had hoped to bring about a league of Italian princes; but with the Papal States and Tuscany in revolution, and the Pope in exile throwing himself on Austria, that had proved an empty dream. Resolved to carry on alone, Charles Albert made a further disastrous attack on Lombardy, which resulted in his defeat by Radetzky at

[1] Griffith, 214.
[2] Bolton King, *Mazzini*, 133.
[3] Trevelyan, *Garibaldi's Defence of Rome*, 101.

Orsini as a deputy to the Republic of Rome, 1849
From a contemporary print

the second battle of Novara, and his abdication in favour of his son, Victor Emmanuel II.

The temporary destruction of the only considerable Italian army produced a marked hardening in the attitude of the Catholic powers. Austria was free to begin a long advance down the Adriatic coast which eventually brought her as far south as Ascoli and Foligno. King Bomba of Naples paraded his army on his northern borders and did what he could to aggravate frontier incidents. Spain fitted out an expedition which was always just about to land in the mouth of the Tiber, but somehow never did. Tuscany abandoned her republican pretensions, and prepared for the return of Archduke Leopold from Gaeta, hoping, as it turned out, vainly, to avert an Austrian intervention. A host of enemies was bearing down upon the new Republic of Rome; the Republic appointed Mazzini its dictator, and prepared to sell its life as dearly as it could.

The Romans placed great hopes on France, the most powerful of the Catholic countries, and the only one which had not yet declared itself. France had, it was true, a long and jealous tradition as the champion of the Pope. On the other hand, rivalry with Austria was equally well established as the major premise of her foreign bureau, and it was certain that she would not permit the power of Austria in Italy to be increased. Moreover, France was once more a republic: a jaded and a *rusée* one perhaps, but still able to contrive the virginal blush of liberal principles; surely she would not allow her innocent young neighbour to be ravished by a set of experienced old tyrants? Finally, thought the Romans, their chances had recently been very much improved by the election of Louis Napoleon as President. From what they knew of him, he seemed to represent the modern spirit; cutting out old shams and formalism he was going to institute a strong, centralized government founded directly on the wishes of the people. They knew that their independence was a central feature of his plan. Had he not, at the nadir of his fortunes as an exile in New York, reaffirmed to Count Arese that he would do something to help Italy when he came to power in France? He had proved himself a man of action. Who would not prefer the inspirited and chancy ventures of the former Carbonaro to the "mellifluous sympathy"[1] of Lamartine?

[1] Trevelyan, *Manin*, 81.

The Italian expectations of Louis Napoleon were due to a misunderstanding. For that the Italians were not to blame, since it was his fate, whenever it was not indeed his policy, to be misunderstood. At the outset of his career he had stated his purpose plainly, and since leaving Italy in 1831 he had pursued it without the slightest deviation. It was the eccentricity of the means he chose that obscured and confused his ends.

After Hortense, his mother, had rescued him from the Austrians in Italy, for the next few years he was at pains to keep his name before the public. Then, in 1836, he crossed the French frontier from Switzerland and entered Strasbourg. Dressed in a blue artillery uniform with a colonel's epaulettes, wearing the star and broad riband of the Legion of Honour, and a general's cocked hat, and escorted by the shrouded eagle of the Empire, Louis Napoleon waited in the officers' mess of the garrison artillery till dawn, when he rose and said, "Gentlemen, the time has come!", to which they responded sleepily, "Have no doubt of it; France follows!" He led them out and was arrested.

There followed his exile to America, his mother's death, and his establishment on a lordly scale in London. Sometimes his extravagance went too far for the English taste; he was well to the fore as a knight in real armour at the Eglinton tournament; and in August 1840 he startled his dinner guests by requesting them to dine again with him on that day twelve-month in the Tuileries. To make good his invitation, he landed near Boulogne with fifty-six men and many cases of glittering uniforms. He entered a barracks where amid scenes of wild enthusiasm he promoted all the corporals to be sergeants and the sergeants to be captains, presenting each with the appropriate epaulettes, until his proceedings were terminated by the infuriated Colonel. This time he was put on trial for his life. In a defiant address he spoke of the cause of Empire, of the defeated of Waterloo; and many of the beribboned veterans assembled to sit in judgment on him audibly choked back a sob. Nevertheless he was sentenced to life imprisonment in the damp and gloomy fortress of Ham where he spent six tedious years, and whence in 1846 he made a spectacular escape with the aid of his physician and his valet, disguised as a workman carrying a plank.

Back in London he bided his chance to advance his schemes in a less obvious manner. He distributed his *Manuel d'Artillerie*, not only throughout France, but to all British officers of his acquaintance, and was rewarded with election as an honorary member of the Army and Navy Club. He resumed his pleasurable pursuits, which included Miss Rowles of Chiselhurst, Miss Seymour, Miss Burdett of Burdett-Coutts, not to mention Miss Howard, who busied herself with raising funds for his impending election campaign in France.

For at last his hour had struck. Suddenly, in February 1848, Guizot's government collapsed. In June, the serious disorders inherited by the Second Republic were bloodily repressed at the barricades by General Cavaignac, a veiled reactionary, at the enormous cost of 10,000 persons killed or wounded. When an uneasy calm had been restored, Louis Napoleon reappeared in Paris, where he had gained a seat as deputy in the republican Assembly. Exploiting the derisive unconcern of his colleagues, he stood for President of the Republic in the forthcoming election, which was decided by universal suffrage. At the polls in December, Lamartine, who favoured himself as the popular candidate, secured only eighteen thousand votes; Louis Napoleon five millions and a half. Some of his supporters in the provinces simply supposed that the Emperor had come back. "How should I not vote for him," said one of them: "I, whose nose was frozen off at Moscow?"[1]

Such was the state of things in France when Pio Nono's call for help was heard from Gaeta. Louis Napoleon had no more changed his youthful feelings about Italy than he had changed his determination to be Emperor, but the one was dependent on the other. As soon as he was Emperor, Italy should be among the first to feel the benefit: until that day, like everything sacred and profane, Italy was a pawn in his battle for advancement. He said as much, within a few days of his election, in reply to the question of his old friend Hortense Cornu. "Tell them that my name is Bonaparte, and that I feel the responsibilities that name implies. Italy is dear to me, as dear almost as France; but my duties to France come first, and I must watch for an opportunity."[2] That opportunity had not yet come.

[1] Fisher, *Bonapartism*, 83.
[2] Thompson, 168.

VII

In Mazzini's Rome, corrupting means were not allowed to dishonour worthy ends. The liberal mildness of the government was its greatest weakness. Unlike Garibaldi, who was all for "closing the holy shop",[1] Mazzini was too wise to offend religious sensibilities if it could be avoided: the holy *Bambino* continued its rounds of ceremonial visits to the sick, though now it was known as "*il bambino democratico*".[2] Reforms were hampered with impunity by functionaries who did not wish to be reformed, and resistance to the confiscation of church lands was actively supported by Antonelli. Many felt that the "bigots" were let off too lightly. In consequence the semi-military brigades sent out to enforce the law resorted to outrages by way of extra punishment. It was all very well for Garibaldi's high-spirited legionaries, recently arrived from South America, to ransack monasteries in search of love letters belonging to the monks, but it did not stop there. A class of extreme republicans arose who received no more than a rebuke for crimes of violence, lust and outright robbery.

The worst of them was one Callimaco Zambianchi. Exiled from Forli in 1832 he had spent fourteen years in France studying the history of the Terror. Returning at the Amnesty, he put into dreadful effect what he had learnt, during the disturbances in Bologna in the summer of 1848. Arrested and imprisoned by Farini, the Republic most mistakenly listened to his claim for release and honourable employment. With the rank of captain, he was now commanding a column of *Finanzieri*, or security troops, down at Terracina, almost on the Neapolitan border and not far from Gaeta, where his wholesale ravages were providing an excellent weapon to Antonelli in his efforts to bring the Republic into disrepute.

Zambianchi had to be stopped. In March 1849 Orsini, in view of his probity and reputation for intrepid action, was chosen for the task. He wrathfully pursued his over-exuberant fellow-countryman to Terracina, and ordered him back to Rome. As

[1] Griffith, 215.

[2] Trevelyan, *Garibaldi's Defence of Rome*, 151 n.

Zambianchi took no notice, Orsini appealed to the local garrison for help. But the colonel would not risk a battle with the terrible Zambianchi for fear of a slit throat, and so Orsini had to return inconclusively to Rome. On 9 April the Ministry of War announced that in order to secure the government's authority, the strength of the *Finanzieri* was to be increased to two battalions. Captain Felice Orsini was transferred from the battalion Alto Reno to take command of one. The other was entrusted to Captain Callimaco Zambianchi.

It was unthinkable! Two men, two Forlivese, the one of honourable family, the other from the dregs: the loyal soldier and the mutinous brigand, the instrument of chastisement and the scoundrel, now of equal rank, appointed brother officers in the same corps, and that the worst corps in the army! What a muddling, two-faced, chicken-hearted lot were in the government. The Triumvirate!-old Armellini, a bumbling lawyer: Aurelio Saffi, another Forlivese, a young man of modest, melancholy purity, all mildness and philosophy: and then, Mazzini. Mazzini certainly compelled respect; he was tireless and inexorable; but he was a scholar, not a soldier. What they needed was a man of action like good old General Pepe. Orsini, never a man to mince his opinions, wrote and told them so, using expressions of "indifference and disdain". "If you know me, you must be aware that I never feared governments or individuals; what I tell you is dictated by patriotism and the cause. I desire nothing from you, neither do I fear."[1]

Perhaps the government were impressed by the fierce sincerity of the scarcely known young deputy. At all events they dropped the question of the *Finanzieri*, and found him a mission bristling with far greater obstacles and a high degree of personal danger at the greatest distance possible from Rome. At five o'clock in the afternoon of 19 April, one of Mazzini's personal aides came to summon Orsini to the Triumvirate. As he entered defiantly, ready to justify himself, Mazzini rose, gave him a piercing look from his dark eyes, and shook him briskly by the hand. He then spoke with the utmost gravity, in a manly way, without a trace of the expected haughtiness. He explained how the moderation of the government was being abused on every side. He reminded Orsini that the Romagna had a deplorable

[1] Orsini, *Memoirs and Adventures*, 77–8.

record of brigandage and feuds. At Ancona the *reduci*, republican extremists returning from the war, under guise of rounding-up their Catholic rivals, were terrorizing the whole region. The trade of the vital port was at a standstill; public officials did not dare to do their duty; twenty-eight Sanfedists already had been slaughtered, and the murders were increasing at the rate of six a day. The commissioners so far sent had done no good, and no news was being received from them; the mission was so difficult that no one could be found to take it on.

It was a case (and here, with a faint smile, Mazzini made his only reference to Orsini's impudent letter) for a man of action and decision. Orsini knew the district of Ancona, and was himself known and respected there. He could count on full support; a force of a hundred men would follow him, and a further fifty would be ordered up from Ascoli. He must go at once; the situation was becoming hourly worse. Foreign governments were alarmed, and at a time when the Republic could least afford it, menacing despatches were coming in from France and England. A British gunboat was standing by to take off the consul, Mr. Moore.

Orsini demanded unlimited powers in writing. This was as much his habit before accepting any undertaking as it was to write a strong report about it afterwards. Mazzini agreed, drumming impatiently with his fingers on the table. Two hours later Orsini galloped out of Rome. After a breakneck journey through the Apennines, with relays of horses, he clattered into silent Ancona at four o'clock in the morning of 21 April. As he rode, he rather regretted his decision; feuds in the Romagna were always bad; and he did not know to what extent Zambianchi was behind it all. On the other hand, Orsini had been entirely conquered by Mazzini's personality and charm. And there could be no denying it, the title of Commissioner Extraordinary of the Roman Republic had an agreeably important sound.

He decided to remain incognito at first, to assess the situation, and so gave out that he had been sent on business connected with the customs and finance. He had no difficulty in discovering the culprits. The name of the Red Man was in every mouth, and the ruffian swaggered about the streets with his lieutenants while the citizens shrank away to clear his path. What to do about them was another matter. All doors were barred at sundown, and after dark death ranged unhindered. The police had either been corrupted, or cowered behind locks and bolts. The Governor was powerless: his motley force two hundred strong, made up of *Carabinieri*, port artillery, coastguards and National Guard were all intimidated, and the latter, who were the most numerous, included members of the gang. Nobody thought that the Red Man could be defeated except by regular troops. But as days went by the soldiers promised by Mazzini did not come; instead a shower of messages urging action exposed the real nature of Orsini's duties. The Red Man was well aware of them, and as Orsini went round the brothels and casinos making his inquiries, his life was once saved only by the failure of a pistol trained upon his back.

He sought out his predecessors. To his surprise he found the two commissioners living unmolested and in comfort. He soon saw why. The Red Man, they assured him, was not a bad fellow after all; he and his followers had many grievances; they needed understanding, and tactful treatment. They went on to suggest that the gang should be enrolled as a special company of security troops, paid and armed by the Republic: such a course would, they felt certain, appeal to the honour even of smugglers and assassins. Also, they would be more easily distinguishable once they were in uniform. Disgustedly, Orsini packed the ex-commissioners off to Rome.

As he saw it, there were three small factors in his favour. The old fortress of Ancona was an impregnable base; the *Carabinieri*, though only twenty-four in number, were loyal soldiers; and finally, the Red Man in his insolence had grown unwary. On these three points he built a plan, revealing it to the Governor only two hours before he put it into execution. At 2 a.m. on 27 April the twenty ringleaders were surrounded in their dens and were marched off to the fortress, where the drawbridge was pulled up behind them. At five a general call to arms was sounded, and the Governor harangued the National Guard in the City Square. At the same time a state of siege was declared, with orders for a curfew and the lighting of the streets at night, and the carrying of weapons was prohibited. A proclamation by Orsini in a strong yet reasonable tone was posted up to reassure the citizens. By the time the followers of the arrested bandits learned what had occurred it was too late to do anything except chalk threats of vengeance on the walls. In the evening there was some trouble in the suburbs at the Porta Pia, where it was said armed rebels from the country were coming to release their friends and leaders. Orsini shut the gate, and ostentatiously announced that anyone who approached would be met with grapeshot from the cannon in the embrasures on either side. No one came.

So far, so good. There remained the question of dealing with the captives. A council of war had been convened for bringing them to summary trial, but it was quite impossible to get anyone to testify against them, let alone to act as judges. Anticipating this situation, the Red Man had concluded that Orsini would attempt their deportation. He overawed his jailors, who were so unnerved at having him among them even as their prisoner that they obeyed his orders and refused to let down the drawbridge. So the rebels became masters of the castle, where they now held the commandant and his family as hostages. Their confederates in the city, furthermore, had had time to recover themselves. A deputation of the National Guard, drunken and terrified, waited on Orsini at Government House and represented that they would be heavily outnumbered in any attack upon the fortress.

That night a detachment of the guard went to the castle with victuals for the inmates' supper. The hungry janitors, seeing no harm in this humane and routine measure, let them in. Whereupon Orsini and his twenty-four *Carabinieri* slipped from the shadows and attached themselves to the rear of the procession. After an interval they reappeared, each *Carabiniere* accompanying a shackled felon, like the conjuring trick of the thieves in the pack of cards. In midnight silence broken only by the rattling of their chains the desperadoes were put on board a vessel waiting in the harbour, were taken down the coast to Fermo, and sent to the government fortress at Spoleto.

Next day, the twenty-eighth, ten more arrests were made. Orsini, determined that the ends of justice should no longer be defeated at Ancona, had summoned six magistrates from neighbouring towns on pain of dismissal from their posts. Protesting uselessly, they came; the trial began. The next necessity was to persuade the civil service back to work. Many officials had pleaded the terror as an excuse for retiring to their country villas; the Director of Postal Services was sunning himself at Porto Recanati. They too, threatened with instant superannuation, returned to duty. Order was so far restored that by the twenty-ninth, only eight days after his arrival, Orsini was able to rescind the state of siege before it should injure trade. The British Consul, Moore, came round in person to offer his congratulations, and to ask sheepishly for the release of one of the prisoners, who proved to be an Englishman.

Before leaving Ancona, Orsini rectified an injustice of another kind. The Austrians were once more battering at Bologna with their artillery, and the delegate sent behind their lines to discuss the terms of truce had been detained as a hostage, contrary to the rules of war, on the advice of Monsignor Bedini, the Papal Legate. Orsini had for his fellow guests in Government House at Ancona two brothers of Bedini, a niece of Pio Nono who was the wife of one of them, and her small daughter, all having come from Sinigallia to shelter from the Red Man. He took them into custody, and personally conducted the gentlemen to comfortable confinement in the castle, while the ladies were looked after in the town, until the sudden release of the Bolognese delegate when they too regained their freedom.

On 9 May Orsini returned to Rome, where the praises of his chief and a degree of local fame were very welcome to him. He had, however, made the inexperienced mistake of doing too well. In a matter of days he was on his way to another equally invidious appointment at Ascoli, some eighty miles south of Ancona in the eastern foothills of the Apennines.

Whereas at Ancona the trouble had been caused by the returning soldiers, at Ascoli it was fomented by disgruntled Papalists, strongly resentful of the sequestration of their lands. With the connivance of the Papal court at Gaeta, Monsignor Savelli, from nearby Teramo in the kingdom of Naples, was playing upon the ignorance of the peasants by devices such as the Weeping Madonna of Fermo, which, in response to a judicious use of soap and water, blanched with sympathy for the sufferings of the Church. Provided with officers and equipment by King Bomba, rebels and brigands had been tacked together into an army of two thousand commanded by a colonel of the former Gregorian Centurions. Led by priests and friars crucifix in hand they had entered the province of Ascoli to carry on a holy war of plunder. The better regiments of the Republic had recently been recalled for the defence of Rome. Faced by the usual hotch-potch of customs men, *Finanzieri*, *Carabinieri* and the National Guard, the insurgents were having everything their own way.

As at Ancona, Orsini acted boldly. He proclaimed martial law, and condemned three leading members of the clerical party to death by shooting. When the victims were receiving their last religious comforts he suspended the sentences, thereby gaining good currency for barter, with which in the first instance he tried unsuccessfully to obtain the freedom of his old friend Colonel Ribotti, long a prisoner of the King of Naples. He joined his odds and end of soldiers into a single regiment which he called, not thinking them worth more, the battalion *Mobilizzata*. He led them out of Ascoli to attack a force of eight hundred rebels, but made little progress since the enemy held strong positions on inaccessible cliffs and crags, and he had to retire at dusk for fear of ambush by other bands concealed in woods and mountains.

After that the initiative was taken from him. The Austrians entered Bologna on 16 May and swept down towards Ancona. As the Austrains advanced the rebels increased both in numbers and audacity, and on 31 May Orsini had to conduct a desperate seven-hour defence of Ascoli. Meanwhile the rebels filtered round his flanks, cutting off one by one the mountain passes leading back to Rome, and by getting astride the road from Ancona to Ascoli intercepted the trickle of supplies from the port to the beleaguered province. Seeing the danger of being hemmed in between the Austrians coming south and the rebels working north to meet them, the colonel of the only remaining regular unit left for Rome. Orsini contemptuously took over his command, giving himself the magnificent title of High Commander of the Expeditionary Forces in the Province of Ascoli. To maintain his troops he sold the goods of absconded Papalists, and made requisitions through the local mayors from all those who had insulted or defied the republican banner.

On 3 June Ascoli became untenable and he had to withdraw to villages successively further north, making a strong point out of each. His force, reduced to a few hundred, was openly disintegrating. His greatest asset, the mounted *Carabinieri*, were convinced that the Republic was about to fall, and so not only did not want to fight, but did not even want to get back to Rome. Orsini blamed their cowardice on their leader Captain Freddi, whom the government had posted to him, to his great disgust, with high commendation for valour and devotion. Freddi, a former captain of the Papal Guard, was the son of the Colonel Freddi who had arrested Orsini and his father at Bologna in 1844. He now professed, so long as things went well, an obsequious loyalty to the Republic. It did not in the least deceive Orsini, who well remembered how the odious youth had jeered at him as he passed in chains through Forli on his way to prison at San Leo. His regret at losing the *Carabinieri* was tempered by relief at getting rid of a man who maddened him. He left them behind as castaways in his retreat, whereon they went to the nearest place where there were Austrians, and surrendered.

On 16 June Ancona fell; therafter Orsini was harried day and night on every side by Austrians and rebels. He was still opposed to all capitulation. "In order not to go to sleep"[1] he made a furious sortie, planning to break through to Rome; but his officers refused to follow him, and he resigned command. When the enemy arrived to capture him he hid among his subalterns; presuming that he had fled, the Austrians were not much interested in the others, whom they congratulated upon an excellent fight and permitted to go home. Orsini thus managed to obtain a pass in the name of 2/Lt. Francesco Pinelli for Terni where, he said, he lived. He set out on 19 June, alone and in disguise, and passed through the Austrian lines at Foligno. At Rome he succeeded with great difficulty in penetrating the cordon of the French besieging army, and reported to his government a week or so before the end of its existence.

VIII

In the early months of 1849 Louis Napoleon found his promises to Italy and the difficulties of his new office as President of the French Republic coming ever more strongly into conflict. Two

[1] Ghisalberti, 88.

years of intricate manœuvring still stood between him and absolute power. The friends of Italy in the Assembly—Ledru-Rollin and his democrats, Jules Favre the lawyer, Louis Blanc with his socialistic blueprints, Raspail the humane reformer—were in all other respects his enemies. Nor was he secure enough to act alone. His following was not powerful at the most important point, the mob of Paris, which four times in the last half-century had made and unmade governments and kings. He was entirely dependent on the Catholic vote. In the coming month of May there would be the elections for the National Assembly; a Catholic gain was forecast, and it was essential that they should be pleased with him.

It was not sufficient for the Pope to be restored; it was necessary that Louis Napoleon and no one else should do it. It was here that the last hope of the Italian patriots went awry, for the quarrel between the French and the Austrians, instead of centring upon Austrian aggression, became a race to destroy the Roman Republic. On 24 April 1849 Louis Napoleon sent General Oudinot to occupy Civitavecchia, and to discuss with Mazzini the question of the Pope's return on terms. But neither side would hear of any terms. Contrary to his orders and mouthing out the jest that Italians never fight, Oudinot advanced on Rome. The gate which he attacked, although several centuries old and marked clearly on his maps, proved to have been walled up many years before, a contingency which should always be provided for in Italy. He was soundly beaten and retired to Civitavecchia; Mazzini, still convinced there was some mistake, prevented Garibaldi from driving him into the sea. The French prisoners were carefully tended, and returned to Oudinot laden with gifts of cigars and snuff wrapped up in tricoloured tracts.

An ignominious retreat from Rome was the last thing Louis Napoleon could afford; on 7 May he was defeated in the Assembly by Jules Favre; now more than ever only the Catholics could save him. While he was reinforcing Oudinot at Civitavecchia, he sent Ferdinand de Lesseps to parley with Mazzini. de Lesseps, the future builder of the Suez Canal, was a personable young man; Mazzini liked him, and they came within sight of an agreement. But early in June Oudinot, who now had 30,000 men and a train of siege guns, felt himself strong enough to break the truce. During the night he occupied the villa Corsini, house of the four winds, which stood on the vital hill outside the walls overlooking Mount Janiculum, the key to Rome. de Lesseps was recalled to France next day.

With an overwhelming army at the gates, with three other Catholic armies on the march from Austria, Spain and Naples, without any hope of assistance from abroad, the situation of the Republic was already hopeless. Yet Mazzini would not hear of a surrender. For him it was a battle of religions, of the old against the new, and Rome was a symbol sacred to them both. Rome of the Caesars, Rome of the Popes, through the ages the complacent seat of tyrants, Rome was held in contempt by the liberal provinces of Italy; only by falling gloriously to join them in their ruin could she rise again to be the focus of their unity and freedom. Therefore, "since we were destined to fall, it was our duty, in view of the future, to proffer our *Morituri te salutant* to Italy from Rome".[1]

The advance of Oudinot brought Garibaldi back from Naples, where he had been harrying King Bomba's army. "He has come! He has come!" yelled the crowd all down the Corso. His shaggy, sunburnt, dusty warriors in their scarlet blouses and black-plumed rancho hats rode nonchalantly to their convent billets, tethered their horses, roasted huge quarters of oxen over open fires, unrolled their saddles into mattresses, and went to sleep, as if declaring the siege officially begun.

Men from many nations and all parts of Italy took part in the defence. There were Durando's Volunteers, repatriated from Vicenza, many of them extreme *reduci*, now refurbishing their uniforms—often black velvet trousers under a black velvet blouse with tucked waist and pleated skirts, large black buttons and a fold-down collar fastened by a tricoloured bow, and a soft black hat pinned up on one side with a spray of ostrich feathers. In contrast were the Papal regulars, deserters from their exiled master, but loyal Romans all; they wore tight white trousers with gilt frogs and facings to their tunics, pipe-clayed bandoliers, shiny black wallets on their backs, and on their heads the formal stiff-peaked *shako*. The Lombard *Bersaglieri* arrived, a regiment of aristocratic volunteers, the heroes of Milan, wearing

[1] Trevelyan, *Garibaldi's Defence of Rome*, 112–13.

their ever-famous grey felt hats trimmed with cock's feathers of black and green; disciplined and seasoned troops, they marched in severely at attention, ignoring the frantic *evvivas* of the crowd, who then began to think them supercilious.

There were also the "unbrigaded citizens" of Rome, dressed in whatever took their fancy, armed with whatever they were able to pick up. Three hundred students from the university were among them, and a thousand National Guard. They were joined by the Trasteverines, who came pouring from their Tiber-side slums with double-barrelled shot guns, and knives between their teeth, leaving their elders and their womenfolk to squat before their hovels, and spit as each round went screaming over, and say, "There goes another Pio Nono." Conspicuous, too, were the international Bohemians, the innocents of every revolution; abandoning their traditional mode of life—scribbling, daubing, sculpturing all morning, arguing all afternoon, drinking and loving promiscuously at night—they left their attics and *locandi*, and fought all day upon the walls; always returning (that is, if they did return) to spend the evenings as before. Included in their ranks they had at any rate one Frenchman, the architect Laviron. Exiled from Paris since the days of June 1848, on hearing of Oudinot's attack he flung down his callipers, and set out for Italy. He died as he wished to die, by a French bullet at the gates of Rome.[1]

The fighting was mostly in the northern suburbs, on Mount Janiculum, where every morning Garibaldi held his conference of officers, with lashings of black coffee and cigars. In Rome itself life was desperately normal, as if what had previously been humdrum were now precious. Rationing was strict and orderly; the paper money worked; the National Guard protected foreigners in cafés. Everyone took a hand at digging trenches, led by the ladies in voluminous summer frocks, with lips compressed, prodding defiantly with their tiny slippers against the shoulders of rusty spades. Later, when the wounded started coming in, the ladies turned to nursing. Princess Belgiojoso, an exquisite Milanese, the fashionable Parisian hostess of Victor Hugo and of Heine, set up a hospital in a convent, where she was soon to be seen seated primly in a printed apron on a hard-backed chair reading Dickens by the light of an oil-lamp to a dying poet. She

[1] Herzen, III, 86–8.

was assisted by Margaret Fuller, the gallant American wife of an Italian patriot, and by no fewer than 6,000 volunteers, including a number of prostitutes released by the government from houses of correction in conformity to liberal principles. The Pope's Palace on the Quirinal became a convalescent home; Margaret Fuller spent her afternoons in the little pavilion used by the Pope for private audiences, within sight of the white tents of the French, watching the antics of the gardener, who produced a watery pyrotechnical display from His Holiness' fountains for the diversion of the wounded heroes of his country.[1]

Ugo Bassi, now a red-shirted chaplain to the Legion, exhorted his hearers to believe that Rome, which he had formerly called Babylon, was instead the City of God. From time to time cheering about the town announced that Garibaldi was making an appearance, and everybody ran to see him, splendidly statuesque with his chestnut mane, his sapphire eyes, his flowing white cape, on his magnificent milk-white charger, escorted by his enormous Moor, Aguyar, in a blue cloak, mounted on a coal-black horse.

It may be thought that there was something extravagantly operatic about some of this, and so there was. Duty officers, for instance, did not need to visit all their outposts; they only had to stand beneath the walls, and listen to the sentries carolling arias from "*Gerusalemme Liberata*" to the stars, to know that all was well. The unbending Lombard *Bersaglieri* certainly thought the heroics overdone. "Accustomed for some time past to judge of these matters with the eye of regular troops, all this array of warriors in glittering helmets . . . reconciled us but little to the scanty numbers of real, well-drilled soldiers."[2] Nor was the point missed by the keen and cynical eyes of foreign correspondents. Koelman, a Dutch artist, accompanying Garibaldi to inspect a barracks, was surprised that the sentry, who was sprawling on a carved oak bench, made no attempt to rise at the General's approach. William Story, an acute American, noticed that the swarthy gangs employed on digging trenches would, as soon as they thought themselves unobserved, relapse into idleness, "leaning picturesquely on their spades,

[1] Margaret Fuller, III, 211–12.
[2] Trevelyan, *Garibaldi's Defence of Rome*, 122.

or sometimes pitching a shovelful of gravel into a wheel-barrow".[1]

Yet the deeds that were done on the perimeter make the charge of histrionics seem unworthy. There was nothing false about the bravery of the men who went in wave after wave up the fatal hill to attack the villa Corsini: who re-won it for a time, and defended it at barricades made of the dead bodies of their comrades, until they were driven back at last, leaving five hundred killed and wounded to redden the white dust of the intervening roadway only six hundred paces long. If they were all operatic more or less, it does not mean that the dangers they confronted were unreal. It means simply that the Italians in their supreme moment reverted, as all peoples do, to their natural method of expression.

Orsini would have wished to be in the thick of the battle. He would have liked to be with his friend Angelo Masina, as he stormed on his horse up the steps of the ruined Corsini, and there met his death; or with Giacomo Medici in his marvellous last stand at the Vascello. But he returned too late from his out-post duties at Ancona and Ascoli. He was appointed major on the General Staff, and could only use his military skill to prolong the inevitable end. On midsummer night the French broke through the walls, "a very fatal go", as young Arthur Clough of the *Illustrated London News* described it in his letter home. On 30 June Orsini was at his place in the Assembly when Garibaldi strode in amidst cheers, his figure matted with grime and blood, his sabre so bent that it protruded half-way from its scabbard. Brushing aside Mazzini's determination to fight on, Garibaldi announced that the time had come to save what could still be saved. Accompanied by his Amazon wife Anita, who, though pregnant, had left her children in Nice and had come to join him, he set out at the head of a company of 4,000 on his historic march towards Venice: a march which was to end in the swamps of the Comacchio with the betrayal and execution of Ugo Bassi, with Anita dead, and with his own phenomenal escape.

After Garibaldi left, despair and gloom settled down on Rome. The Triumvirate had resigned. Taking advantage of Orsini's rectitude some suggested that he should accept the

[1] Trevelyan, *Garibaldi's Defence of Rome*, 115.

dishonoured task, but he refused. On 3 July the French entered, by arrangement. In their red trousers and blue jackets, dog-tired, their heads bowed to the hoots of their fellow republicans, the unhappy *troupiers* tramped along the Corso, the instruments of "one of the meanest deeds that ever disgraced a great nation".[1]

[1] Bolton King, I, 340.

CHAPTER THREE

Del Modo Di Cospirare

I

ORSINI might easily have gone with Garibaldi. For a man of his temperament the prospect of remaining under arms against the Austrians was alluring, while accustomed as he was to disguises and to quick decisions he would have had a better chance than many of surviving. The thought of Assunta held him back. She, showing not the least desire to emulate Anita Garibaldi, was waiting placidly in Florence for her husband to come to join her. There was also the question of where his loyalty lay. In defeat as in victory, Mazzini was still his Chief; to desert him now for Garibaldi would be a form of treachery, for the relations of the two were anything but cordial. Garibaldi, fighting like a lion throughout the siege, had gone out from Rome an even more romantic hero than before. If he lived, he could be counted on to crop up on other shores, on other battlefields; to gather round himself another army. Mazzini was a far more tragic figure. The Republic had been the temple of his hopes and dreams. More gaunt than ever, with his hair turned grey, he prowled about the streets. Though hopelessly conspicuous, his moral stature was so great that neither the French, nor Austrians, nor Pio Nono wished to lay their hands on him. In the end, he took ship at Civitavecchia for Marseilles, and eventually returned to London.

Orsini could not hope for such indulgences. Furnished by their clerical protégés with lists of wanted republicans, the French were making numerous arrests. Fortunately, the British and American consuls, Freeborn of England, Brown of the United States, rose to the occasion and doled out diplomatic passes. Brown went so far as to defy the French who came to examine his Legation, which was crammed full of refugees, confronting them at the head of the stairs with a sword in one hand and the Stars and Stripes in the other. Orsini availed himself of the less bellicose services of Freeborn, and so escaped to Florence on 10 July.

Assunta was glad to see him, and for a day or two they sauntered peacefully, staring at the trinkets in the silversmiths' windows on the Ponte Vecchio, or watching the waters of the Arno turn crimson as the sun went down behind the round surrounding hills. Orsini talked incessantly about the fall of the Republic and about their future movements; as he talked, Assunta studied him closely, for the first time with detachment. Behind his handsome beard his mouth was set and grim; in his brilliant eyes, even when he smiled his faint, peculiar smile, there was always a kind of barrier, an habitual vigilance and restraint. Vain and excitable he was; there would never be a resting place for him. She did not see how she could communicate the intimate comfort she wanted to extend, and he so badly needed to receive. She loved her native Florence, and hated the thought of leaving it. She begged him to give up politics, as he liked his plotting to be called, to settle down and make a home. Their money was all spent, and his uncle had warned him he would not send any more to be wasted in the same senseless way. He could practise law. He was not yet thirty, it was not too late. . . .

Orsini struck attitudes. Of his sacred duty to his country, of the malice of his enemies, Assunta seemed not to have the least idea. There could be no denying that she had a trivial mind. As for a home, why, the Archduke Leopold was returning to Florence with an Austrian escort; there could be no home for them in Tuscany. The more he raved, the more he played into her hands. He knew the Minister, she said; he ought to go and ask. The Minister listened civilly as he outlined his case, demanding asylum as both his mother and his wife were Florentines, and he had become a property-owner by his mother's will. But, as he expected, when he promised to live quietly in the country, the Minister shot him a shrewd and bird-like glance. Within ten days the Orsinis were on their way to Genoa.

Genoa was a clearing house for refugees. They thronged the cafés and the quays, gossiping, spreading rumours and indulging in recriminations; on Sundays they joined in the old Italian custom of milling about the piazzas as though on the point of a desperate uprising when in truth they were waiting for their dinners. Among them, Orsini noticed, were several of the villains he had put in prison at Ancona. Released on Garibaldi's order to take part in the defence of Rome, they had at once rejoined their leader Zambianchi, who had put a blot upon the record of the Republic by a hideous massacre of priests in the Trastevere. Subsequently they had mingled with the exiles, and were still at large, swearing to avenge themselves upon Orsini. Finding that both Zambianchi and the Red Man were in Genoa he collected witnesses and went to have it out with them, as was his invariable rule when dealing with such people. Much of their former truculence was gone; some of their comrades who had returned to Ancona had been shot by the Austrians, while others who remained in Rome were later, quite justly, executed by the Papal Government for murder. Though they complained in a maudlin way that he had treated them as common criminals, whereas all that they had done had been from ardour for the democratic cause, Orsini was not troubled any more. Zambianchi afterwards secured a place, unworthily, in the Immortal Thousand who sailed to Sicily with Garibaldi; the Red Man disappeared.

While in Genoa, Orsini complied with the observance, almost compulsory for members of Young Italy, of calling upon Mazzini's mother. The old Jansenist, who received him suspiciously at first, soon became much struck with him: not only because, as she said, any friend of Giuseppe's was a friend of hers, but because Orsini, with his strong physique, his magnificent dark head, quick animation and formality of manner intoxicated every woman, old or young. She showed him Mazzini's sunny green and white bedroom which she had kept aired and dusted every day for twenty years, training thyme and verbena, his favourite flowers, against the trellised balcony. She undertook to forward letters between Orsini and her son, letters revealing that Mazzini still had many tasks for him to do. But Orsini must not stay in Genoa; it was too crowded, and Mazzini's agents were too closely watched by the police; he should go instead to Nice. Orsini sung the advantages of Nice to Assunta; its paradisial climate, its peaceful atmosphere so ideal for the man of letters he was now aspiring to become, its better situation for the hemp business in which his uncle promised to establish him. They arrived in March 1850.

Nice was long since established as a health resort for the comfortably-off from every nation. In addition, being a remote half-independent canton of Piedmont, it was a refuge for the better class of exiles from every country which had been caught up in the convulsions of 1848 and 1849. Earnest figures with sallow complexions and deeply furrowed faces could be seen at all times, talking rapidly as they weaved in and out between the gigantic push-and-pull bath-chairs on the Promenade, or muttering together in little groups under the palm trees in the winter gardens.

Although less expensive than the larger cities of Piedmont, Nice was far from cheap. A room on the front, with service and light included, cost fifteen shillings a day, while a good plain meal in a *trattoria* came to one and six. Partly for this reason, Orsini lodged with a fellow advocate in the northern suburbs. After a year he moved into a villa with a charming prospect a mile or so out of Nice, towards Cimiez, where Assunta was at last able to settle down to keeping house.

They had for their neighbour Luigi Folli, with whom in Genoa Orsini had started a friendship for once unconnected with politics. Folli, a wealthy young man of twenty, was the son of an old family of landholders from Codogno in Austrian Lombardy. In 1848 his parents had found it wise to remove themselves to Montevideo until times became more quiet. Folli had now returned, and was in Nice awaiting permission to reoccupy his parents' mansion in Lombardy, the villa Vanicella, and the family factories of gorgonzola cheese: such permission was eventually forthcoming, for the Austrians classed him as politically harmless on the grounds that he was rather deaf. In the meantime his open-handed, gentlemanly hospitality was a great comfort to Orsini. They shared a passion for horses, and often rode together on the splendid mounts from Folli's stables.

The transactions for opening a hemp factory at Nice in liaison with Orso Orsini's long-established business at Imola were completed through a respectable banking firm, Vedova Colombo e Figli, which had retained its original name although the widow in question had been dead a hundred years or more.

The present head of the house, Abraham Colombo, was a staunch friend of all Italian exiles, and managed the affairs of many of them: and so in due course the concern known as Monti-Orsini et Cie. came into being. From the first it failed to live up to its imposing title. Orsini was not diligent in business, and left the direction to his good-natured friend and former adjutant in the battalion Alto Reno, Joseph Fontana of Modena, who had lost his right arm in the fighting at Mestre, and now came from Marseilles to be his partner. His own share of the work was confined to writing to those of his revolutionary friends who were in commerce, like the Modenese banker Achille Sanguinetti and Carlo Lefebvre of Genoa, asking them for contacts.

Although Orsini did not apply himself as keenly as he should perhaps have done to the retting of tow or to the manufacture of ropes and sacking, his life was far from idle. His first interest while in exile was to keep himself fit to renew the fight for Italian freedom. Every morning he was up at dawn: after a quick turn with the foils at six o'clock he went up into the mountains to study tactical problems with imaginary troops. After dinner there were hurdle-jumping and other equestrian exercises, and at five it was time for sabre and pistol practice. He made it a point of honour to read every day some military history, trigonometry and algebra, in order to keep abreast of the theoretical side of the soldier's profession.

He did not neglect his literary output, but here again there was a certain monotony of topic and approach. Soon after he arrived in Nice he planned a full and fearless history of Italy during the last five years, to be preceded by an introductory sketch, in two volumes, of the events between 1815 and 1846. He sent a synopsis of it to a publisher in Switzerland,[1] but as the publisher rejected it he wrote instead a military topography of Italy, a task more in accordance with his interests, and of more immediate practical use. The result, a lengthy affair of 422 pages, not without a certain technical value, was published in Turin in 1852 earning the sum of ten pounds for its author.[2]

[1] The synopsis acquired some notoriety after Orsini's death, and was published in the *Eco d'Italia* in New York in 1859.

[2] *Geografia Militare della Penisole Italiana*, Felice Orsini, Pomba, Turin, 1852, reprinted 1861.

Finally, charges by the Papal Government that he had been guilty of extortion and bloodshed in Ancona and Ascoli led him to print a vindication of his conduct absolving Mazzini as well as himself from blame.[1]

He kept an eye upon the conduct of his fellow patriots. He mourned the misdeeds of young Antonio Mordini, who allowed himself to be kept by a *signora*, very much his senior, of doubtful associations. He warned them all against Farini, whose *History of the Roman State from 1815 to 1850* he considered meretricious. Farini, he assured them, was a traitor; an infamous fellow who, when called in as a doctor to attend the daughter of a friend, made use of the opportunity to seduce her, although she was the fiancée of another patriot. When Achille Sanguinetti got entangled in a love affair, Orsini stood by him as his second in the duel. He was always in great demand on such occasions for his knowledge of the etiquette. He remained in close touch with Mazzini, whom he revered as a revolutionary giant of temperamental genius. "Pippo is displeased: he can do nothing at such times," he would say to excuse the crotchets of his leader.[2] When Mazzini changed his London lodgings to avoid the droves of visitors to the Great Exhibition who were inclined to treat him as an extra spectacle, Orsini, not knowing his whereabouts for a week or two, was inconsolable.

In September 1850 Mazzini, as head of the Italian National Committee, started a scheme for financing republican ventures by the sale of bonds redeemable on the liberation of the country. Naturally, the bonds were condemned by all the governments of Italy, and in Lombardy the Austrians made their possession tantamount to treason. Orsini, who was rated "no lukewarm friend", was given the concession for Piedmont. Bundles of notes and manifestoes were smuggled in from France, and Matilda Biggs, one of the four cigar-smoking Ashurst sisters who had taken Mazzini under their management in London, arrived to assist him in the distribution. Excuses and half-promises crumbled before her brisk efficiency, and between them they got rid of quite a number, Orsini handing over forty pounds to Mazzini's mother in Genoa.

[1] *Memorie e Documenti intorno al Governo della Republica Romana*, Felice Orsini, Nice, Caisson et Cie, 1850.

[2] Ghisalberti, 131.

At the same time Mazzini, always alive to wider issues, had formed a Central Committee of European Democracy, with Ledru-Rollin of France and Arnold Ruge of Germany as his fellow members. It was hoped that the Hungarian, Kossuth, would join them on his return to Europe from America, and it was thought desirable to add a Russian representative. The choice fell upon the distinguished liberal, Alexander Herzen, who was then in Nice. Orsini, armed with a letter from Mazzini and a whole arsenal of supporting propaganda, and accompanied by Mrs. Biggs with a wad of Italian bonds (for Herzen was a man of means), went round to call on him.

Herzen refused to join the Central Committee of European Democracy. He went further. He said, "It seemed to me that its basis lacked depth of thought and unity, that there had been no necessity for its foundation, and that its form was simply a mistake." He finished by saying that the manifestoes drawn up by Arnold Ruge in the name of Divine Providence were singularly inappropriate, since Ruge was known to him primarily as an uncompromising atheist.[1] Feeling very uncomfortable Orsini folded up his propaganda. He had never heard anything like it. The Herzen circle fascinated him; its tolerant mockery of his principal was startlingly illicit, like rites of black magic performed upon the altar. Soon he found himself embroiled in a highly Slavonic domestic tangle, in the course of which he met the woman to whom one day he was to owe his life.

II

Herzen, the son of a very influential Russian nobleman, had like Orsini been a rebel from his early years. When still a student at Moscow University he had been banished beyond the Urals for leading a particularly disrespectful roundelay at a carouse held on St. Nicholas' day, the nameday of the Czar. On his return, he had eloped romantically with his sweetheart cousin, Natalya Alexandrovna. For a time, the young couple lived happily in poverty, and before long Herzen was jotting in

[1] Herzen, III, 172–5.

Giuseppe Mazzini says farewell to Italy on going into exile
From *Vita di Giuseppe Mazzini*, by Jessie White (Mario), 1886

his notebook, "family life begins with the child".[1] In 1846 his father died, and Herzen went to clear up the estate. Instead of conferring liberty, as the custom was, upon one or two of the most faithful serfs, he insisted on freeing them all. Word got about, moreover, that he could not tell one from another, and other serfs came from miles around to receive their manumission. The Russia of the "pewtery-eyed" Czar Nicholas was clearly not the place for Herzen. He applied for the Imperial permission to go travelling, and obtained it with extraordinary ease.

In Paris in the dreadful days of June 1848, disillusionment with the French Republic made Herzen bitter. At intervals, from the windows of their house, he and Natalie could hear deliberate volleyings as the prisoners were shot. The news that Louis Napoleon had been elected President was the end of both liberal and domestic hopes. Life with Natalie had been sustained by certain intellectual ideals, and these had now come crashing down. Herzen's bitterness poured itself out on Natalie in cruel scorn. Her life became a misery. The situation wanted only, as the Russians say, for "a grey cat to come between them".

When he first arrived in Paris, Herzen had met the famous German poet, George Herwegh, a friend of his friend Bakunin. Known as "the Poet Laureate of Democracy", Herwegh's rise had been meteoric. Dark and sleek, he was at all events sufficiently self-centred for his role, though not perhaps so frank and simple as a man of the people ought to be. The son of a restaurant keeper, he had deserted during his military service and published his first book of poems in Switzerland. The poems were not of the kind that age well, but they were in tune with the spirit of the times, full of defiance of authority, and of ecstatic nationalism; they were promptly banned in Germany, and Herwegh's triumph was assured. He was able to return, with no one daring to lay a finger on him in his royal progress, with banquet after banquet, reading after reading, to Berlin, where the King himself found it necessary to receive him.

Near the palace in Berlin there lived a banker's daughter, Emma Siegmund, who yielded to none of the other young ladies of her period in her worship of great men. She sported the style which was *de rigueur* among the brides-in-spirit of Franz Liszt,

[1] Herzen, II, 88.

long hair swept back from an accentuated forehead. As Herwegh was all the rage, she decided that he was her poet, the successor to Goethe and to Heine, and prevailed upon her father to give a party for him.

Emma Siegmund was, it seems, "a very plain young person, with a loud voice and rather *Junker* manners". Though not unintelligent, her culture was scattered rather than refined. None the less, she was very determined. In place of beauty she offered the penniless maestro wealth, comfort, every indulgence, "a sack of gold, a tour in Italy, Paris, Strasbourg pies, and Clos de Vougeot".[1] George Herwegh accepted her, after insisting on every detail of the dowry being delivered in advance.

After a sumptuous honeymoon, Emma settled him in Paris, in "a study with soft sofas, heavy velvet hangings, expensive rugs and bronze statuettes", where, to her vexation, he wrote nothing. She redoubled her endeavours. She praised and fondled him in public shamelessly. Turgenev, calling one evening, found Herwegh stretched out on the ottoman while Emma stroked his feet. She endlessly related his disgusting little foibles—how he bought her a beautiful camelia, but could not bring himself to give it up, and hid it in his study until it was quite dead. "He is a poet," she would explain. "All great poets are capricious children all their lives, and they are always spoilt."[2]

In the convulsions of February 1848 the German workmen in Paris, not wishing to be left out, decided to liberate the Duchy of Baden. But who was to be their leader? George, thought Emma. On the fiery steed so prominent in his verses, he should win resounding victories, and have his statue in the *Unter den Linden* opposite her father's house. The revolutions in Paris, in Italy, Vienna and Berlin seemed to be going ahead without much violence, and if it were only a question of making proclamations, George could do it very eloquently. After all, if Lamartine could be a dictator, why not Herwegh? Emma went shopping in the rue Neuve-des-Petits-Champs and bought herself a riding habit in red, gold and black, the German tricolour, with a black beret and cockade to match. She soon had everything arranged.

[1] Herzen, IV, 28.
[2] *Ibid*. 31.

But instead of welcoming their exiled brother Germans, the soldiers of the Duke of Baden, with obtuse Teutonic zeal, opened fire on them. Herwegh fled to a nearby village, where a kindly peasant concealed him in a barrel until Emma came to fetch him, and drove him in a cart across the frontier. Back in Paris, the defeated revolutionaries blamed all upon their leader, charging him with faulty preparations, with running away, and with embezzling the funds advanced by the Provisional Government of France. They further complained that while they straggled back hungry, wet and cold, Herwegh was going-it at a luxury hotel and wearing (here they spat with especial emphasis) "yellow morocco slippers".[1]

Herwegh was discredited. Yet for all his spiritual infirmity he possessed one incomparable gift, the power to arouse the vital instincts, fierce and undiluted, of almost any woman. Emma, for instance, cared nothing for her own social probity. Although her banker father had been ruined by the revolution, she struggled to maintain the level of Herwegh's comfort as before, knowing that of all things he most had a horror of being poor. She borrowed right and left: she sold or pledged belongings: one by one her valuable rugs, her bronze cupids and amorinos disappeared. "She not only denied herself necessaries, but even had no underclothes made for the children, that he might dine at the *Frères Provençaux*."[2]

Herwegh was ungrateful. He spent more and more time at Herzen's, groaning that his sensibilities could not stand Emma's gruff contact and loud voice. Gradually his spell engulfed Herzen's wife, the unhappy Natalie; she too could deny him nothing. Herzen was hampered by his liberal views on marriage, and in June 1850 allowed himself to be persuaded that they all should go to Nice. Convinced that there was no escaping from the Herweghs, he loaned Emma £500 and agreed that she should have the top floor of the house which he had taken there.

It was in the autumn of 1850 that Orsini appeared with Mrs. Biggs and Mazzini's roll of papers about the Central Committee of European Democracy. He did not think much of Herwegh, but Emma greatly took his fancy. He grew very devoted to her, to the astonishment of Herzen, who unkindly put it down

[1] Herzen, IV, 35.
[2] *Ibid.*, 39.

to "a sort of physiological absurdity; what there was in common between the handsome, ardent young Southerner and the ugly, lymphatic German woman, I never could imagine".[1] Orsini saw in Emma virtues which passion obscured from Herzen. He enjoyed her friendly comfort, of which his Assunta offered all too little. He admired her loyalty and courage. Her romantic extravagance amused him, and he listened indulgently while she insisted that there was a magnetic affinity between them; while she peered into her crystal, rapped her table, and predicted that one day soon he would be lying near to death in the strongest castle in Italy, and that she, Emma, would then come and save him.[2] Perhaps most of all, he was touched by the freedom of her confidences, when she told him with unbridled tears and yet without reserve, how much it cost her to maintain her wifely dignity by repelling the advances of her spouse.[3]

One evening early in 1851, Herzen had a desperate scene with Natalie. Breathless, his face distorted by rage and jealousy, he asked her certain questions which she, sobbing, confirmed. He turned to kill her, but on seeing her distraction fell on his knees in tears beside her, and dabbed eau de cologne about her swooning temples. At one again in everything, about one thing they had no doubt. Herwegh must go. Next day Herzen hired a private coach and packed all the Herweghs off to Genoa.

Herwegh kept writing, threatening suicide. Natalie was terribly upset, but Herzen at last induced her to reply that she agreed, and that Herwegh's suicide was the best way out. How Herwegh went about it they learnt a few days later when Orsini, who had been to Genoa on business, returned to Nice. He said that he had called on Emma, who explained she could not offer him a meal as she was starving herself to death to share her husband's chosen fate. "We have touched nothing for thirty-six hours," she continued; "do persuade him to eat something, save the great poet for humanity." Orsini went out swiftly to the verandah, and came back as swiftly with the news that Herwegh was standing in the corner eating *salmis*. Emma, overjoyed, rang the bell and ordered soup; at that moment her husband tottered in. "George," said Emma, "I was so delighted, hearing from Orsini that you were eating, that I ordered soup."

[1] Herzen, IV, 80. [2] Orsini, *Memoirs and Adventures*, 129.
[3] Ghisalberti, 277 n.

Herwegh looked huffed. "It's of no consequence. Death by starvation is too painful; I shall poison myself instead." His wife rolled her eyes towards the ceiling, and glanced meaningfully at Orsini. The poet helped himself to soup.[1] After this incident he appeared to give up his persecution of the Herzens. Sending Emma back to Nice with the children, he moved from Genoa to Zurich, where he lived with, and on, a discarded mistress of Louis Napoleon.

In December 1851 news reached Nice that Louis Napoleon had seized absolute power in France by a bloody *coup d'état*. Though they had long expected it, the event struck all Herzen's circle with a shock of indignation, and no one more strongly so than the Frenchman, M. Mathieu. A lawyer by profession, M. Mathieu had been a minor official in the provinces during the February republic, and called everyone *citoyen*. He vanished across the frontier, the River Var, which lay a few hundred metres from the bottom of Herzen's garden, and in a couple of days came back announcing that all France was in revolt: he must launch an expedition, and Orsini must raise an Italian contingent in support. Orsini certainly had a directive from Mazzini stressing the importance attached by Ledru-Rollin to such a venture, but aquick reconnaissance in spired him with grave doubts of its success. Nevertheless, M. Mathieu was not to be deterred, and as he could not be allowed to go alone, the two set off together.

The night after they started, Herzen was aroused at four o'clock by two ruffians wearing red woollen mufflers, with huge horse-pistols protruding from the sashes round their waists, and short clay pipes embedded in their beards like birds' eggs in their nests. They explained that Mathieu, relying on Herzen's love of liberty, had sent them to ask for money with which to buy a boat. Since Mathieu was on dry land, Herzen was at first perplexed by his request. But knowing that conspiracies give rise to their own logic, and trusting in Orsini, he gave them what they asked.

Next day the two principals reappeared, Orsini looking calm and spruce, Mathieu all in tatters and caked from head to foot in mud. There had been some mistake, he said. The watchword agreed on to deceive the gendarmes had been the lowing of a

[1] Herzen, IV, 58–9.

cow. While Orsini sat keeping watch under the frosty mountains and the stars, he, Mathieu, had been mooing steadfastly all night. Whenever he heard an answering call he had struggled towards it through the bogs and briars, only to find in every case that it proceeded from a cow. At last they had met some men who had a boat, and Mathieu had hit upon a new and better plan. They would return to Nice and mount the attack afresh upon the sacred shores of France, this time by sea.[1] By means of an elaborate trick Mathieu was, with great difficulty, restrained. As it happened there really had been a revolt in Var, and how M. Mathieu came to miss it no one but Orsini ever knew. Within a few days the refugees came streaming into Nice, as Herzen said, "like yellow leaves driven before the wind".

At the end of 1851 Herzen was expecting his mother, his younger son and the boy's tutor to come from Paris by the steamer from Marseilles. Tremendous preparations had been made: Christmas lights shone from the windows of the big house, the garden was a forest of fairy lanterns. At dusk he drove down to meet the ship. His party was not on board. It was, he learnt, a rescue ship. There had been a storm, an accident; the steamer had sunk with heavy loss of life.

Herzen was more or less demented: Natalie, never strong, went into a decline. One morning as Herzen was dozing in his study, a letter in a well-known hand arrived, stating on the envelope that it contained a challenge to a duel. Herzen disapproved of duelling, and he could not possibly leave Natalie to go to fight a duel with Herwegh. Ducking his head in a basin of cold water he went to consult Engelson, his somewhat overcharged compatriot who, with his no less overcharged wife, was living in the house.

To his amazement Engelson already knew about the letter. It appeared that Herwegh had warned Emma he was going to send it, and she in dismay had passed on the news. In his rage Herzen said many things about Emma that were totally unjust. He said that Herwegh had sent her back to Nice to spy on him. That he had caught her planning the division of his property against the day when Natalie should leave him and go to Herwegh. That she was an unsexed woman who obscenely pandered to her husband.

[1] Herzen, III, 246–54.

A few days later Orsini called on Herzen very early in the morning. He was conciliatory without being unsevere. He admitted that Herzen had great provocation, but said it was wrong to blame a poor woman who had done no harm except from excessive loyalty to her husband. Herzen would not agree with him. Pale, and his eyes a little brighter, Orsini said that all the circle had declared Herwegh's impudence inexcusable, and to prevent a duel, proposed to call a Court of Honour. He had therefore laid the facts before Mazzini. Herzen could not see what Mazzini had to do with his affairs, nor indeed why Orsini should discuss them with his friends. But there was that morning something more than usually panther-like about Orsini's manner, and as Herzen already had one duel on his hands, he let it pass.

Mazzini behaved with tact. He wrote to say that a Court of Honour should certainly be held; in the meantime he passed Orsini's letter to a friend of his in London, General Haug, whom he knew to be on intimate terms with Herzen. Haug was a German regular officer exiled since the '48, and had served with distinction under Garibaldi. Imperious and impulsive to a degree he was, with his cadet background, considered a great expert in affairs of honour. He now wrote frantically to Herzen urging calm, saying that he was leaving immediately for Nice.

Natalie meanwhile lay feverish in her bed. One day she demanded to see Herwegh's letter. "How vile!" she exclaimed. She wrote an answer in an unexpected tone of power and scorn: her letter was returned from Zurich with the seals intact. "If that's it," cried Natalie, "it shall be read to him!" She clapped her hands, and as if by magic Orsini and the other exiles poured into her room, followed by General Haug still dusty from the road.

"Let me die in peace," she pleaded in her faint low voice, "trusting that you will carry out my last request. That man has sent me back my letter." Her champions were deeply moved. Orsini's face shone with admiration. Haug stepped forward, took her hand and said throatily, "Your letter shall be read to him, I stake my life on that."[1]

The others felt that Haug, the newcomer, had been too quick to take upon himself an honour intended for them all. Furthermore, experiments in a chemist's shop with a duplicate letter

[1] Herzen, IV, 85.

and a pair of scales showed beyond doubt that Herwegh had steamed Natalie's letter open, added some abusive missive of his own, and sealed it up again. Such caitiff conduct demanded sterner punishment than that prescribed by Natalie. Orsini coached the Russian, Engelson, in a plan for Herwegh's summary extirpation; but Engelson could not refrain from blurting it out to Herzen, who had to cancel it for fear of causing shock to Natalie.

A day or two later, the doors of the sick room were thrown open. Vogt, the doctor, made his professional departure. The mirror was veiled, orange blossom was strewn about, and soon the room was all in white except where Natalie lay surrounded by bright flowers. When it came to Orsini's turn to take his leave, Herzen was moved to Latin vehemence. Clasping Orsini's hand upon the body of his wife he swore "Vendetta! O Vendetta!"[1] Natalie was buried by moonlight among spring flowers on a breezy hill between Esterel and the Corniche. There was no priest, but each of the exiles picked a dark red rose from an enormous wreath upon her coffin.

True to his promise, Haug tracked Herwegh to his hotel in Zurich. As he entered the suite Herwegh snatched at the bell rope and yelled for the police. Haug slapped his face. And as the echo of that prodigious slap spread through the conspiratorial halls of Europe like the ripples of a stone dropped into water, the scandal ended. Haug, wishing to expose Herwegh yet more thoroughly, showed Herzen with great pride a statement he proposed to publish in the press. Herzen, much disturbed lest it should compromise his own superbly damaging account, managed to get the manuscript away from Haug and burn it, while Orsini shook his head with a funny little smile, repeating, "O, il generale! Il generale 'Aug."[2]

Soon afterwards the group broke up. Haug and Herzen went to London; the Engelsons left Nice for Genoa. To Orsini's inexpressible disgust Emma forgave Herwegh and went back to him in Zurich, dressed horribly to kill with a cloud of artificial curls.[3]

[1] Ghisalberti, 264.
[2] Herzen, IV, 102.
[3] Ghisalberti, 277 n.

III

Life seemed drab to Orsini after they had gone. Yet although he had thrown himself with zest into their entanglements, so small a thing as the death of a favourite cat he had brought to Nice from Genoa was enough to remind him how much he was cut off from Italy. He was an Italian. Nice was cosmopolitan. The news from his unhappy country made it plain that his life in Nice was mere frivolity.

In Lombardy, Marshal Haynau and his Austrians had embarked on a reign of terror. In March 1849 the people of Brescia, taking courage from Charles Albert's attack, rose against 20,000 troops. During the fighting, "the heads of young children cut from their bodies, women's arms, and fragments of human flesh, were thrown into the midst of Brescian troops".[1] Haynau had a hundred leading citizens dragged up the steep hill to the castle, where they were flogged and finally shot. Women were bound, while their menfolk were covered in pitch and set on fire before their eyes. It was small compensation that a hunchback who was being burnt to death caught one of his tormentors in a grip like steel and clung to him till they were fused together by the flames: or that a year later, Marshal Haynau, visiting Barclay's Brewery in Southwark as a quiet well-dressed military man, was seized by the burly draymen and beaten up.

When the Milanese hissed a prostitute for flaunting the Austrian colours, Radetzky caused sixteen of them to be publicly whipped, including two young women[2]; a proceeding altogether blackguardly, in the eyes of Palmerston, because some of the male victims were gentlemen. In Mantua in 1852 some two hundred citizens were tried and tortured as a result of the Mazzinian bonds; while the priest Tazzoli and the other Martyrs of Belfiore were hanged in a little valley outside the gates.

The puppet rulers bound themselves into a league of Catholic repression, cemented by the sweeping ultramontanist claims of

[1] Pepe, II, 91.

[2] Labadini, *Milano ed alcuni momenti del Risorgimento Italiano*, 30.

the restored Papacy. The Romagna, once more under its priestly government, was an anarchy surrendered to the brigands. King Bomba of Naples exulted in his element. He decreed that cookery teachers must take an examination in church catechism, and made children at school learn such things as "the promise of a prince to limit his sovereignty is null and void". Worst of all was Duke Charles III of Parma, a shameless young rake who slashed his citizens in the face with his cane if they did not take off their hats. His courts re-echoed to the sound of whipping: men were beaten for singing patriotic songs, for possessing a newspaper from Turin, for persuading an Austrian officer to get drunk. In the first five months of his reign in the little Duchy there were three hundred public whippings.[1]

Orsini knew it all, in impotence and seething rage. He could concentrate no longer on his books. He found relief in music, which he had taken up when Emma chided him for having insufficient graces. He got himself a teacher, an excellent old Italian who had once studied with Rossini; and under his censorious rule of tuning fork and metronome set out to master the tonic solfa. For two months at the end of 1852 he scarcely left his house. After five months he started making compositions of his own, to the equal astonishment of his teacher and his friends, who had no idea of his tenacity of purpose.

Orsini had little inclination for the affairs of Monti-Orsini et Cie, and as his partner Joseph Fontana used the premises chiefly as an arsenal for a secret army, the business soon declined. Its disintegration was speeded by a severe financial setback sustained by Uncle Orso. The failure of a Romagnuol merchant, whose shares he had backed at the instance of Pio Nono when Bishop of Imola, left him with liabilities amounting to £4,000. As the man had since found employment with the Papal Government, Orso went to Rome to see the Pope, but obtained no assistance beyond a dissertation on the shortcomings of his nephew. Being unwilling to incur the pontifical displeasure, and seeing the folly of financing the concern of a wilful young man who misappropriated the funds for unlawful purposes, Orso discontinued his support, with the result that Monti-Orsini et Cie was wound up in 1853 at a heavy loss.

Forced to scrape and pinch to keep her home together,

[1] Bolton King, I, 367, 378.

Assunta grew increasingly dissatisfied. Orsini as a handsome army officer, or as a member of the Roman government, was one thing; Orsini as a bitter, impoverished refugee was quite another. She was not permitted any share in his unprofitable pursuits, and there was no place for her in his club life with the other exiles. She was very jealous of Emma Herwegh, whose company he openly preferred to hers; while he was insanely resentful of the few distractions she managed to discover for herself. Their only remaining realm of contact was the sexual, and that, being unsupported, became a battleground of force on his part, fraud on hers. Since his secret correspondence was conducted in her name, she knew that he had taken to conspiracy again as a man reverts to drink. He was always looking for letters from Mazzini. The moment he had his orders he would vanish like a will-o'-the-wisp, uncertain of return.

Children, thought Assunta, were the way to keep him. Her plan might have succeeded. Orsini was highly excited at the thought of having a son, and he was not entirely joking when he told his friends he was expecting the Messiah, the wonder-child of Italian liberation. He was ready to teach his son all his own skills, and to bring him up in the craft of a conspirator. The boy would be dandled on the knees of illustrious patriots of all nations. His text-books would be crammed full of ciphers and messages in invisible ink. Father and son would tumble about, locked together in the proper holds of wrestling; or would gallop bareback off into the wilds beyond the Corniche to engage in desperate games of Liberals and Centurions. In the process Orsini would have exorcized much of his own restlessness. It was through no fault of hers that Assunta failed; the child who saw the light on 9 April 1851 was a daughter, Ernestina. Another daughter, Ida, was born on 12 March 1853.

In Italy small boys were lords and masters in the family. Whether naughty, sulky or merely spoilt, they were pampered objects of delight to one and all. But what was permitted to boys, and perhaps expected of them, was by no means the same for girls. Their upbringing was in the care of women. When they came of age they remained, in the eyes of men, the reflection of man's weakness, faintly evil, though deliciously seducible. Orsini left his daughters to their mother. He did what he could, in his way, to provide money for their welfare, as if from a sense of duty towards children who were a disappointment to him.

Orsini's long-awaited summons came at the beginning of February 1853, when Mazzini ordered him, in attractively occult terms, to Genoa, to hear from his special agent Maurice Quadrio about "a most dangerous undertaking". Assunta was expecting the birth of her second child, but when Italy beckoned, women had to wait. With a consolatory pat upon her shoulder, Orsini disappeared.

Mazzini, the philosopher of Fulham Road, the former dictator of the Quirinal, had now become a master spy. From his littered first-floor sitting room (Italians in London never lived on the ground floor), where the shiny couch served as a bed, where brass fire-irons gleamed through a haze of cigar smoke, where greenfinches fluttered from wicker cages always left open as an emblem of freedom, messages written on scraps of tissue paper in his tiny Greekish script flowed across Europe raising the assassin's arm and adjusting, all too frequently, the hangman's noose. His dealings with Ledru-Rollin and Kossuth had widened his field; his web spread further and further from the narrow meshes near its heart in northern Italy. As he strode about Brompton nodding to policemen, sometimes as Signor Ernesti, sometimes as Mr. Flower, he brooded upon his universal revolution, stylized, strait-laced and vehemently anti-socialistic. At any time his unmistakable figure might loom up and vanish unaccosted in the securest citadels of tyranny.

The plot outlined by Quadrio to Orsini was the most ambitious Mazzini had ever planned. The days of 1848 were to come again, and once more Milan was to lead the way. During the Shrove Tuesday Carnival on 6 February, the Austrian General Staff would be massacred at dinner. At a signal flashed from the spires of the cathedral, the great castle of Francesco Sforza would be seized, and its armoury emptied. The populace would rise. Kossuth had promised an Hungarian general to suborn his nationals in the Austrian army. Battalions of exiled patriots would advance from north and south, from Switzerland and Piedmont. "Pippo" himself had already reached Lugano, only thirty miles from Milan, and proposed to cross the frontier in an Austrian troop train disguised as a Jesuit priest.

It was to be a *dies irae* for all tyrants. In Paris, Louis

Napoleon, renegade Carbonaro and blood-stained usurper, was to be murdered as he left Nôtre Dame with his beautiful Spanish bride, Eugénie de Montijo. In Vienna, a doom was ready for Francis Joseph. In Rome, Pio Nono was to be shot while riding in procession. In Parma, the flagellant Duke was to have a clean knife stabbed into his black heart.

There were to be diversions everywhere, and especially—here Quadrio gripped Orsini by the arm—in Bologna. Orsini and Joseph Fontana must start at once. They would find Aurelio Saffi, their fellow Romagnuol and former Triumvir, already there. With a seraphic smile upon his face, with a folksong and a snatch of Dante on his lips, he had descended from the Apennines into the enemy's lair. They were to help him raise an army to act in concert with Milan.

To his concern, Orsini found the forthcoming insurrection being freely discussed in the murky underworld of Genoa, generally with adverse expectations: and short as he considered his own notice to have been, Fontana, who had received none at all, had consequently not left Nice. Nevertheless, with a hasty, scatter-brained Modenese called Giacomo Ricci Orsini set off down the coast to the southernmost confines of Genoese territory near La Spezia. Thence they crossed into Modena in the neighbourhood of Ricci's home, and began their risky journey through the mountains to Bologna.

From the first, they had the dogged attention of the Ducal forces. At the summit of each snowclad pass, in the valleys at the crossing of each icy torrent, there were patrols. At every barrier and *Dogana* they appeared to be expected. Their credentials were requested, were leaved through with an ominous indrawing of the breath, were taken inside to be further scrutinized for tell-tale pricks or fraudulent blemishes. Reluctantly endorsed for the destination of Bologna, they were returned to the travellers, who were told not to linger on the way. As they left, Orsini saw the officers dodge into their cabins and start tapping energetically at their telegraphic apparatus. For an agent of his calibre it was worse than being arrested; it was humiliating.

When they came down from the mountains towards Modena they learnt that everything was over. All the intended murders had gone wrong (though that of the Duke of Parma was accomplished a year later). In Milan a handful of desperate men had gained the castle, but instead of going for the muskets in the racks they tried to bring a defective cannon into action, and tinkering uselessly were quickly overwhelmed. There had been no popular uprising beyond the stabbing of a few soldiers drinking their *grappa* in the taverns. The general promised by Kossuth turned out to be a corporal deserted from the Austrian Army. Weaselly, pallid, brash, he loitered ineffectively in the Piazza posing as a Colonel of Hussars, and was smuggled back to Switzerland by three girl conspirators whom he afterwards betrayed. The leaders, Dr. Piolti di Bianchi and Mazzini's personal aide Pistrucci were in hiding. The Piedmontese republicans had been prevented by their government from marching; Mazzini had remained at Lugano. Saffi had left Bologna and was making his way to safety.

Orsini, by this time held under surveillance in an inn at Sassuolo, decided to retrace his steps. Without reserve he flung himself upon the conscience of a noisy group of students. They did not fail him. They gave him a fresh passport, and when the dreaded tramp of feet resounded in the courtyard they let him out from a back window.

He rejoined Ricci, and with a mountain guide they took to the bleak five-thousand-foot ranges of the Apennines. The night was dark, the cold was bitter, and it was snowing heavily, so that they were constantly losing the line of telegraph poles, their only landmark. When they had climbed uncertainly for hours, Orsini thought of turning back. The guide gripped him by the wrist. "By heaven, no!" He pointed down to where a snarl of snow driven before a whipping wind had laid a treacherous downy drift across the trail behind them. They forced the frozen door of a mountain hut, and there huddled until dawn. Then they stretched their shrunken limbs to the descent, crossed the frontier of Piedmont at Sarzana, and joined Saffi in hiding in a villa. Disguised in the gorgeous head-gear of the National Guard of Piedmont they went by sea from La Spezia to Genoa, where they vanished in the crowded docklands.[1]

They had no choice but to hide from the hitherto friendly Piedmontese. Since the defeat at Novara, that pugnacious kingdom had acquired leaders highly representative of the national

[1] Orsini, *Memoirs and Adventures*, 101–4.

character. Victor Emmanuel II was a brutish little man with popping eyes and dirty clothes, who chased women with the same rugged greed as he hunted steinbock.* As Queen Victoria gamely said after getting up at four o'clock to see him off at Windsor, "We're bound to like him when we know him better."[1] His people however had no such reservation. To them he was their soldier-king, the son of Charles Albert who had gone honourably to his ruin against the Austrians. His minister Cavour, likewise "somewhat careless of the smaller moralities",[2] was a shrewd and clever statesman. They shared tight, down-to-earth ideas on the future of Italy and the future of Piedmont.

Far from abandoning the ideals of national unity and the eviction of the Austrians, they ultimately meant to harvest for their own increase the crop sown by Mazzini, and to enlist under their national banner all disappointed dreamers, whether federalist or republican. But for the present they were very much on sufferance. They must first earn the indulgence of foreign powers, and then, by acute diplomacy, convert that indulgence into the armed assistance without which, the Turin realists knew, the Kingdom of Piedmont could never grow into the Kingdom of Italy. Their greatest ally was a reputation for military and commercial reliability, and for good sense in affairs of church and state. Respectability was very precious to them; and respectability demanded an abhorrence of Mazzini, whose aims and methods no sound government could contemplate without a shudder. So they harried the Genoese republicans, ostentatiously policed their frontier, kept out refugees, and deported dangerous aliens.

As the following of Victor Emmanuel and Cavour increased, that of Mazzini waned. The failure of 6 February 1853 was disastrous to him. To the severe reprehensions of *The Times* were added the howls of orphaned families. "Give Mazzini three men and four stones, and he will announce a national revolution," grumbled his former adherents.[3] Yet the more he

* Mr. Cesare Milano of Savona, great-grandson of Orsini, assures me that Victor Emmanuel's fame in this respect is still remembered in Piedmont, where he is admiringly known as "the father of our country".

[1] Thompson, 172.

[2] Bolton King, I, 201.

[3] Griffith, 257.

was criticized, the more he showed a scholar's rigidity and bad temper. The ways of Piedmont were not his ways; they were not in the canon of Young Italy, and could not be trusted. The flame of rebellion must be kept alight month after month, year after year until victory was won.

Orsini, a good party man and loyal to his chief, was one of the last of the die-hard, ever-ready martyrs. On his return to Nice, after receiving Assunta's chilly greeting and kissing his two baby daughters, he began at once to furbish up his weapons. He did not have long to wait. South of the border of Piedmont the bitter sinewy men who laboured spectrally in the caverns of the Massa copper mines, or hewed and quarried on the marble mountains of Carrara, had been excellent revolutionary material ever since the day when they had been taken from the mild Tuscan rule and handed over to Austrian-dominated Modena. Orsini was to cross the frontier near the ruins of Etruscan Luni, which give the name Lunigiana to the district. Modena, Bologna and the Romagna would join in the resultant rising, and soon the whole of central Italy would be in turmoil. Joseph Fontana, whose missing arm precluded him from violent enterprises, represented to Mazzini on his friend's behalf the imprudence of undertaking such a venture without diversionary support. Mazzini, obdurate, impatiently demanded a plain yes or no, and Orsini finally agreed. He received forthwith his formal commission together with seven thousand francs, the cost, it is to be supposed, of freeing Italy.

He set out for La Spezia again, and rounding Portovenere into the gulf viewed with misgiving the distant coastline where he was required to create a revolution single-handed. What movement could he hope for from those empty, towering peaks? What assistance, or what treachery, waited on those impassive olive slopes? Once ashore he felt less disheartened. The area of operations proved to be a wide shore of sedge and dunes, enclosed on every side between the mountains and the sea. Given an initial success, it would be difficult for the Austrians to bring up reinforcements. The leader of the Modenese, a marble sculptor from Carrara,* was mature and sensible, and had served as a major under Garibaldi. He promised at least a hundred men to work from inside the frontier, while Ricci, who

* Ferdinando Fontana, aged twenty-seven. *Not* Joseph Fontana.

was once again Orsini's adjutant, undertook to find a hundred more from among the National Guard at Sarzana, near his home; Ricci added that a lot of arms, taken by the Piedmontese from Lombard exiles after Novara, were stored in depots round about. There were also a number of former officers at Nice, Genoa and Turin to provide a core of seasoned leadership.

Orsini hoped to form a foreign legion out of disaffected elements of the second-rate Austrian occupying forces. He had with him proclamations from Kossuth, and he got Emma Herwegh in Zurich to send him German manifestoes designed to convert the officers and terrify the men. He arranged for twenty thousand cartridges to be secretly manufactured at La Spezia. He drew up Orders of the Day enjoining orderly and moderate conduct after victory, and signed them with a flourish as Commander-in-Chief of the National Insurrection in Central Italy.

Speed was essential. On 1 September 1853 he ordered his men to assemble in a hidden valley near the frontier at eleven o'clock that night. Arriving with Ricci at the rendezvous, Orsini found five young men who identified themselves as Modenese ready to act as guides and as messengers to the contingent at Carrara. By degrees, with much crackling of undergrowth and whispering of passwords, a further twenty youths turned up in ones and twos from the Piedmont side. But though they waited and waited, there was still no sign of the main body bringing the bulk of the arms and ammunition from Sarzana. As time passed interminably Ricci, accusingly questioned, remained confident that there could be no mistake. When two o'clock drew near, Orsini pulled out his magnificent gold watch and reproachfully shook his head. Twenty-nine men with fourteen muskets between them were not a striking force. At that moment, however, a steady tramping on the road from Sarzana announced the approach of a sizable, organized formation. In great excitement guides were sent out to fetch in the reinforcements; but the elation changed abruptly to dismay when they returned to say that a company of Piedmontese regulars were marching with grim assurance straight towards the camp. There was only just time to hide the weapons, send word to Carrara, and scatter.

Orsini with his three lieutenants, the sculptor from Carrara, Ricci, and an artist from London who had joined the expedition as Mazzini's envoy, took refuge in a deserted hovel where two days later they were surrounded by seven gendarmes with levelled carbines. In vain they protested that they were unarmed, and had never had the least intention of doing violence to the Piedmontese. They were rigorously searched. Orsini's letters from Mazzini, his proclamations from Kossuth, his special Orders of the Day were discovered in the thatch. His suitcase, his metal pocket book, and his gold watch were seized as possible items of further evidence. He was put in chains, and taken to Sarzana. After a rough examination he was sent on, still in chains, to Genoa, and lodged in solitary confinement in the condemned cell of the jail.

During the next six weeks in prison Orsini reflected bitterly upon the perfidy of the Piedmontese. Had the rising succeeded they would have been the largest gainers, since all central Italy would have joined their flag. As it had failed, their severity went far beyond a mere maintaining of appearances, and they took a delight in heaping insults on him. They called the insurgents terrorists and brigands; they gave full details of the plot to Naples and their other reactionary neighbours; they claimed in the press that Orsini had broken down and made a full confession. His angry demands that they should turn him over to the Austrians who could not treat him worse went unheeded.

Many of his friends, even Joseph Fontana, began to blame him for the failure. Some, who were banished from Piedmont and so lost their last foothold on Italian soil, reviled him as an imbecile for not destroying his papers; some accused him of rashness, blind arrogance and want of preparation; others, of cowardice for not going forward at all hazard.

To complete his sorrow he learnt that Colonel P. Fortunato Calvi, while on a Mazzinian mission in the Italian Alps, had been betrayed to the Austrians, and that his life was now despaired of. In 1848 Calvi, a Venetian, and originally a regular officer in the Austrian army stationed at Vienna, had formed an army of five hundred irregulars, and for six weeks defied ten thousand Austrians in the *Passo della Morte* and elsewhere in the mountains of Cadore. Afterwards he had taken part in the defence of Venice. A price of ten thousand florins had been set upon his head. He was of all men the one Orsini most admired.

It seemed to Orsini that no further misfortune could befall

him, but it was his own wife Assunta who performed the ultimate outrage. Sentenced to summary exile he obtained permission to visit his family in Nice, and on 29 October was taken there under a close escort. Seeing her errant husband returning in the hands of the police, Assunta shrugged, laughed mockingly and turned away. When he begged her to go with him to England, she refused point-blank. After a night in the local jail he was taken back to Genoa, and put on board the steamship *Marie Antoinette.*[1]

IV

Orsini's first day in London was a Sunday in November, a day equally distressful to the exiles of all nations. "On Sunday everything in England is locked up," said one of them. "The whole of London is transformed into a sort of huge cupboard. Silence reigns in the streets, the only movement is in the parks. The children walk decorously, not one bowls a hoop nor tosses a ball in the air."[2]

He found lodging with a certain Signor Cesarini, a faithful though excitable Mazzinian at whose establishment the Chief occasionally dined, in a squalid quadrangle leading off Brewer Street, euphemistically known as Golden Square. The house was a tall, shaky, echoing building, with peeling wallpaper and intricate plaster convolutions like dirty icing sugar on the ceilings. Orsini slept badly. At last he groped in the darkness for the candle, and looked at his gold watch which he had fortunately recovered from the Piedmontese police. The watch said eight o'clock. He wound it up, he placed it to his ear incredulously; he then fell back in bed. At nine o'clock the gloom was still intense. At ten he heard at intervals a moaning cry, "O-hoo! O-hoo!", coming from below. His quick suspicions instantly alert, he got up again, wrestled with the

[1] The foregoing passage is taken from Orsini, *Memoirs and Adventures*, 104–8; Orsini, *Memorie politiche*, 101–8; Luzio, *Felice Orsini e Emma Herwegh*, 18–21.

[2] Herzen, VI, xix.

grime-fast window sash, and finally admitted a chilly yellowish fog which smelt of coal gas. "There's something funny going on here," he told himself.[1]

Dressing hurriedly, he creaked his way downstairs. In the street he found that the mysterious call came from a cocky-looking fellow wearing a peaked cap, falling ringlets, a red and green silk scarf, a double-breasted waistcoat of rat-hued corduroy with large pearl buttons, and a blue serge apron, who stood blowing on his hands beside a barrow laden with hot eels, pea soup, sheep's trotters, whelks and pickled tripe. Orsini made a careful choice, looking inquiringly at the man to learn the price. The man asked for a "flatch". When Orsini held towards him a handful of small change, he spat cordially and removed a halfpenny.

As Orsini wandered off into Soho, grey muffled shapes slid purgatorially past him in the fog. Cabs clopped along, spattering him with mud. Dray horses in blinkers whinnied steam. At a street corner he slipped on an oozy patch of pavement, and stumbled into a covey of young mudlarks. Pointing at his foreign beard, they began to shriek in chorus. He brushed past them, but they pursued him, chanting. When he turned on them angrily they ran away, and pelted him with the half-frozen balls of horse dung that lay everywhere.

Finding his way to Windmill Street, he entered the *Café d'Étoile*, where all the jetsam of the world were accustomed to assemble with glasses of hot gin or pots of porter. Teachers of languages, worn-out doctors, portrait painters, makers of artificial flowers and gewgaws, would-be patenters of fountain pens, informers and common sponges crowded there, "waiting for a revolution, for which they were no longer adapted, and money from relations, which they would never get".[2] Proud patriots mixed with dubious gentlemen who spoke of their "misfortunes". Martially dressed Hungarians boasted to obsequious German street musicians. Resentful Frenchmen, those who looked forward to an Orleanist restoration, and their opposites, members of the *Marianne* longing for the bloody reckoning promised by Felix Pyat, grumbled together about the English. Right at the back an elegant Italian major, who

[1] Orsini, *Memoirs and Adventures*, 109.
[2] Herzen, V, 2–3.

always had so much money and time to spare that he was thought to be an agent of the French police, raised his billiard cue and neatly potted his compatriot's ball.[1]

Continuing his dismal exploration, Orsini came at last to "Lessesstair Skooar", the renowned centre of his new world, a derelict swamp presided over by a statue of a horse whose rider had fallen off and lay neglected in the mud.[2] He saw a policeman underneath a lamp-post, majestic, unafraid, armed only with a bull's-eye lantern in his belt. He observed the English in amazement. He watched them going into a church-like place to drink buckets of insipid beer behind stained-glass doors, as their incredible custom was, each to his own appointed pen or loose-box according to status and degree.

Most of his acquaintances lived among the better class of refugees in Kensington or Brompton. They looked older and a little seedier, the sockets of their eyes more hollow and fanatical than when he had seen them last. Bickering sectarians, "their world was the smoke-laden atmosphere of dingy committee-rooms; they declaimed or applauded furious harangues".[3] Some earned their living scouring up hunches for newspapers such as Justin McCarthy's *Morning Star*. Some came to a mournful end, like the Neapolitan who was determined to expose King Bomba by touring England and America with a set of rusty instruments of torture. He advertised widely, spent his last penny on a hall, and, since he could not speak English, induced a professional lady lecturer to speak for him. When the day came the hall was bare. Ruined and at last disillusioned, he ran to his lodgings where the lady lecturer found him with a bullet in his brain. Others were more fortunate. Father Gavazzi, for example, whose fluid rhetoric charmed Palmerston and Ruskin, was able to fill the Princess Theatre. Panizzi was still at the British Museum. Aurelio Saffi taught at Oxford. One Italian even became a master at Eton (though naturally he was not a Mazzinian). Another, knighted by Gladstone, held a comfortable position on the Civil Service Examination Board.

Orsini had to find work like all the rest. He had not only himself, but his family in Nice to think about. He had arrived

[1] Holyoake, *Sixty Years of an Agitator's Life*, II, 8–9.
[2] Justin McCarthy, *Reminiscences*, I, 117.
[3] Griffith, *Mazzini*, 246.

in London with thirty shillings in his pocket, and his uncle, either through vexation at finding him once more in trouble, or else for fear of losing favour with his clerical friends, had cut off his allowance. He resolved to talk things over with Mazzini.

"Pippo" was at his most charming. His smile more serene than usual, he was, he said, just pondering how to get rid of a particularly nasty meal without offending his landlady who had cooked it. He made light of the Sarzana episode. It went to prove what he had always said about the Piedmontese; they could not be trusted. He could perhaps make some ground against them, through the columns of the *Italia e Popolo*; beyond that the affair was only worth forgetting. He would not hear of Orsini settling into a permanent job. A little bit of teaching, possibly; and if he liked to give a lecture or two, in Birmingham say, under the auspices of the Society of the Friends of Italy, well and good. But Orsini must think of himself as a soldier on active service. Their country must come first, and he, Pippo, had many things afoot. He would provide for Orsini's upkeep in the meantime.

As he grew accustomed to the oddities of the English, Orsini became aware of their underlying gruff good-heartedness. Joseph Catteral of Preston, an excellent industrialist he had known at Nice, insisted on taking him not once but twice to Westminster Abbey, hoping it reminded him of Florence. The Society of the Friends of Italy were more than cordial; they glowed with enthusiasm for the cause; they invited him to their member-of-parliamentary homes, and lifted him clean out of the ruck of Soho refugees. He had moreover what, he explained to Emma Herwegh, was the great good luck to be attacked by *The Times*, seeing that "in England, except for some priests and old aristocrats who believe in it, opinion concerning that paper is unfavourable".[1] Sure enough, the liberal *Daily News*, the *Morning Post* which belonged to Palmerston, and the remainder of the press struck up in his defence. The seditious popery then being manifested by the Irish drove even *Punch* to chime in on the side of the anti-clerical Italians.

Orsini was a notoriety. On 22 February 1854, the anniversary of Washington's birthday, he was invited by the American Consul Mr. Sanders to a banquet attended by all the fashion of

[1] Luzio, *Felice Orsini e Emma Herwegh*, 22.

the revolutionary world. Mazzini was there, and Garbaldi, just returned from the United States where he had been making tallow candles on Staten Island. There was Ledru-Rollin, gigantic, raddled and grey-haired, a literal-minded Frenchman who believed that every proper Revolution must begin in Paris, and thought England was going to the dogs simply because the Tories were opposed to all reform. There was Louis Kossuth, beautiful and pensive, whose marvellous eloquence had won all hearts, so that when he came to London he was met at the station by the Lord Mayor's coach. Having had departmental training he knew that the universal revolution expected by the others was a myth. His interest was Hungary first and last, and he had nothing left but dying hopes. There was Worcell, the champion of Poland in her perennial Russian bondage. Once a glittering young aristocrat, he had gone to exile abandoned by his lovely wife; he was now a distinguished, absent-minded, frail old man, forgotten by his Czarist children, and destined to die miserably of a weak chest in the London fog. As befitted such a gathering, the dinner was superb; but to the disappointment of the press, the conversation, though rich, at no time touched on politics.

Yet for all his growing fame, Orsini was unhappy. He poured out his heart to Emma Herwegh.

> "Bless the simpletons, I laugh at them all, but that does not take away my sadness, nor fill the emptiness I feel, nor make my country free, nor end the worries which give me no peace, which have come upon me from the bosom of my family, whom I have loved, have pardoned, have rescued and taken out of danger, only to go and finish badly.
>
> "[At Nice] I found Assunta, as always, insensible; however, I love her and hate the idea of having to separate from the mother of my children with whom I have lived for years. Back in prison at Genoa I wrote her a most affectionate letter which I arranged to be posted a few hours before I was put on board. She wrote to me here, and makes no mention of it. I have replied with a long letter saying that if my wife is to fail me in any of three qualities, that is to say, discretion, virtue, or affection, I will not return to her. That I will take away my children; that I will assign her so much a month (provided that I earn anything) on condition she no longer keeps my name. How much this step has cost me you could not believe. I have days of great sadness: I leave the house in the morning and

wander about until the evening: I am ready to expose myself to any danger whatever if I could only be certain of being killed outright: I am tired of this life in which I have nothing but sorrow."[1]

Restlessly, he planned to go over to Nice and fetch away his children, or at least to move to Birmingham to escape the expense of London. His day by day uncertainty about Mazzini's orders, to whom he was now in the position of a hired attaché, prevented him. He became consumed by an urgent concupiscence, appropriate to men expecting to be suddenly deprived of life, or to women passing middle age. "I feel however a most strong desire for love, and if I have to leave Assunta I cannot but find me a companion with whom to share everything up to the last days of our lives. Shall I find her? How? It is very difficult, and I am far, far from it at present."

How, indeed? Cautiously he studied the sexual habits of the civilization of which he now formed a part. He was astonished at the numbers and the beauty of the London prostitutes, so much less timid, so much less obviously riddled with diseases than those of Italy. He suspected that they had them none the less, and that the coldness of the climate kept the effects in check. In any case, prostitutes could not provide what he required. There were, he knew, many possible amateur partners, for Italian patriots with their fiery good looks had a certain *cachet* among the emancipated set of women who made that sort of thing a point of honour. But such alliances were carried on either brazenly or in chilling secrecy, involving, instead of a passionate pursuit and a fate-impelled surrender, a matter-of-fact licentiousness the thought of which appalled him. Still less attractive were the high-principled women who crowded round Mazzini, like Emily Ashurst (Hawkes, divorced, Venturi) for all her raven hair and classic beauty. They were too chaste, and masterful. "I think then," he concluded, "that the women have not much heart: everything consists in the appearance: so long as that is safe, anything is permitted, even within the well-to-do families."[2]

He reverted to his youthful pattern of behaviour in the courts of love. He looked for a diaphanous idyll, a haunting Laura to worship with romantic awe. Surprisingly, he found her decently

[1] Luzio, *Felice Orsini e Emma Herwegh*, 21–2.
[2] *Ibid.*

embedded in a comfortable English household. She "possessed beauty and inexpressible grace, united with innocence, virtue, and modesty, a complete education, rare wisdom, a profound sentiment of the beautiful, good, and noble".[1] The latest object of his nympholepsy—her name was Miss Louisa and he called her Héloise—was a fundamentally sensible girl. Probably she was very like Assunta, or the girl who had tried to make a Jesuit of him, or the girl who had jilted him when he was first arrested in Bologna. At all events, when in due course he went to say farewell before departing on another mission, Louisa instantly saw through his thin pretences, and guessed that he was going to Italy. She did not however weep, and throw herself into his arms; nor did she proudly pin her gage upon his breast. No. She scolded him in French; she a pert twenty, he a balding conspirator of thirty-five. "Listen to your sincere friend's advice—love your country, make sacrifices for her liberation, but do not throw away your life like a fool!" He could not do her bidding. But her words, unlike the similar warning given him by his uncle a dozen years before, stuck in his memory as the acme of all wisdom.

Meanwhile Mazzini was maturing plans for his next rising. The disadvantage of repeating previous failures never seemed to strike him. The doughty Milanese as usual would provide disturbance from within. The supporting attack was to be a three-pronged affair; from the Swiss Valtelline, where the arms he had assembled for use in Milan the previous February still lay hidden; in the Lunigiana, where Orsini's weapons were likewise undiscovered; and in Sicily. He and Orsini would lead the first; Giacomo Medici, who was in Genoa, was well-placed to lead the second; as for the third, as if by a miracle, the very man had just appeared. "Garibaldi is here," Mazzini wrote excitedly on 16 February 1854, "and ready to act. Garibaldi's name is all powerful among the Neapolitans, since the Roman affair of Velletri. I want to send him to Sicily, where they are ripe for insurrection and wishing for him as a leader."[2] But Garibaldi was not so ready to act as he supposed.

As soon as the hero reached the West India Docks in his coaling steamer, the good ship *Commonwealth*, Orsini and two

[1] Orsini, *Memoirs and Adventures*, 111.
[2] Trevelyan, *Garibaldi and the Thousand*, 22.

of his friends from Nice, Herzen who now lived at Primrose Hill, and General Haug, Garibaldi's comrade in the Roman war, went down to greet him. Garibaldi, wearing a striking rig, received them in wide nautical fashion and invited them below to luncheon in his cabin. Over a gourmet's course of oysters from South America washed down with the wine of his native Nice which he had treasured throughout his two Atlantic voyages, he indulged his tallest yarns, and explained how Italy could best be conquered. "What is better than my idea?" he beamed: "what could be better than gathering round a few masts and floating over the ocean, hardening ourselves in the rough life of sailors, in conflict with the elements and with danger? A floating revolution, ready to land on any shore, independent and unassailable!"[1] His face grew serious. What a pity it was, he went on, that poor Pippo got so carried away. Pippo did not know the people in the way that he did. Now was no time to quarrel with Piedmont and to hark about Republics; all that counted now was unity. These senseless plots were nothing but plain murder. He, certainly, would not go to Sicily; at least not until he was invited to lead a movement actually in progress.[2]

Medici similarly declined to lead the rising in the Lunigiana. Medici, a well-bred Lombard, blue-eyed, fair-haired, a gay and limpid lover, was the *beau idéal* of the Risorgimento. He had been a veteran of the pampas, a buccaneer while yet unbearded, a poet, and the desperate defender of the Vascello, the Verdun of the siege of Rome.

Orsini was the friend both of Garibaldi and of Medici. What, then, was he to do? Mazzini keenly felt his increasing isolation. As he wrote to Emily Hawkes a little later, "Love of country, which is life, religion, fever for me, is a sort of dilettante-parading habit with all those who have sworn with me. There is no earnestness, no depth in them."[3] Orsini's soldierly sense of duty bound him to his chief, from whom he drew his pay. For proud Orsini in Mazzini's debt, for Orsini, lovelorn, eager for death or glory, there was only one course of action open. He offered to go back to the Lunigiana, with or without support in other theatres.

[1] Herzen, III, 77.
[2] *Ibid.*, IV, 147–8.
[3] Gangulee, 63.

V

On 18 March 1854, Tito Celsi crossed the grey waters of the Channel on the packet steamer to Ostend. He was a merchant from Ravenna, respectably dressed in black. His chin was clean shaven, firm and round; he had a bushy English-type moustache and side-whiskers. His frame, which must once have been powerful, was held in as if shrunken by some wasting illness. His eyes, dark and of an unusual luminosity, he kept modestly downcast. As he stood by the rail, away from the crowd, he fumbled in his waistcoat pocket, withdrawing his hand in faint annoyance, as though remembering that he had left his watch elsewhere.

At Brussels Tito Celsi called at the Legation of the Papal Nuncio, where passport formalities were handled for nationals of the Papal States. For some time he chatted with the staff, telling them technical facts about the hemp trade, and amusing them with stories of celebrities whom clearly he knew quite well, like Archbishop Falconieri of Ravenna, and the Pope himself when Bishop of Imola. Then turning to his trifling business he mentioned to the first secretary that his passport was old and in places undecipherable from much commercial travelling; it sometimes led to delays and ridiculous doubts which a man of his probity found very disagreeable. The first secretary, all creased smiles and solicitude, ordered a new one to be made out, and personally applied the Papal firmat with a thump of special confidence.

Celsi went on through Paris to Geneva, where the Mazzinian agent Maurice Quadrio engineered a meeting in a lonely house with a little, aspish fellow, a Hungarian. Celsi was introduced as Mazzini himself, while the Hungarian, whom Celsi was told to call Fissendi, was in reality none other than the corporal who had posed as Kossuth's Colonel of Hussars in the affair of

February 1853. Celsi gave Fissendi money and instructions for going again to Milan. Passing through Zurich, he gave duplicate orders in case of accident, this time to an Italian. That done, he entered Piedmont over the Mont Cenis, and so came to Genoa, where he lived in quiet style in a villa outside the town.

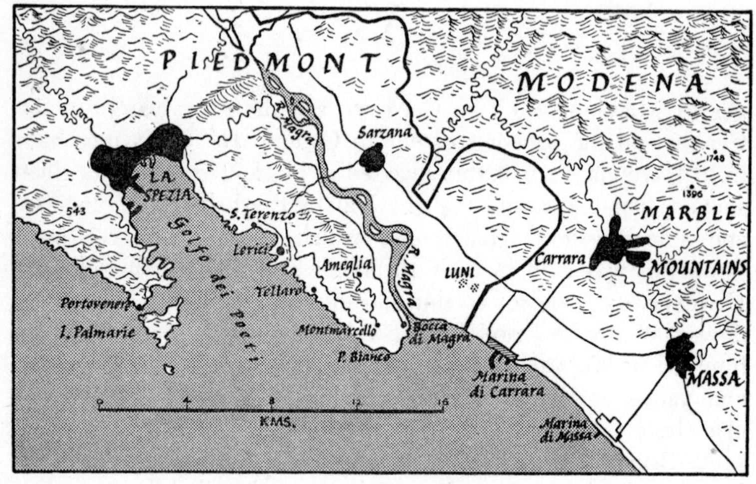

THE GULF OF SPEZIA AND THE LUNIGIANA

Both his former confederates, the ebullient Ricci and the sculptor from Carrara, were at large and came eagerly to greet Orsini. Everything, they assured him, had been ready for the last five months. Roughly the plan was as before, namely to support a rising of the Carrarese, intended to spread through Modena to the Papal States, by bringing arms and men across the border of Piedmont from the province of La Spezia. This time, however, Mazzini had adopted Garibaldi's notion of a floating revolution, and less was to be left to chance or human frailty. Orsini would bring arms in a chartered sailing boat from Genoa to the gulf of Spezia, would link up with Ricci and whatever forces he was able to produce, land on the sandy *marina* of Carrara, and go to the aid of the sculptor, who by that time would have a movement under weigh. Orsini would then take unified command.

On Saturday 6 May Ricci went by steamer from Genoa to La Spezia, and on Sunday evening was in the hilly wilds overlooking the town. On his own authority he had taken with him ten exiles from that region, whom he sent off into the surrounding countryside to rouse support. The speed of the operation, Ricci thought, would not give time for secrecy to be impaired. It was a faulty move; the young men, deliriously pleased at getting home, made off to frolic with their girls and brag to their friends in the piazzas of their villages.

That same Saturday night Orsini and the sculptor made sail from Genoa in the arms ship, only to be driven back to port by a violent storm. As delay was extremely dangerous they set out again at dawn, but the waters of the shining Riviera coast had been lashed to a grey fury, and off Portofino they were forced to heave-to. For several days they tossed about, miserable and helpless, and not until Thursday evening did they gain the shelter of Portovenere at the entrance to the Gulf of Spezia, after a voyage lasting five days instead of a dozen hours. By that time Ricci's helpers had attracted considerable attention. The Piedmontese police made movement difficult, while in Massa-Carrara where there were rumours that two American arms ships were approaching, the ducal troops were confined to barracks ready to march at one hour's notice.

The Gulf of Spezia, the *Golfo dei Poeti*, is, according to D. H. Lawrence, "the most beautiful place on earth" especially at this season of spring. All round the bay blue water laps on sunny sands, on rocky coves, on the palm-clad waterfronts of brightly coloured fishing villages. Inland, the olive groves climb up in one unbroken sweep to rounded hill-tops, yielding at the summit a distant view of shining peaks. On the western side of the gulf the promontory of Portovenere, divided by a channel from the island of Palmaria, provides a natural refuge from the open sea; its little church upon a rock stands stubbornly out into the waves as if enjoining calm. It was from Portovenere that Byron made his Olympian swim across the bay to lunch with Shelley in his snowy villa on a tiny cape between Lerici and San Terenzo.

Just now however the bay was in the grip of one of those "white squalls" which struck the *Ariel* during her fatal voyage.

The surface was chopped into vicious flecks. Clouds scudding low on the water broke into swirling mists against the hills. As night closed in the banks of olive trees tossed shrouded heads in ragged chorus. Along the shore the stringy palm leaves rustled like streamers in the wind.

Whatever the weather, there was no more time to lose. Driven before the westerly wind Orsini's arms ship sailed through the straits of Portovenere and on across the gulf towards Tellaro, where the donkey track along the coastline ended. From that point for a mile or so down to the Modenese border on the flat Carrara beaches, the eastern shore became a craggy, tapering headland, high, heavily wooded, inaccessible, falling away steeply on its further side to the mouth of the River Magra. Here they tacked up and down in the darkness, scanning the cheerless cliffs for the gleam of a swinging lantern which was to be Ricci's signal. There was no lantern. At last the sculptor asked the captain to go in closer so that he and a companion could swim ashore and make their own way across the frontier to Carrara where they still had much to do. The captain at first refused, for fear of coastguards; but being anxious to get rid of his illicit cargo as soon as possible, he finally put them ashore by dinghy. The vessel then returned to Portovenere for the night.

On Friday morning, since it was imperative to find Ricci, and yet too risky for Orsini to go to look for him, the captain set off along the tortuous pathway connecting Portovenere with La Spezia. He came back glowing. He had found Ricci in San Terenzo; everything was arranged. As the beaches of Carrara were so shallow that the ship might run aground, Ricci would meet them off the headland after dark with longboats, and they would transfer the load at sea.

They put out from Portovenere at dusk, once more crossed the gulf, and spent another nervous evening tacking to and fro. The sea remained rough although the storm had lessened. At 11.30 they heard a plash of oars, and two longboats came up with answering signals containing Ricci and fourteen companions, all chattering volubly. Hardly waiting for them to bob alongside, the captain and his crew began to heave the arms chests over into the boats in a series of sickening crashes. To add to the commotion Ricci fell in, and was narrowly rescued with a rope.

Luck went with them, they were not interrupted, and at last Orsini formally transhipped himself. The captain towed the longboats round the cape, through the strong current at the mouth of the River Magra, before he cast them loose. He then swung round, and beat off at all speed for Genoa.

Alone in a choppy sea the boats rocked on uneasy oars towards the Modenese beaches, glimmering and ominous.

A voice piped up. "Where are we going?"

"You know very well," Orsini answered tartly.

"But the men and the ammunition that should have come from Sarzana—they are not there!"

"How is that?" Orsini demanded. There was a host of explanations. It turned out that Ricci had been unable to get through to the frontier by land with his reinforcements and supplies owing to the vigilance of the Piedmontese police. He had therefore decided, without warning either Orsini or the Carrarese, to collect Orsini and the weapons by sea, and make an independent landing. His fourteen men were all his army. The entire invasion consisted of two boats. Ricci sat shivering miserably in the bows, denying everything.

Orsini swallowed down his wrath; he had, from past experience, expected something of the sort. At least he had the weapons under his own control. At least the sculptor could be relied upon to assemble two thousand men on his side of the frontier.

"Never mind. Follow me. We will attack the first troop of *Carabinieri* we meet."

The first voice wailed again. It belonged to a doctor, who, so a tablet in Lerici relates, lived on till 1908 and was a valiant soldier in the cause of freedom. "We will not die as the Bandieras did!" At this a chorus of assent broke out in both the boats, echoing over the water. "No, by Heaven, we will not die the death of the Bandieras!"

Mutiny and confusion, all at sea. "No one can imagine what I suffered," says Orsini, "except a military man." Clearly, the attack must be abandoned for the present. He turned the boats about, and painfully made back towards the cape, restraining his now hysterical followers from firing at the shadows of the rocks which they were convinced were coastguards. He landed them in a cove, a smugglers' den, telling them to keep quiet and wait for orders. He took one of the boats. In three hours of stiff rowing against the tide he covered the mile to Tellaro, landed at dawn and went on by road to San Terenzo. He managed to get word to the sculptor delaying the attack on Massa until that night. He then chartered a fishing boat to pick up Ricci and his men and take them well out to sea until everything was ready.

A reply from the sculptor confirmed the arrangements for the attack on Massa, promising that at any rate sixty of the two thousand Modenese originally hoped for would be at the rendezvous. While Orsini was digesting this, still more disastrous news arrived. The coastguards, hearing rumours of contraband being landed at the mouth of the Magra, had sent a corporal and two or three men round in a boat to make inquiries. Finding himself outnumbered four to one by desperadoes with a whole arsenal of arms and ammunition, the corporal had resourcefully cried out, "Riflemen to the centre." Whereupon Ricci and his companions had abandoned the arms chests and scrambled up the cliff into the olive groves. The captain of the fishing vessel going to fetch them had been just in time to witness the inglorious engagement; he had at once absconded with the ten pounds he had made Orsini pay him in advance.[1]

The reaction of the authorities to the incident was formidable. Most of the fugitives, including Ricci, were quickly rounded up. Troops pouring out from La Spezia and Sarzana pounced on the weapons. The Modenese were on the march in Massa and Carrara. As far away as Florence Austrian battalions were issued with field rations and live ammunition. Gunboats from Tuscany and Piedmont cruised threateningly up and down the gulf. If Orsini were captured by any of his pursuers, he must expect short shrift. For more than a week he lay up in the hills, changing his position once by day and once by night, watching through his glass as cordons beat and tramped the undergrowth, occasionally firing a random shot in an attempt to start him like a hare. Gradually he worked his way

[1] Orsini, *Memoirs and Adventures*, 112–18; Orsini, *Memorie politiche*, 110–21.

down to the sea at San Terenzo. Even though forty soldiers routed through the house where he lay hidden the good fisher-folk did not betray him. When all was quiet again they took him concealed beneath their nets and lobster pots to Genoa. At Genoa Orsini borrowed money from his friends, got to Marseilles, and thence to Geneva, where he reported to Maurice Quadrio, his superior.

The special agent let his hooded hawk's eyes play fastidiously on Tito Celsi's half-overgrown disguise, his ragged clothes, his flapping shoeleather. Tito Celsi was in bad shape. Quadrio started to upbraid him for his failure, almost accusing him of cowardice for not carrying on in spite of all. Quadrio added that the supporting rising in Milan had not come off because the two messengers sent into Lombardy, the Hungarian and the Italian, had both been arrested. That also, apparently, was Celsi's fault. Replying hotly, Orsini muttered something about "closet theories". Really, it was too bad, he wrote rebelliously to Emma Herwegh, his one true friend; "if Napoleon himself had been in my place he could not have done it."[1]

Quadrio went on to say that it was useless to recriminate about the past. The great thing was to profit from one's errors. The struggle must continue without respite. Pippo, the Chief, had now come to Geneva to direct the long-delayed invasion from the Swiss Valtelline. He would require—he looked Tito Celsi up and down contemptuously—a military commander. Wearily Orsini attended to his make-up, bought maps of the Grison Alps and Northern Lombardy, procured himself a copy of *The Campaign of the Duke of Rohan* who had done well in those parts. On 11 June he arrived in Coira.

Everything was just as he expected. Although the rising had been due a month earlier, nothing had been prepared; it was also plain that the local people to whom he had been given references would take no part in it. He reported to Mazzini urging haste, without in the least ruffling that inspired serenity. Very well: this time Mazzini should take the blame. Orsini climbed about in the watershed of the Alps where so many of the great rivers of Europe, the Inn, the Po, the Danube and the Rhine begin their course, deciding through which passes the various assaults could best be launched, and arranging the appropriate

[1] Luzio, *Felice Orsini e Emma Herwegh*, 24.

dumps of weapons. He was utterly dejected, yet at those high altitudes he felt for the first time in his life a kind of philosophical elation. "Those forests, those cascades, the simplicity of manners, the kindness of the inhabitants, made one feel a happiness dashed with a sense of melancholy. . . . I was near my own country, and yet could not enter it. From the summit of the Alps I could see the fertile valley of the Po, and could not descend. I thought of my children, and yet could not embrace them. I saw the clouds roll beneath me, and I had more than once almost decided to cast myself over a precipice and die."[1]

In mid-July, with one assistant, Conti, he set up headquarters at the Albergo del Müller in St. Moritz. It was the summer season. Visitors were flocking to St. Moritz for the waters: the hotels were full of life. But the cantonal police were very active. He found that his alias was of little use to him, for everyone was talking about Tito Celsi. Tito Celsi had acquired a separate identity, if anything more dangerous than his own. As he had to be someone, he joined a group of the Pope's emissaries, who were recruiting Swiss mercenaries for the Papal army. The trouble was he had to sit at table with them; every time he raised his glass to Pio Nono, they capped his toast by drinking to King Bomba. Eulogy rivalled eulogy, and so many loyal healths were called that they often left the table very merry.

Mazzini's hopes relied upon a hundred and fifty exiles whom he had provided with journey money and summoned to assemble at St. Moritz. To overcome the difficulty of distinguishing them from the genuine visitors, he had lightly and characteristically decreed that his "brothers" would all come wearing flowers in their hair, and Conti was duly posted on the Julian Way ready to pick out any so adorned. Now it happened to be the custom for everybody going to St. Moritz at that season to go gaily decked with alpine roses plucked from the wayside. As far as the eye could reach, the Julian Way was a laughing, noisy sea of brilliant nosegays, and Conti had to make his selection very much at random. The first to be hailed with the esoteric password was an elderly German Swiss who ground out a startled "*Ich weiss nichts*". The next proved to have a wooden leg. A third, more likely-looking, brusquely told Conti to mind his own business. People of all nations, women and children, rich

[1] Orsini, *Memoirs and Adventures*, 121–2.

and poor, old and young, were put to the test, but only two young lads responded, Carlo di Rudio and Fumagalli, who arrived famished and exhausted and were sent by Orsini to recuperate in the concentration area in the mountains. When, a few days before zero, Mazzini and Maurice Quadrio came from Geneva, the expeditionary force at their disposal numbered nine.

Nevertheless, Mazzini decided, there could be no turning back. The "brothers" at Como were ready to seize the steamers on the lake. When joined by Aurelio Saffio and his detachment, they would flash a telegraphic signal (why should the enemy have a monopoly of that diabolical invention?); the invasion would begin. Further delay was dangerous. Much had leaked out already; there was reason to think the Austrians at Como in concert with the Swiss were piecing together fragments of the plot. The day of decision was settled for 24 August.

On 20 August the police of the two nations struck. So far from piecing together fragments, their pattern was complete. Forty men at Como were put in chains and sent to the political prison of San Giorgio at Mantua. Most of the weapons were captured on the passes, with some of the nine troop captains standing by at battle stations. In St. Moritz, the first thing that the chief of the Engadine police did was arrest Orsini at the Albergo del Müller.

Although aware it was in a sense a compliment, Orsini felt aggrieved. Why should Mazzini at another hotel in the same place go unmolested? Was he always to bear the blame of both sides for everything? He was tired of going to prison. He approached a Russian lady staying at the inn who took, in addition to the waters, "a very great interest in his fate".[1] She used her influence nobly; appealed to the chivalry of the two stout gendarmes, indicating the embarrassment of her position. The gendarmes regretted: Tito Celsi and his friend Conti were to be packed off by the federal diligence for trial at Coira. While she continued to protest, Orsini turned his scalding eyes upon his humbler helpmate, Martina, the pretty barmaid, in her Swiss lace cap and dainty flowered apron, who was gazing at him with a sweet and pitying smile. He whispered a few words in her ear; she blushed, and nodded breathlessly. He then gave her a

[1] Orsini, *Memoirs and Adventures*, 124.

message of warning for Mazzini, and wrung her warmly by the hand.

When at last the Russian lady flounced away, the gendarmes, limply swilling beer, watched their prisoner finish packing his valise. The weather was hot, and they were in no hurry. Martina set herself at the more sentient of the two, ogling him provocatively, swinging her trim ankles from the corner of his table. Seeing him deeply ensnared, Orsini slipped past the other gendarme out of the door, jumped over streams, ran through woods and fields, and "after three hours at sharp rifleman's pace", gained the fastnesses of Mount Bernina.

He entered a mountain hostelry, sat down, and ordered eggs, considering his future plans. If he went back to St. Moritz he was certain to be taken by the Swiss. If he went across the Italian frontier into Lombardy, he would be courting death. His only hope was to get into some other canton through the mountains, but for that he would need maps and probably a guide. As he sat undecided, a group of huntsmen came in, ruddy, leather-trousered youths with Tyrolean hats and bristly knees, on their way to next day's opening of the chamois-shooting season. Piling their guns and horns, their satchels and their telescopes upon a table, they clapped their hands for wine.

It was, Orsini felt, a good sign that they spoke French, not German. All the same, they looked disagreeably ingenuous, liable to ask questions. They kept looking in his direction, whispering together. Finally one of them addressed him. Was he going to the shoot? Orsini said no, he was a botanist. His reply discouraged them, but only for a moment.

Did he come from St. Moritz? his questioner went on. If so, he must tell them about the people who had been arrested there.

"I don't know anything about them."

"What! Why, Tito Celsi was arrested there. They say Mazzini and Kossuth are taken too, with many other Italian patriots."

As Orsini prepared to bolt, a miracle occurred. The curiosity faded from the young man's gaze, his eyes clouded, he shook his head sadly, his broad face puckered as if he were about to weep. "Poor Italians," he said. He gulped quickly at his wine, and sighed. "I should like to know Mazzini, and Tito Celsi, and Kossuth."

"Indeed?"

"Oh yes, I would indeed."

"Well, I am Tito Celsi. I escaped." Rising, Orsini broke out vehemently. "You have an honest face, you are a young man and a Swiss; young people are seldom evilly disposed and the Swiss are trustworthy." He paused, and said with emphasis, "I need your help."

The effect was instantaneous. Beaming, the young man grasped his hand, kissed him, cracked him on the back. "Rely on me," he said. In the middle of the night he roused Orsini, and provided him with an experienced local guide. There followed hours of slithering in darkness on a knife-edge path; a day of rolling thunder, drenching rain; a night spent shivering in thin clothes in a cowshed near a glacier. Approaching St. Moritz, Orsini from the heights could see the road below him, and on it gendarmes hurrying south in his pursuit. He skirted the town, moving in stages, the guide making sure the coast was clear before beckoning Orsini forward with a handkerchief. In three days they were in the woods of Coira. So hot had been the pace that the guide, a hardy mountaineer of twenty-eight, collapsed. Orsini none the less pressed on towards Zurich. Early on the last day of August he sailed by the lake steamer into those safe confines, went straight to Emma Herwegh, and sank into the soft refuge of her house beside the school.[1]

VI

The eighteen months Orsini spent in raising rebellions on the Italian frontiers were not financially profitable. From Mazzini and the party he received only the slimmest advances, scarcely sufficient to meet the expenses of the various operations. After the first invasion of the Lunigiana his partner in business at Nice, Joseph Fontana, though not directly implicated, had like himself spent some time in jail in Piedmont and afterwards lived in banishment at Marseilles. The assets saved from the foundered firm of Monti-Orsini et Cie. could not immediately be realized. Furthermore, Orsini's relatives at Imola had fallen on lean times. His father Andrea, living in retirement with his second family, obstinately continued to consume the legacy due

[1] Orsini, *Memorie politiche*, 122–32.

to Orsini from his mother's will. His brother Leonidas, recently married to a lady called Orsola Massa, had acquired responsibilities of his own. His uncle Orso's hemp business was suffering from the unwelcome notoriety of his exploits. Between them, under the pressure of the Papal government, they resolved to make him, like his father, their pensioner on parole, disgruntled possibly, but politically inert. Orso, who had already reduced his nephew's allowance, terminated it altogether with a lump payment of 3,000 francs (about £150), intimating that that was all he had proposed to leave him at his death.

With so little money himself, Orsini could do little for his wife and children who were still at Nice. On returning to Genoa after his second, seaborne, expedition to the Lunigiana, he realized in dismay that since he last saw her before sailing for England nearly eight months earlier, he had sent Assunta no more than £50. How she was managing he had no idea. She had nothing of her own; her father had died before her marriage, and her inheritance was long since spent. At last persuaded that no good could come from Mazzini's enterprises, Orsini decided to give in to his uncle, and seek respectable employment in a bank at Paris, where Emma Herwegh provided him with introductions. Before he could do so, however, the talk of the Mazzinian coterie at Genoa confirmed a hideous rumour which had formerly tormented him in London. Assunta was unfaithful to him. She had at any rate one lover within the colony of Italian patriots at Nice.

How far Orsini's conviction was justified must remain open to conjecture. Even at this stage of his career he had many false friends ready, Iago-like, to lead him on, to his own ruin, and later the affair became the cruel taunt of his enemies among the extreme Mazzinians. The biographer Alessandro Luzio has been at pains to shield Assunta from the imputation, while her elder daughter Ernestina always loyally insisted that she was an exemplary wife and mother. Yet the story of her misconduct is persistent.* She was a woman of great beauty but few brains.

* See A. M. Ghisalberti, *Lettere di Felice Orsini*, Roma, Vittoriano, 1936, p.163 n.; also Alessandro Luzio, *Felice Orsini e Emma Herwegh, nuovi documenti*, Firenze, Le Monnier, 1937, p.75. Luigi Folli, writing to Emma Herwegh in August 1855, observes, "A few days ago I was in Genoa and learnt that Assunta is continuing her licentious life. It wanted only this for poor Felice."

There were, besides, the promptings of her amorous nature, for Assunta was a lusty girl. After Orsini's untimely end she outlasted two further marriages and only death prevented her from contracting yet a fourth, to a dashing Royal Dragoon, nearly half a century later. What should she do, deprived in her prime of the manly comforts so agreeable to her by a wild unmanageable outlaw who had uprooted her from the Florence she adored, and left her to bring up a family alone in exiled poverty? Deprived by a virile, fascinating husband who took no pleasure in her company and openly preferred a boisterous German? The emancipated notions prevalent in Nice attracted her. Flagrantly unfaithful himself, what right had he to criticize?

Whether or not Assunta really had a lover is of secondary importance. The main point is that Orsini firmly believed it to be the case. A revolutionary on patriotic grounds, he was in all other things as old-fashioned as only a military man can be. What, done by a man, he would condone as a harmless diversion became, when perpetrated by his wife, a dishonest act, an eternal stain upon his honour. A single infidelity he might have pardoned, had Assunta soothed his rancour and shown a suitable contrition. But he did not give her any opportunity to do so; he neither wrote nor went to see her. With fierce pride, thinking of his children, he arranged a hasty loan on her behalf with his friends at Genoa, Carlo Lefebvre, Giacomo Medici, Achille Sanguinetti, payable at Nice through the bankers Vedova Colombo e Figli. His rage was terrible. Sometimes hard and controlled, sometimes broken down by suffering, his desire for violence and revenge kept flowing out in beacons of bright anger. One day he cleaned his duelling pistols; the next, a prey to self pity, he bought himself a phial of strychnine, easily obtainable in Genoa that summer as a cure for cholera. He abandoned all idea of going to Paris with Assunta. To assuage the worm in his soul he flung himself into Mazzini's operation in the Valtelline.

Afterwards, when he gained the peace of Emma's house in Zurich, oceans of righteous indignation overwhelmed him. To serve his country faithfully in forlorn adventures, the hired minion of a leader he no longer trusted, and get nothing for it but abuse: to be a wanderer in foreign lands, exiled from his children, abandoned by his kith and kin, betrayed by his wife—

it was too much. Without action he would lose his reason and would end a suicide. He must get away from it all, forget it all: he would renounce the world and follow his own star. Yet where could he go? There was not a foot of soil in continental Europe where he was not hunted. In England he would have to endure the petty jealousies, the insults of his fellow-countrymen. As for America, America, Garibaldi said, was the land of forgetting home. The more he talked it over with Emma Herwegh, the more it seemed that the only thing for him to do was to set out for the wars.

In the Crimea, Russia was fighting England, France and Turkey. Austria, hard-pressed in her ramshackle domains, hung fire, reluctant to affront Czar Nicholas who a few years earlier had handed a rebellious Hungary back to the Empire, purged and prostrate. Cavour, hoping to steal a march on Austria at the peace, was fitting out a Piedmontese contingent for the Allies. Several of Orsini's friends were thinking of joining it. Young Domenico Cariolato was going, who at the age of twelve during the battle of Vicenza had saved a child by throwing himself upon a bombshell; and next year, taken prisoner at Rome, had made the French general Oudinot laugh at the sight of a warrior so young and so determined. Joseph Fontana, too, was talking of it: if Fontana, with one arm, could go, why not Orsini?*

But if he did go, it would not be in the ranks of the hated Piedmontese. He would go as a free lance, a simple mercenary. In that event, which side should he join? Mazzini thought it atrocious, as he thought all Cavour's designs, to shed Italian blood on behalf of Louis Napoleon, tyrant and traitor of Rome. Orsini agreed with him: on the other hand, Orsini liked the English and did not want to fight against them, while Emma was strongly anti-Russian, predicting that Russia would one day engulf Europe with a devastating new political system.

Russian, English, French, Austrian, or even Turkish—what did it matter so long as it was a disciplined, well-constituted army where he could at last become a proper regimental officer

* Cariolato was later one of the Immortal Thousand who invaded Sicily. In 1866 he became adjutant to Garibaldi and was decorated by King Victor Emmanuel II. Fontana ended his career as a major-general in the Italian army.

carrying out sound military orders, could at last be freed from madcap plans, from impossible commissions? At worst—he would die the death of his own choosing, a death of honour on the battlefield. At best—who knew?—at best from soldier of fortune he might rise to be a *condottiere*, drawing patriots of all nations to his band as Calvi had done in the mountains of Cadore. Then, when Italy no longer lay torn by dissension and by greedy interests, he would return, a liberating hero equal in fame to Garibaldi. He told Emma, "When my country fights, I shall be there. Give me armed men who will follow me, really follow me, then I will take responsibility for the deeds which I myself shall order."[1]

Mazzini had moved from St. Moritz to a place near Zurich, where Orsini went to lay his case before him. The idea was not a new one to Mazzini: he had often talked over with Kossuth the possibility of seducing Hungarian and Italian troops in the Austrian army by means of agents disguised as officers. He admitted that he too was deeply distressed at his repeated failures. So, while far from happy that his lieutenant should take the initiative in this way, Mazzini did not try to hinder him, but generously offered money.

Orsini stayed in the Herwegh's house at Zurich the whole month of September 1854, getting ready for his journey to the east. Herwegh, full of self-importance, was busily employing himself as philosophical midwife to the major operas of Wagner, who saw more in him than most people did, largely because Herwegh proved a willing listener.[2] Wagner could not get on with Emma; he suspected her of gossiping about his supposed affair with the wealthy and beautiful Frau Wesendonck. Consequently, Herwegh was not much at home. He bore no grudge, however, against Orsini for his unsympathetic attitude in the matter of Natalie Herzen. Rather, he seemed to welcome Orsini's presence in the house, and left him alone a great deal with Emma.

Emma greatly enjoyed preparing knights for war, and probably found Orsini a more convincing knight than her husband had once been. She scurried happily about. She took Orsini's telescope to be put right by the best lens-grinder in Zurich,

[1] Luzio, *Felice Orsini e Emma Herwegh*, 24.

[2] Wagner, *My Life*, II, 559–60.

and made sure that it was ready on the instant. When it came to passports, she spotted immediately the marked facial likeness between her husband and her friend. She fetched Herwegh's passport, and altered two letters in the name: so that, by a stroke of genius, Felice Orsini, *alias* Tito Celsi the Ravenna merchant, became Georges Hernagh, a Swiss watchmaker.

It happened that there was at Zurich then another leading Mazzinian, Peter Cironi. Cironi had fallen in love with Emma. Mistaking the nature of her antics with Orsini he grew jealous, and resolved that his rival should be put, like Uriah the Hittite, in the forefront of the battle. One day he mentioned casually that Mazzini was still receiving signals from Milan. It was necessary for an experienced man to go there, get to know the leaders and report upon their chances of success.

To go to Milan, the scene of so many abortive risings, was certainly to court destruction. But Orsini in his Othellan mood did not fear death. A strain of Byron ran constantly in his head:

What is death? a quiet of the heart,
The whole of that of which we are a part;
For life is but a vision.

Why not pay one final visit to the land he loved? Why not perform this last most dangerous service before he parted from Young Italy for ever?

When he called on Mazzini for his instructions, he found that they went beyond anything Cironi had led him to suppose. Not merely was he to make a journey of reconnaissance, he was to be the bearer of a deadly letter, one of several which may still be seen, as Luzio says, "hidden like little sticks of dynamite among the dusty records of Lombardy-Venetia".[1]

Taking advantage of the weakness of the foreign garrisons in Italy owing to the war in the Crimea, Mazzini aimed at nothing less than a new Sicilian Vespers. The Milanese were to organize a Company of Death similar to that of the mediaeval Lombard League, consisting of eighty of the bravest and the best, divided into groups of five. Each group would closely watch a number of Austrian officers, generals and those of field rank being divided out by name. They would study their habits,

[1] Luzio, *Biografico*, 85.

their walks, their taverns, their conference rooms and love affairs. Then, armed stealthily with daggers, at the height of the New Year festivities they would murder them. The follow-up was to be very much as usual. At a single toll from the cathedral bell the people would rise, start building barricades, etcetera. Arms would pour across the frontier, diversions would break out in Brescia and the Romagna, in Rome the entire French garrison would be obliterated. As usual, Mazzini was to be with them on the day. Such were the contents of the message which Orsini was to carry on his person through the Austrian domains and present to unknown, unproved confederates in Milan. Hastily he committed them to memory.

On 28 September 1854 Orsini made his peace with the world. He wrote to his uncle, his brother and his brother's wife, renouncing all his inheritance in favour of his children. He entreated them to remove the poor innocents from their mother and bring them up at Imola as true Orsinis. He explained that the necessity of using a false name prevented him from making a more legal form of will. He added a word or two about the education of "Ernestina, who also answers to Lucy, aged but three; and Ida, only one".[1] He enclosed a letter, to be read to them when they were old enough, expounding the advantages of rectitude and outlining his sacrifices and misfortunes. He further enclosed two heart-shaped lockets containing fragments of his hair.

He wrote a farewell letter to his father, sending messages to his step-brother in South America and to his two step-sisters, omitting only his step-mother with whom he had never been on cordial terms. He was uniformly vague about his intentions. He said, variously, that he was going to Russia, Asia, or possibly to Ireland to seek his fortune. He told everyone that if they heard nothing for four months they were to act as if he were dead. Assunta, at Nice, having had no news of him since February except for the loan he had raised for her in June, was anxiously sounding Carlo Lefebvre and Mazzini's mother for his whereabouts. He arranged for her to be told, once again, that he had finished with her; that if she gave up his children, and dropped his name, he would ask his family to settle a small pension on her. The letters, though written in Zurich, were

[1] Orsini, *Memoirs and Adventures*, 137.

posted in Geneva, and were forwarded through the banker Colombo at Nice.[1]

On the evening of 1 October Emma Herwegh took Orsini to the coach station in Zurich and despatched him, in the gathering valedictory gloom, on his journey over the St. Gothard. He was travelling as Georges Hernagh but was still known to the Mazzinians as Tito Celsi. His profusion of identities helped to increase his sense of disembodiedment; of timeless vagrancy.

He arrived in Milan early on 7 October by the diligence from Turin. He dropped his bag at an hotel, and strolled about the city until dusk. He then made his way to an insalubrious back street, the Contrada della Maddalena, to call upon one Paolo di Giorgi, who played the cymbals in an orchestra. di Giorgi received him with extreme reserve, having had no notice of his coming. Eventually it was agreed that Celsi should call again the following evening.

When he arrived, three young men he had never seen before were present, who listened with increasing agitation. They thought the plan bore all too close resemblance to that of February 1853, and the savage sentences incurred in that disaster were all too freshly in their minds. Once since then Mazzini had severely compromised them, in the Valtelline affair. What guarantee had they that this time he would be able to carry out his promises? At a final meeting they insisted that Orsini put the instructions down in writing, to avoid all possibility of error. Orsini hesitated. It was contrary to every instinct he possessed; yet if he refused, his mission would fail entirely. In the end he wrote out the orders clearly, signed his name Celsi, and half-deleted it as a faint concession to his better judgment. He then gave the young men an inspiriting talk, shook their hands, sent off his report to Mazzini, and went on his way without saying whence he came or whither he was going.

Not until some months later did he realize he had walked into a trap. One of the leaders of the Milan Committee was the sublest police spy in Italy, Giuseppe Bideschini of Palmanova. He was the heart and soul of the plot, constantly enlarging its scope and widening its membership. He excelled in ruthlessness. He pressed for the killing of Louis Napoleon, a pet project

[1] Ghisalberti, 160, 164–5 n.; Luzio, *Biografico*, 82–4.

of Mazzini: he reserved to himself the supreme task of assassinating the Emperor of Austria. With his own hand he drew up the constitution for the Company of Death, defining the duties of each of his confederates. It was he, with his passion for regularity, who insisted on having everything in writing. He kept an operations file wherein one conspirator after another, writing in invisible ink between the lines of a large music score, transcribed the most treasonable papers, confirming the entries with their signatures.

In the middle of January 1855 Bideschini's net was full. By arrangement with the police he fled from a supposed arrest. The music folio was found, also a recipe for invisible ink. On the application of a little iron sulphate the murderous inscriptions sprang to light outlined in staring blue between the black staves of music. Bideschini had been wonderfully methodical. Beside each ciphered document was its relative key, a page reference to the writing of some patriotic author, an aria of Metastasio or a stanza of Manzoni. To make things still easier for the police, he had persuaded the plotters to avoid using works of which there were several differing editions.

As a matter of fact the police had no need of such consideration. The cipher experts of their *gabinetto nero* were so familiar with the codes used by Young Italy that they were able to correct or fill in the frequent errors made by Mazzini owing to haste and frenzy. The frightful evidence was sent to old Marshal Radetzky, the military commander, who in turn passed it at the end of February to the judicial authorities at Mantua. Over a hundred arrests were made at a single sweep. Bideschini received a reward of 30,000 Austrian lira, adopted the slippery title of Conte dall'Olio, and roamed about Lombardy with a woman of bad life.[1]

All unaware of the storm brewing in his wake, Georges Hernagh, his last service for Mazzini now performed, was blithely enjoying a conspirator's holiday. After leaving Milan he spent a pleasant non-political week-end at Codogno with his rich young friend Luigi Folli, who sent him on as far as Brescia in his own carriage. On his way to Venice Orsini visited at leisure the old battlefields of '48; Vicenza, where his friend Andrea Liverani had fought and died beside him at the Porta San

[1] Luzio, *Biografico*, 85–94.

Lucia, and Treviso. Stripped of all illusions, he saw for the first time how dispirited the people had become, how divided among themselves, and how they endured the foreign occupation not merely with patience but with some contentment. The attempted insurrections from outside had been a pursuit of an *ignis fatuus*, presuming as they had upon the long since faded inspiration of the days of '48. By dire contrast, how smart were the police, linked by electric telegraph from every corner of the empire to their central bureau in Vienna. As for the Austrian army, it struck him as magnificent and up-to-date, much better than the army of Piedmont: hour after hour he watched the garrisons at their drill with keen professional admiration.

Though liable at any moment to arrest, he was lightheartedly absolved from fear. At Peschiera he hung about the new fortifications of the Quadrilateral fortress showing more interest than was sensible. In Milan unknown to him the police, acting on the information of Bideschini, were already looking for Tito Celsi; yet when forced to return there to get a visa for Trieste he, as Georges Hernagh, boldly interviewed the chief of police in person. Approaching Venice, he argued hotly with the sentry who denied admission to his old barracks in the fortress of Malghera, whence he had set out for the assault on Mestre. His audacity was born of recklessness. The strain of his past adventures, his loneliness, his intense personal sorrow were rendering him, though not at all insane, a little off-centre mentally. The whole of his journey had a haphazard, hallucinatory tinge. Throughout, he was battling with the idea of suicide. He carried in his pocket his little phial of poison.

When the time came for him to board the steamer for Trieste the sea once more threw up a violent tempest, as though churned to its depths by demonic surges. The storm upset the normal peace of Venice. Gondolas bumped and yawed in confusion on the Grand Canal; the tall-funnelled paddle-driven *vaporetti* lurched noisily against their mooring platforms. Orsini, embarking at the Riva Schiavoni, slipped on the gangway and fell into the lagoon. "Everyone cried out save him, but nobody moved," he told Emma gaily[1]; he suffered no damage, except

[1] Luzio, *Felice Orsini e Emma Herwegh*, 27.

that he had to return to his hotel to change his clothes, and obtain another copy of the *Guide de l'Europe*. But he had again drawn unnecessary attention to himself.

During the crossing, as he lay prostrate on his bunk, his gaze became fixed on the saloon, where every now and then a wispish little figure was flung sprawling across from side to side with the heaving of the boat. Repulsive at any time, the man's features were further convulsed with terror. His beady eyes were bloodshot, his hair stood up on end, his cheekbones were deformed, protruding on one side and crushed in on the other. In his hand he clutched a little book, and his loose lips jabbered, as if muttering some heathen form of prayer. Once in a while his jaw gagged open in an involuntary spasm, revealing a set of ochre fangs. With a sinking heart Orsini placed him. It was Moses Formiggini, a Modenese Jew who had once had business dealings with his uncle. He knew that the man, between his bouts of nausea, had dimly recognized him too.[1]

Arrived in Vienna, Orsini mooned about as he had done in Lombardy, watching the soldiers on parade. Finding himself, for no obvious reason, in the heart of enemy territory, he remained curiously insensible to the risks he ran. He went over the Imperial Palace. He visited the tombs of the Emperors, to lay curses on the oppressors of his country. He attended the Imperial Opera for a performance of Bellini's *La Sonnambula*, the Sleepwalker. He sat within easy pistol shot of the much-bedizened royal pair, and studied them reflectively. "Two German types without expression," he decided; "a phrenologist would merely discover matter, useful only to produce more matter."[2]

His afternoons were spent at the Café Français, where he was incautiously easy in his confidences. Formiggini, the Modenese Jew, was often there. Most of the Jews in Italy, who were themselves downtrodden, were comrades in misfortune with the patriots. But it was all too plain that Formiggini could not be trusted. He had too many attributes of the natural informer. Fortunately, like many of them, like Titus Oates and

[1] Orsini, *Memoirs and Adventures*, 143–4.
[2] *Ibid.*, 144.

Whittaker Chambers for example, he was more than a bit fantastical. If he were properly humoured there was just a chance that he would keep his mouth shut. So Orsini spent many torturous hours with him, cat-and-mousing around the real identity of Georges Hernagh, and what Formiggini meant to do about it.

Then there was Antonio Vernazza, a Dalmatian, a mean inquisitive fellow with an exaggerative streak. He quickly guessed, from Hernagh's lack of German, that he was an Italian, not a Swiss. Vernazza also noticed Hernagh's military preoccupation. Had he by any chance, he wondered, the honour of associating with Garibaldi? Flattered, Orsini at once confessed that he was indeed Italian; his real name must, he said, remain a secret; but he let it be known that it began with Felice and ended in—INI. Later Vernazza mentioned, jocularly, a reward he could easily get from the police. Orsini paid him money. He likewise lent eighty florins which he could very ill afford to a trickster by the name of Schaf. His circle of acquaintance at the Café Français was completed by a Spaniard and a Turk. Finding that a Swiss who knew no German was too much of an oddity, he took lessons in that tongue from a lady called Maria Ottendorf with whom, occasionally, he spent the night.

By way of carrying out his plan of joining in the war on one side or the other, he called first at the Russian then at the Turkish embassy, without success. Next, always better at instrumenting the designs of others than fertile in inventing them himself, he made strenuous efforts to obtain an Austrian commission, "with the intention of getting up a propaganda in the Italian regiments, so as to attempt a diversion when an Italian revolution should take place. Kossuth and Mazzini having previously expressed themselves in favour of this being done".[1]

The Swiss Fieldmarshal Salis, he discovered, whose relative had been one of the officers enlisting Papal mercenaries at St. Moritz before the Valtelline affair, was sometimes known to favour the gazetting of his fellow-countrymen in Austrian regiments on the recommendation of a Swiss waiter at the Ristorante "Alla Citta di Londra". Orsini approached him, and received a very friendly answer. General Salis regretted however

[1] Orsini, *Memoirs and Adventures*, 145.

that immediate Austrian commissions were not granted to aliens in time of war, and consequently it would be necessary to take the examination for a cadetship. That did not suit Orsini. Even if his German were good enough to get through the exam, it would take him too long to reach the commanding rank essential to his scheme. He therefore wrote politely thanking the Field-marshal, and enclosed a magnificent gold-edged calling card engraved with the name Georges Hernagh.[1]

Orsini was still in touch with Peter Cironi and the Mazzinians through Emma Herwegh at Zurich, who, catching the conspiratorial spirit of the thing, had assumed the pseudonym Mathilde Herder. It seems in fact as if she were to some extent directing his activities, for she sent him books suitable for propaganda including a fat socialistic work which, when later perused by the police, was pronounced excessively Proudhonian, although as its leaves were uncut nothing could be made of it against Orsini. Assunta, still pursuing her inquiries after her vanished husband, at length wrote to Emma, who forwarded the letter to Orsini in Vienna.

He was furious with Emma. What did she mean by sending him Assunta's letter? Had he not expressly told her that having made provision for his children he had finished with Assunta and was not to be entreated? His life was ruined, his dreams were shattered, and he stood stripped naked as a tree in winter. Emma must do as she thought best about answering Assunta. He would have nothing more to do with it.

Yet, for all his fuming, he could not dismiss Assunta's pleading from his mind. After months of not knowing where he was, or even whether he were alive, she said, she had suddenly been ordered to give up her children and renounce her name. How could he be so cruel? She had no more money from his family. She and the babies could not get enough to eat. Orsini felt in full force the torments of remorse. It was, he told himself, all a ruse by that deceitful vixen. All the same, she was his wife: they had once been lovers. He could not bear the thought of his two babies and their mother abandoned to loneliness and want. He sent her an antedated letter which he arranged to have posted in Trieste, so that it appeared to have been written long before hers had arrived. It contained a little money from his own

[1] Luzio, *Biografico*, 98.

dwindling resources for her immediate needs, pending a monthly payment from his family, which he now promised to arrange at once even though she had not carried out his terms. He told her to look upon it as a present for the children from the father they would never see again. Soon his existence would embarrass her no more: she would be free to take what would become her legal right, and go her own way, without fear of being made to blush at meeting him. Thus a settlement was reached. Assunta, who had flatly ignored Uncle Orso's shamefaced attempts to enforce her husband's orders, lived on at Nice with Ida and Ernestina, where Orso resumed his support of them through the banker Colombo.[1]

But Orsini had not yet purged his soul. After posting his letter to Assunta he felt listless and inert. One night, tossing sleepless on his bed, he leapt up with a racing heart and what felt like a hammer beating in his head. In stark clarity, the clarity preceding total darkness, he realized that what he most feared was happening; he was on the brink of madness. If he, Georges Hernagh, Tito Celsi, lost his mind, what babbling incriminations would result both of himself and others! He fought down an impulse to batter himself against the walls. He strove to concentrate his swimming faculties on some fixed object, the brass knob on the foot of the bed, the flowered jug on the washstand. Little by little he managed to control himself without alarming the remainder of the household.

Next morning was a Sunday. He remembered it was just about the anniversary of his first day in England. A year of senseless dangers, furtive fear, loneliness, failure, private bitterness and affronts had brought him from London to Vienna. As he had done in London he left his *pension* early and roamed the streets all day. Towards evening, feeling the same symptoms coming on, he went to an *albergo* where he had stayed for a few days after his arrival and had friends among the staff. He went to bed; at his request an Italian doctor was called in, who gave him a sleeping draught. Orsini slept soundly, and awoke to find the doctor once more at his bedside.

"When are you going to bleed me?" Orsini asked. The doctor looked at him steadily, then said, "You don't need bleeding. You need moral peace."

[1] Luzio, *Felice Orsini e Emma Herwegh*, 30–2; Ghisalberti, 160 n[2].

"Moral peace? What do you mean? Who says I have not moral peace?"

The doctor shrugged. "I am a doctor. I find out the cause of your malady. Apart from that I am not in the least interested in your affairs. Rest, calm down, divert your mind. Otherwise you will be really ill." He made a bow, snapped together the lips of his little bag, and left.

Moral peace! How, when they were all trying to trap him, lock him up? Why would they not leave him alone, let him go into a monastery? Why could he not make them pardon him, take him back to his own country, back to his little ones, to Emma and his friends, to everyone except Assunta? No matter. He was strong and cunning: he possessed titanic forces: no one knew what he was capable of: he saw everything clearly: he would get well despite them all: he would never let them lock him up.[1]

He who had been burdened for so long with hopeless responsibilities would be responsible no more. He would slough it all off; he would be carefree. The doctor had told him to divert himself. He put on airs. He dallied in Viennese society; he made a conquest of a lady in the highest rank. To the watchful Dalmatian, Vernazza, who suggested it was not in character for a little Swiss watchmaker like Georges Hernagh to fly so high, he haughtily replied, "You do not know my noble lineage." His conduct was so exorbitant that when in due course the police began to trace his steps, they rated him in their reports as Count.[2]

Then, suddenly, the bubble of his vanity burst. What was he, Felice Orsini, the most hunted patriot in Europe, doing lingering week by week in the enemy capital? The Italian regiments of the Austrian army were far away in Transylvania. He must be off to join them as a simple soldier. The trouble was, he had no money for the journey. Disbursements to his blackmailers, his doctor's fees, his luxurious amour, had left him almost penniless.

For once luck favoured him. One evening at the Opera he recognized an old friend, Count Ernesto Galvagni, chief of police at Rome in the days of the Republic. Out of scruple for

[1] Luzio, *Felice Orsini e Emma Herwegh*, 32–3.
[2] Luzio, *Biografico*, 99.

each other's safety they made no signal during the performance, but afterwards they met joyfully in the street. Before they parted, Galvagni lent Orsini sixty florins in exchange for a draft on Joseph Fontana at Marseilles. He also swore never to reveal Orsini's presence in Vienna, a promise which he stuck to, although it was to cost him dear.

Georges Hernagh left Vienna on 7 December, passed through Budapest, and in ten days was hundreds of miles away in the frozen grasslands and mountains of Transylvania. His sense of safety was illusory. No sooner had he gone than the editor of the supposedly pro-Italian *Corriere Italiano*, Felix Mauroner, informed the police how Moses Formiggini had one day brought to his office a man looking for a job whom he first introduced as a Swiss called Hernagh but later admitted was an Italian agitator. Under questioning Formiggini quickly squealed out that Hernagh's real name was Orsini. Vernazza the Dalmatian also told all that he knew, and more. In consequence Hernagh, while dining at an inn in Hermannstadt, was arrested on orders from Vienna.

Orsini felt that his position, though serious, was not yet desperate. He did not know that his true identity had been discovered, and as he was so far from home still hoped to conceal it. Nothing was found on him relative to his mission, and in fact he had broken no law since entering Austria. He resolved to put a bold face on it, and find out how much was known.

His first statement to the police was a marvellous muddle of truth and make-believe. He said he was Georges Hernagh, the son of a Swiss pastrycook who had died at Messina. He had fought with the Papal army at Vicenza and had later been taken prisoner by the French in Corsica. He had emigrated to America, but had recently returned to Zurich and earned his living as a travelling watchmaker. Bowed down by family cares he had thought of suicide, but had thrown his pistol into the Danube. For a time he had half intended entering a monastery; finally he had decided to seek his fortunes in the war, whither he was now bound.

His story was soberly taken down. Little to his surprise however it was discredited at police headquarters. He was transferred to Vienna, and still in disguise was taken to sit for his portrait to a French photographer. When he saw it was useless to deny Mazzinian connections he wrote to Peter Cironi in Zurich announcing his arrest. As he knew the letter would be held up by the censors, he inserted further lies about his family—this time he said they were in Florence—but his prevarications created no confusion and he was forced to change his ground. Before the court of primary investigation he sought to establish an impression of integrity, of defiant resignation. Saying that evidently all dissimulation was in vain, he impulsively declared he was Orsini. He tendered an account of his career, relating with convincing candour everything he knew they knew already.

Of his five arrests, this was the first by the dreaded Austrians. He was relieved at the calm and soldierly way in which his judges treated him, far better than the Piedmontese. He noticed their contempt for the underhand ways of the presumptuous *sbirri*. They seemed to admire his patriotism. He begged them not to send him back to the Papal States; he would rather be shot in Austria than waste away in the inefficient dungeons of Cardinal Antonelli and his clerics. His judges conceded only part of his request. They sent him with a heavy escort by the fastest trains to the Imperial and Royal Court of Justice Resident in Mantua, where Italian prisoners of state were tried, and hanged, on charges of high treason.

CHAPTER FOUR

Mantua

I

AT Mantua, the River Mincio makes a southerly bend from the east in its reluctant passage from Lake Garda to the Po, widening as it does so into three sluggish lakes surrounding the city on all sides except the south. The lakes, placid, teeming and mosquito-ridden as antediluvian swamps, yield gradually to land through acres of rushes, tall and thick, the haunt of lazy-plashing fish and surreptitious waterfowl.

The natural strength of the northern approaches to Mantua was emphasized by the fortress of San Giorgio, standing on a narrow promontory between the city and the lakes, the citadel of the Gonzagas who had lorded it there in the fifteenth century. It was a foursquare building of red brick, with turrets rising at each corner, crowned by pantiled cupolas flatly pyramidal like Japanese straw hats. The construction was so massive that although the towers soared to a hundred and sixty feet, the appearance of the whole was squat. The castle walls fell sheer into a moat twenty feet deep and eight yards wide, which remounted to ground level by a vertical brick counterscarp. The moat was sometimes full and sometimes empty, according to the level of the water in the lake.

Backed directly by the city, the castle faced north-east, towards the San Giorgio bridge with its quarter of a mile long causeway traversing the central lake. The road from the bridge to the city gate skirted the moat on its northern flank, dividing it from the lake. It was by means of a sluice beneath this road that the moat was filled. The remainder of the castle, to the south and west, was closed in by the rambling Gonzaga palace, which was now used as a magazine. Access to the castle was from behind, where a closed stairway spanning the moat dropped down to the Galletta Square.* The square in turn was entirely hemmed in by barracks and offices of administration, except for a single archway admitting to the heart of Mantua. As a main bastion of the vital Quadrilateral, Mantua was heavily garrisoned by the Austrians.

Though many had tried, no prisoner had successfully escaped from the castle of San Giorgio in all its dismal history. In the great days of the Gonzagas an intrepid Milanese had lowered himself into the moat, only to swim helplessly about until rescued by the magnificent chatelaine Isabella d'Este, who showed him every kindness, lighting huge fires, chafing his frozen limbs, and putting him to bed in her own bedroom with a large ball and chain fastened to his ankle. On account of its security the Austrians had used it, after 1848, for the examination of all prominent political offenders in occupied Lombardy and Venetia. In the winter of 1852–53 nine of the Martyrs of Belfiore † were disgorged to the executioners from the restricted gullet of San Giorgio, leaving behind them desperate messages to humanity scrawled upon handkerchiefs with fingers dipped in their own blood.

Two years later, on Tuesday 27 March 1855, at half-past eleven at night, a closed van turned through the archway into the Galletta Square, rattled over the cobbles, and came to rest outside the entrance to the castle. Guards jumped out and helped Orsini to alight. He was half dead from privation; his nerves were shattered, and he was so racked with dysentery he could scarcely stand. Yet sick as he was, instinctively he looked about him. It was raining. Water dripped from the eaves as steadily as ticks of the clock of fate. The only other sound came from the hollow footsteps of the sentries pacing up and down. A single torch was flaring in the courtyard. Its light cast shadows on the streaming yellow walls of the encircling buildings; behind them he could see the grim shape of the fortress towering up into the darkness. For once his courage failed him. His usual decision and confidence were gone. "How,"

* Now called the Piazza Castello.

† There were eleven in all.

he could only murmur brokenly, "however shall I get out of here?"[1]

Leaning on the guards he passed through an iron grille and ascended the inclining corridor up which, in days gone by, ambassadors had ridden their horses over the moat into the Ducal audience chamber. A second gate clanged to behind them, as they turned off to the left, and started up a winding flight of bare stone steps. Orsini counted eighty of them. At the top he was received gravely by a tall individual with grizzled hair and military moustaches. His features were greyish and stiffly folded, but his air of respectability was betrayed by the singular badness of his teeth and by the roughness of his voice. This was Francesco Casati, the head jailor. Born in Milan, the son of a jailor, he knew his business, and held the Austrian Cross of Merit. When he barked commands the turnkeys trembled.

Under Casati's cold, suspicious gaze, Orsini was thrust into a little guardroom and minutely searched. His clothes were then returned, his particulars noted in the register, and he was led along and locked into a cell. Before the removal of the warder's lamp left him in darkness, to his surprise he found he was provided with a pair of sheets, two blankets, a large towel and a wash basin, in addition to the usual trestle bed, straw mattress, chair and table. Next morning he received a visit from the prison doctor, who said his condition was feverish and put him on an invalid diet. Orsini decided that the prison routine, though strict, was exceptionally efficient.

The form of justice dispensed by the Imperial and Royal Court at Mantua was more in the nature of an inquiry than a trial. There were no bewigged dignitaries, no panoply of law, no judge or jury, counsel or reporters. A single judge-advocate shot questions at the prisoner in a private room; his secretary wrote question and answer down; two Italian witnesses were forced to attend, ostensibly to see fair play; but if they were wise they kept silent and signed their names when told to do so.

In addition to the liquidation of the most dangerous rebels, the idea was to unravel the whole tangled skein of conspiracy throughout the Empire. A high degree of centralization was imposed. Time and again there would be a lengthy wait while

[1] Orsini, *Memoirs and Adventures*, 149.

application was made to Vienna for the antecedents of the accused or for cross-checking of his testimony, without his knowledge, from the results of other cases. A trial might linger on for years, being constantly reopened as fresh strains of evidence flowed in. At last, when no more could be gleaned, sentence would be passed in the presence of the prisoner and the whole proceedings would be sent off to Vienna. Some months later they would be confirmed; after that, it all depended. If the times were quiet, the lesser sentences, such as five years' solitary confinement for failing to report a suspect, might be rescinded or reduced with paeans of admiration for the Emperor's clemency. Capital sentences were not usually commuted: they would remain in force until the situation demanded an example, when the example would be taken from his cell and hanged in the open air at two days' notice.

Until recently the trials had been conducted by military tribunals presided over by one of two Austrian officers, Captain Straub, young, handsome and cruel, or the no less terrible Captain Kraus. Straub, at any sign of recalcitrance would sigh, and mention cell No. 12, a little room at the very top of the castle, so high that screams could not be heard, where Casati the jailor stood watch in hand beside a wooden horse, counting the vicious strokes delivered with slow ceremony and precise observance of the regulations. Kraus, in his own way, was even more effective. He wheedled his prisoner, became his confessor, his better reason, on occasion his desperate hope of pardon. Having obtained an eager and often over-full confession, he handed the victim over to be shot in an obscure quadrangle of the palace, used by the Gonzagas as a cemetery for their hunting dogs.

The excesses of 1853, however, and especially Mr. Gladstone's condemnation of the government of Naples, had roused the conscience of Europe, and since then there had been a closer regard for the proprieties of justice. The flogging bench fell into disuse. Casati, it is true, still listened at the door of the question chamber and applied sanctions of his own, bribes of white bread in place of the staple black, or the confiscation of the prisoner's bed, but such abuses were comparatively minor. Under the new technique the prisoner was treated honourably, and almost as a partner in an intellectual exercise of which the object was to compose an abstract sufficiently coherent to satisfy headquarters. After each day's hearing he would be required to sign his deposition; next morning he was asked if he had anything to add. The document so compiled was regarded as a sort of holy writ, used to point out contradictions and to wring further confused admissions. There were frequent discussions off the record, when the inquisitor debated the advisability of certain answers, hinting in confidence that extra information had come into his hands. From time to time he would talk about the prisoner's probable fate, stressing that all would be decided in Vienna and that he himself would have no hand in it.

Expressive of the new spirit in the judges was the dandified Herr Picker of Vienna, who always removed his hat on the entrance of his victims and afterwards escorted them politely to the door. But though facetious, Herr Picker was not particularly astute, and the interrogation of Orsini was entrusted instead to Baron Sanchez. Sanchez was a not unsympathetic personage. The son of a Spanish colonel in the Austrian service, he had spoilt his military career by a youthful enthusiasm for wine and women, and had arrived in his present office frankly as a means of earning money. He was a plump, bald-headed, fatherly little man, with gold-rimmed spectacles, twinkling blue eyes and ridiculous moustaches. Married to an Italian wife he spoke Italian fluently and was always angry with his children for their refusal to reciprocate by learning German. At the same time he was a shrewd lawyer, ruthless and incorruptible. After the affair of 6 February 1853 his prosecutions had sent seven Italian patriots to the scaffold and more than a hundred to the galleys.

When Orsini had been three days without fever, the doctor pronounced him fit for trial. At nine o'clock on 12 April he made his appearance before Sanchez. At first the questions were a repetition of those already put to him in Vienna. After formal identification he was asked about his visit to Milan the previous October. As he rattled on about the innocence of his movements, hoping to discover what was known against him, Sanchez stopped him with a single quiet question.

"Does the prisoner know the Contrada della Maddalena in Milan?"[1]

[1] Luzio, *Biografico*, 117.

Taken aback, flushing involuntarily, Orsini managed to deny it. To his great relief Sanchez did not press the matter; in fact he made a gesture of dismissing it, as if it were of no importance. The letter written by Orsini to Cironi from his prison in Vienna was next produced. He felt at ease again; he had expected that letter to be intercepted. But as he was explaining its harmless contents, another paper was put into his hand. He looked down at it. When he at last looked up again, his dark eyes were glassy. It was his instruction to the Company of Death in Milan, complete with the signature "Celsi" clumsily crossed out.

"That also is my handwriting," he replied. There was dead silence in the room.

Orsini laid the papers on the table. "So," he said briskly. "Instead of dying for my country on the battlefield, I shall die for her on the scaffold. Sooner or later it must have ended thus."

Sanchez looked shocked. "No, no! You've been taken by surprise, that's all. Take your time, and think."[1] He then read out in conversational tones complete police records of Orsini's movements since his first arrest in Bologna in 1844.

Orsini kept his head. He realized that much of this was only surmise, needing his confirmation, and that in order to complete his case Sanchez had to keep him talking. And in talking, too, lay his only hope, not of altering the foregone outcome of his trial, but of establishing in Sanchez' mind a false impression of his character which he might turn to advantage later on.

He said that he cared nothing for his life, and dreaded only torture. Upon Sanchez indignantly poohpoohing the suggestion, Orsini freely told him that, in that case, he had no further need of a dose of poison hidden in his gloves. By this simple confession he established the truth of his suicidal tendencies, showed a spirit of co-operation with his judges, and put the vigilant Casati in the wrong. Casati, sent to search the cell, came back protesting that the tiny capsule could never have been discovered earlier, since it was so carefully sewn into the lining that it seemed to be part of the glove itself.

Speaking frankly and at length, Orsini told the truth about his mission to Milan, mentioning by name those who were already compromised beyond redemption. On the other hand

[1] Orsini, *Austrian Dungeons*, 45.

he maintained that he was no more than a messenger and knew nothing of other accomplices whose names were put to him. In the same way he talked openly about the risings at Sarzana and in the Valtelline where he had been caught red-handed. But of the Portovenere affair, where there was no direct evidence of his presence, he said that he had been in London at the time.

When he was on firm ground he loudly challenged the police to prove the opposite of his assertions. He hotly denied going to Bologna in February 1853. Strictly speaking that was true, since he had turned back at Modena; but it did not justify the rest of his statement, that he had stayed in Nice where his wife was about to have a baby, and only vaguely remembered seeing in the papers that there had been a rising for which Saffi was responsible. When a question floored him he fell back upon his dignity. He was not an informer, he was a patriot who was proud to lay down his life for Italy; they might kill him if they chose, but he would answer no more questions.

Sanchez hastily moved on to other matters. What was Orsini doing in Transylvania at the time of his arrest? Was he not on another mission for Mazzini, connected in some way with the projected rising in Milan? Orsini stuck obstinately to his previous answer: betrayed by his wife, cast out by his family, he had wandered off to seek death or glory in the Crimea. He poured scorn upon the evidence of his cronies in Vienna, Formiggini the Jew and Vernazza the Dalmatian; was not Formiggini in a madhouse now? By what right was the word of such base men preferred to his?

Sanchez thought his explanation disingenuous, but though he prolonged the trial by many months he could do nothing to disprove it. What, then, had been the real purpose of Orsini's vagary? Vienna, who knew so much else about him, were utterly perplexed. They were deeply perturbed at the thought of having men of his antecedents roaming their capital, and suspected some widespread intrigue, quite possibly threatening the person of the Emperor. Sanchez foresaw great credit and advantage if he could find out anything. Fortunately for Orsini, no one could believe that he himself did not really know what he had been doing in Vienna. Fortunately, because only their uncertainty delayed his execution.

The further Sanchez delved into the mystery, the more

baffled he became. No clue could be wrung from the Milanese conspirators. Though all the governments of Italy, with the creditable exception of Piedmont, willingly ransacked their files on Orsini, they could shed no light on it. His uncle and brother in Imola, closely questioned by the Papal police, merely repeated his own story, displaying the letters he had written them. Count Galvagni, who had lent Orsini money in Vienna, was brought to Mantua for examination, where he vainly denied the whole transaction. Sanchez' colleagues took the view that Galvagni, having been Orsini's associate at the time of the Republic, obviously knew his nefarious intentions and was probably passing on Mazzinian gold. Sanchez dissented. Orsini, he pointed out, unknown to Galvagni had already admitted borrowing the money. Galvagni's denial sprang from mistaken loyalty. No contradiction could be found to Orsini's story: a small loan between friends at a time of stress was not in itself a crime. Largely owing to the stand made by Sanchez, Galvagni's sentence of ten years was later quashed, and he was set at liberty.[1]

As time went by Baron Sanchez took for good coin more and more of what Orsini told him. He believed, after making a sharp corroboration, in the innocence of Luigi Folli of Codogno, which was true; he also accepted the innocence of Mme Mathilde Herder of Zurich (alias Emma Herwegh) which was anything but true. The man before him, thought Sanchez, who prided himself on psychological acumen, was transparently straightforward. The fellow gloried in his patriotism. There were in his story none of the usual shifting shadows or reluctant hesitations. No man could flow on as he had done, touching on names and places at the core of sedition without tripping to incriminate himself or others, if he were not genuine. No. Orsini was a scholar and a gentleman. Devoted to a generous passion, caught at last, he was resigned to meet the consequences honourably. In any event, what did it matter? (Here Sanchez slammed the dossier on the table.) The man was doomed, doomed ten times over. Almost a pity, really. He thought of Orsini's virile head towering over him; of Orsini's wife and children; of the private sorrows he disdained to bring up in his own defence.

[1] Luzio, *Biografico*, 195–201.

Before sending the papers to Vienna, Sanchez asked Orsini to repeat once more how many times he had been in prison.

"Five times, including the present, which will be my last."

"Where?"

"At Bologna in 1844; at Florence in 1847; in Piedmont in 1853; in Switzerland in 1854; at Hermannstadt at the close of the same year."

Sanchez regarded him in wonderment, and genuine compassion. He said, "This love of country is a religious mania with you Italians. Your life is a romance from beginning to end."[1] It was a sad case, really.

II

Casati also treated him with marked respect. When he arrived Orsini had a meagre five shillings in his pocket, most of which was spent on the wooden cutlery and drinking mug he was compelled to buy. As the prisoners had to pay for their own keep, and Orsini was too proud to accept anything from the Austrians, he would have starved had not Casati insisted on supplying bread at his own expense. Casati took to visiting several times a day. He was displeased to find Orsini reading *La Nouvelle Héloise.* He asked Orsini to teach him French, providing him in return with more wholesome literature, Dante, Shakespeare, Byron's poems: but when Orsini asked for a manual of chemistry and physics he looked suddenly suspicious. Orsini changed the subject. He spoke of an historical romance that he proposed to write. Casati sent him paper and a quill pen, perfectly good for writing with, but useless for any other purpose. Orsini gave it up: the man was far too wary. He had, the turnkeys said, a young wife of twenty and thrashed her daily out of jealousy. He noticed everything; one morning in the course of conversation he remarked that Orsini's finger nails were shorter than usual; what had he been up to?

By questioning the guards, and keeping his eyes open when he went to interrogations, Orsini learnt a lot about his prison. What he learnt gave him little satisfaction. The cells were in

[1] Orsini, *Austrian Dungeons*, 58.

the third and topmost storey. They were reached by a single narrow staircase, approachable only through the guardroom, of which the outer door was always locked and guarded on the far side, as were the iron gates below. For this function there was an armed watch of eight soldiers and a corporal, changed every twenty-four hours, and quite distinct from the regular prison staff.

There were twelve cells in all, containing a hundred prisoners, all "live" cases, awaiting trial or execution. Cells 2, 3 and 4, the only ones at the back of the castle overlooking the Galletta Square, were in a separate wing. In them the most important prisoners were housed, Nos. 3 and 4 being solitary confinement cells used either for special security or for punishment. Orsini was in No. 3. The three cells opened into a little corridor where there was always a turnkey to report the slightest sound to his fellows who lived in a small room at the end.

Three out of the six turnkeys were on duty at any given time. Of these, one kept all the keys, so that no cell could be opened, and no one could enter or leave the castle without his special knowledge and permission. The other two made visits to the cells every two hours during daylight, one standing at the doors which were kept on chains while the other inspected the interior.

After dark no one could go out unless escorted by Casati in person. Every evening at 9.30 he made his rounds. The windows of the cells were so high that the prisoners could not see out, and were closed in by two heavy iron grids criss-crossing into the massive walls, with a three foot space between them. In Casati's presence, these were tapped with a long pole to make sure that they had not been tampered with. At half-past one the turnkeys paid a final visit by lantern light; then, after checking that all doors were secured, they took the keys to Casati's bedroom where they were locked up in a cupboard until morning.

Orsini saw at once that an escape by the staircase was virtually impossible, involving the corruption of too many guards, to say nothing of a set of false keys. Even if it succeeded, he would find himself enclosed in the Galletta Square in the middle of Mantua, a garrison city from which all sympathizers had been eliminated by recent purges, and whose gates were closed by curfew from dusk to dawn. The only other exit was the window, with its two enormous grids. Beyond them lay a sheer drop to an unscalable moat which might be full of water, and was in any case patrolled from the neighbouring gate of San Giorgio. Then there would be the bridge, guarded at either end, and finally mile upon mile of open vineyards in the covertless Lombard plain, in the heart of the occupied Quadrilateral.

Despite Casati's soft assurances that no further executions would be carried out, Orsini had no illusions about his fate. Day after day he watched the shadow of the window bars chequering the wall during the short afternoons when the westering sun peeped into his cell. Day after day he watched the lizards scuttling about high overhead. How long would it be? Six months? A year? They used the *forca* now, he heard. You stood on a platform with your back against a post, and they fastened the free end of the rope to a hook above your head. The platform was dragged away, your feet were stretched downward by a revolving pulley, and your neck was broken. Sometimes it failed to work. When that happened, the executioner jumped upon your shoulders—it was better to think of anything else than that. So, though he knew all planning was hopeless while Casati's rigid dispensation lasted, the demands of sanity forced him to be prepared in the event of change.

As a trained conspirator, Orsini was well-versed in the theory of escape. He had read how Baron Trenck in the fortress of Glatz had slashed his suitcase into rawhide thongs, stitched them together, and let himself down from the height of ninety feet, only to stick in the mud ignominiously in the moat below. He had heard about the ladder of woven silk Latude had made by unravelling the contents of his wardrobe in order to climb his chimney in the Bastille. He knew how Casanova had descended from the leads of the Doge's Palace in Venice. He had studied most carefully of all the methods used by Benvenuto Cellini to escape from the castle of St. Angelo in Rome. Every escape was different; according to circumstances, anything from a night stool to a table leg might prove of service. Yet they all conformed to certain principles. Tools must be acquired, and a place to hide the tools—often within the ceiling or the floor. Then on getting out—a point too often overlooked—

there must be a definite plan. In any escape, there were two factors of paramount value; money to bribe the guards, and an external contact. It was these Orsini first attempted to secure.

He applied to Baron Sanchez for permission to correspond with Emma Herwegh. He was, he said, short of money for his food, and Madame Herwegh, as godmother to his younger daughter, was in a sense his only relative now that his family had cast him off. Having verified the facts from the church register at Nice, Sanchez readily agreed. He felt he knew his man. When the letters duly came to him for censorship he glanced through the first one or two, and felt ashamed of doing so. They were short notes, written in French; they breathed pride of country and dignified resignation; they made anxious inquiries after Orsini's children, and pitiful requests for daily needs—books, or some article of clothing, which Sanchez better than any other knew would be without significance in a few months' time. Thereafter he scarcely looked at them, scribbling his mark hurriedly across the sheets. Georges Hernagh—Emma Herwegh? If the similarity of names occurred to him at all, it was as a mere coincidence.

While Orsini was in Vienna, Emma had received occasional letters from him, sometimes tormented, sometimes nonsensical, according to his mood. When they ceased in the New Year 1855 she was not surprised. Had he not warned her he was starting for the east, and that she would hear from him no more? Suddenly, towards the end of May, two letters reached Zurich in Orsini's handwriting. They were full of trivialities, came from Mantua, and bore a curious countersignature *V.S.* Emma could make nothing of them. However, since Felice was apparently in prison once again, she gladly sent off, though she could ill afford it at the time, the small sum of twenty francs of which he said he was in absolute need. She then passed the letters to Peter Cironi, who in turn forwarded them to Mazzini in London.

Mazzini equally was at a loss. How did Orsini come to be in the dreadful fortress of Mantua? "There is not a single line that is not a mystery." About the appeal for money he could do little; furthermore he had not yet got over Orsini's earlier bitter references to himself. "May God forgive them. Orsini, Fontana, and ten others have become as daggers in my heart.

If they only knew what I have suffered in these months from debts and pledges—. . . that I do not know how I shall survive the year—truly, they would pity me. . . ."[1] He enclosed a letter for Cironi to send to Achille Sanguinetti, Orsini's wealthy banker friend in Genoa, begging for his help. The letter was not answered, perhaps because Sanguinetti had never been repaid by Fontana the 300 francs he had lent Orsini for Assunta's support in the previous year. In the end Mazzini authorized Cironi to release from party funds 200 francs (about ten pounds) for the needs of his rebellious follower.

Emma then bethought herself of Orsini's rich young friend Luigi Folli whom she had met once or twice at Nice. She discreetly found out his address from Assunta, without telling her a word about her husband's fate, and wrote to him in his mansion at Codogno. Folli, under observation by the Austrian police, dared not do anything too elaborate. He sent ten gold Napoleons (200 francs), supplementing them at intervals with gifts small enough to pass as acts of Christian charity. So that by July some twenty-five pounds had been raised for Orsini's maintenance at Mantua.

On 12 June a third letter from Orsini came, no less strange than the others in its meek tone of acquiescence. Emma, by this time seriously disturbed, read it out to her husband. "That certainly does not sound like our Felice," Herwegh said. He took the letter, and mused over it for a while. Then he peered at it attentively, holding it this way and that beneath the light.

"The surface has been tampered with," said Herwegh. He took off his smoking jacket, pulled back his cuffs, and put on the moleskin skull cap he always wore for making chemical experiments. He lit his little lamp of Berzelius and held the paper to its flame. Instantly, between the lines of French banalities, other lines written in Italian stood out in dusky red.[2] There were many systems of invisible ink, explained Herwegh, nodding slily. It seemed from Orsini's letter that though the Austrians were on the watch for the more scientific methods, the simpler ones could pass unnoticed. The one in use at present was lemon juice. There was also a useful preparation of melon seeds or almonds soaked in water.

[1] Ghisalberti, 272 n.

[2] Luzio, *Felice Orsini e Emma Herwegh*, 83.

The interesting correspondence thus begun was interrupted by a misunderstanding. Emmas's remittance of twenty francs was held up by the prison authorities, and for some weeks Orsini did not receive them. His anxiety blossomed into indignation. He dashed off a furious complaint against Emma, sending it not to her, but to a mutual acquaintance, a Zurich businessman whom he had met only twice, with instructions to send a copy to her and the original to Mazzini. Emma had never been so outraged in her life. That Felice, of all people, should accuse her of meanness—and should go and write a circular about it! She consulted Cironi, who had now left Zurich for Genoa. Cironi answered stiffly. "F's letter confirms the bad opinion I have always held of him. If you have anything more to do with that man, you might as well put a plaque on your front, 'here is the woman who can be insulted with impunity'."[1] He hoped to hear the end of the man whom he considered, on no foundation whatever, as his rival.

But Emma had an essentially generous nature. The more she reflected on the incident, the more she made allowances for the frightful circumstances in which Orsini was placed, and the more she felt she could not withdraw her hand from one who had no real friend except herself. Orsini, when he at last received the twenty francs, wrote her a handsome letter of apology, and the lemon juice correspondence was resumed. In the next few months the Herweghs, Cironi and Mazzini all had news of the greatest interest to the party. They heard the full story of Orsini's arrest and trial; the villanies of the arch-spy Bideschini; the heroism or cowardice of the Hungarian Fissendi, and the other conspirators arrested in Milan. They received valuable details about the fortress of San Giorgio, and a provisional outline for a plan of mass escape. Escape! However high the walls, or thick the bars, or incorruptible the guards, the first prerequisite was money.

While in cell No. 3 Orsini made contact with his neighbours in Nos. 2 and 4 by tapping out the alphabet upon the walls in the accepted form. The authorities were well aware of this activity. Prisoners involved in the same case were never put next to each other; sometimes spies were planted to extract secrets; and the penalty for discovery was to be chained to the

[1] Luzio, *Felice Orsini e Emma Herwegh*, 85.

wall, on a diet of bread and water. Nevertheless, in solitary confinement the temptation was overwhelming, and the information so obtained quite possibly vital to one or other party. He first tried No. 4, since it was well-known as the worst cell in the castle, darker and narrower than his own. Its occupant responded for a day or two with messages of courage and goodwill, but then fell silent. Had he gone to the galleys, or to the *forca*? There was no means of telling.

Orsini next rapped on the wall of No. 2. After some cautious sparring he found that it contained three cell-mates, and his heart gave a great leap as the wall spelt out the name of Calvi. Colonel Fortunato Calvi! The hero of the *Passo della Morte* in the mountains of Cadore! He had heard nothing of the great *condottiere* since his arrest by the Austrians in September 1853, at the time when Orsini himself had been captured in Piedmont. How much had happened since then! And yet, eighteen months later here they were, separated by a few feet of brick and mortar. Reckless of discovery they went to their respective window bars and talked across the intervening gulf. The windows of cells 2 and 3 were closer together than most of the others, and the deep embrasures acted as a kind of funnel. As Orsini's auditory sense had been sharpened by long months of silence, he found he could hear the huge, booming whispers of the famous patriot reasonably well.

Calvi's process had long been completed. Sentence of death had been pronounced, and confirmation received from Vienna nearly six months previously. Strangely enough, though his lame efforts at encouragement did nothing to disguise his certainty that Orsini's fate was sealed, he displayed a buoyant optimism about his own. Had they meant to execute him, he maintained, they would already have done so. With every week that passed the Austrians were being forced to greater clemency, out of regard for world opinion. Orsini was less easily deluded. The delay was more likely due to the Austrians' wish to make a greater spectacle by hanging others like himself alongside Calvi. All the same Calvi's nearness was a mighty consolation. Though fear of discovery led them to break off their conversation, Orsini spent tranquil hours upon his bed, watching the shadow of the bars creep along his wall, and thinking of Calvi in the next door cell.

In the middle of August an event took place which filled Orsini with reviving hope. One day the rigorous Casati told him that he had applied for transfer, and asked him as one of the more influential prisoners for a testimony of decent treatment. Never was a letter of recommendation more glowingly or gratefully written than the one Orsini wrote for the over-conscientious jailor. At last his luck was changing. Casati was replaced by a man of a much more hopeful stamp; Stefano Tirelli, a low-minded Mantuan, who had been for twenty years in the service of the Austrian police, and had earned promotion by detecting messages concealed in scraps of bread by the priest Tazzoli who was subsequently hanged.

Meanwhile the case against Orsini was becoming more and more complete and his evasions more and more involved. The Hungarian deserter known to him as Fissendi had sung out all about the meeting at Maurice Quadrio's house outside Geneva, just before the sea attack on Massa and Carrara, when Tito Celsi had given him his orders from Mazzini. Fissendi had further identified Orsini from behind a peep-hole in a door. Thus Orsini's stout contention that he had been in London at that time was broken down. Moreover, his claim that he had been no more than a messenger to the Milan Committee was gravely threatened when Sanchez produced a letter from Mazzini, instructing them to give a thousand francs "to Felice Orsini, who knows what to do with it".[1] Orsini was completely taken aback. The date of the letter was 8 December. By then he had been far away on his road to Hermannstadt, and he had never heard of its existence. Sanchez had found out everything about him; even more, it now appeared, than he knew himself.

As was only to be expected, at the beginning of September Orsini was brought before Sanchez once again, and formally sentenced to death for high treason. However, Sanchez said, the file would not be ready to go off to Vienna before the end of January, and therefore the execution, if it ever took place, would probably not do so until May. There was no reason to despair, said Sanchez; after all, while there was life there was always hope. His tactful sympathy was most depressing. Orsini took it calmly; he objected only to the statement that he had confessed his guilt, tucked in by Sanchez as a means of gaining

[1] Luzio, *Biografico*, 178.

extra credit in Vienna. Back in his cell he felt almost relieved that the suspense was over. Calvi next door was in the same boat as he. With two such sturdy fighters close together, surely they would think of some way out? At least, his letters to Emma were not suspected, and possibly Tirelli the new jailor could be worked upon. He rapped on the wall, and climbed up to his window.

"Calvi!" he whispered.

After a long pause, a hesitant voice replied. "Calvi? Calvi is here no longer."

"Not there? Why, where has he gone?"

There was another pause before the deadly words were blurted out. "To his death. They hanged him weeks ago, on the morning of 4 July."

Orsini reeled backwards from the bars and fell upon his bed. Calvi, hanged! He had known that it must end that way, but that it should have happened so silently and swiftly, and so near to him, shocked him beyond measure. He fell prey to prison fever, endemic in San Giorgio because of the unhealthy humours of the lake. As he raved and shivered, the dreamy twilit world of half-reality in which he had lived for the last year engulfed him altogether.

One dark evening he lay tossing while an early autumn gale howled through his cell. He thought he heard distant melancholy music, and perceived a rosy light shining through his window, reflecting the shadow of the bars just as the sun so often did by day. He rose, and pulled himself up by his arms towards the bars until he could see out. Beyond the Galletta Square, in the Piazza Sordello, a funeral pomp wound slowly towards the *Duomo*. What was this, then? It was the last hope of Italy going to burial. It was Calvi, going to his glory. A hundred torches flickered round his glittering bier, and out of the darkness streamed an unnumbered multitude with slow footfalls and hushed voices, his relatives, his friends, his followers from stricken Italy. As the weird music faded within the majestic portals of the cathedral, the tears poured down Orsini's face. Farewell, Calvi! And he himself so soon, so soon would follow him.

Next morning, still fretful, he asked the warder what had happened. The warder told him it had been the funeral of a wealthy banker. The bathos of it pulled Orsini to his senses. Everyone in the prison, it appeared, had known of Calvi's execution save only he, but no one had cared to tell him, because Calvi's case was so exactly like his own. Greedily he collected all the details. Two mornings before Calvi was due to die, he had been roused and taken to hear the reading of the warrant. Asked whether he would save his life by suing for the Imperial clemency, he had answered simply, "No. I shall hate the Austrians to the end of my days." He went out tranquilly to be hanged, dressed all in black down to his gloves, and smoking a large cigar. His place of martyrdom was not in the valley of Belfiore, but at the far end of the bridge San Giorgio, in a little hollow on the left. Halfway across the bridge he stopped the carriage, and leaned out to look back towards the city. On the scaffold he took the cigar from his mouth and tossed it to one of the attendants. Calvi was left hanging until sunset; his body was then cut down and thrown into a ditch. Casati had a coffin made, and gave him a decent burial at his own expense.[1]

Orsini rummaged in his valise beneath the trestle bed, and pulled out a pair of white kid gloves. Emma had given them to him in Zurich, and he had jokingly promised to save them for his execution. He looked at the place where the little phial of strychnine had been stitched inside the wedding finger. He did not resent its loss. In freedom he had thought of suicide often enough, but under sentence of death the idea was strangely unattractive. The thought of the grisly ritual of the *forca* chilled his blood. Already he felt the rough halter round his neck, already he faced the frantic moment. Calvi's message had been one of defiance to the last. Very well, if he were doomed to die, he would die fighting for his liberty.

Now that his process was concluded his strict surveillance was relaxed. He was allowed a glass, and lights till nine o'clock, and a steel pen to write his book. Because of his good conduct, Sanchez said, he was soon to be released from solitary confinement. He received visits from the chaplain, Monsignor Martini, a kindly man who had seen many of his compatriots through their calvary. Martini sat informally on the bed, shared pinches of snuff, and discoursed knowingly on literature. But

[1] Orsini, *Memorie politiche*, 207–19, 222.

his well-meant kisses always reminded Orsini of the final kiss before the hangman stretched the rope.

The new jailor, Tirelli, permitted him to order wine with his meals, to sing, to do bodily exercises to improve his strength. Tirelli, he found, unlike Casati, had weaknesses. He drank a lot. He was familiar with the turnkeys. Discipline slipped, they no longer tapped the window bars at night. Themselves Italians though depraved, they chatted freely with the prisoners, and regarded them with sorrowful respect. Orsini tested their venality one by one; when they recoiled in horror, he laughed and clapped them on the shoulder and poured them out a tumblerful of acquavite. How droll he was, to be sure, they thought, tossing down the acquavite; every inch a literary gentleman! They did not know that the smart silk scarf he wore about his neck was knotted and greased into a fast-running noose, which, if ever the moment seemed to him propitious, he would slip over their heads and so silently strangle them without compunction.

Tirelli had a wife called Giovanna, a sturdy, rawboned woman of thirty-one, a midwife by profession. Giovanna's sexual craving was quite uncontrolled. She looked on the young men locked in the cells as a harem provided for her own enjoyment, and she took her husband's keys whenever she felt like it. She quickly became smitten by the handsome, silent, experienced-looking gentleman who was kept alone under special guard in No. 3. Orsini, by remaining as aloof and untemptable as John the Baptist roused her interest to obsession. Before long he had tantalized her, under promise of elopement, into most desperate ventures.

His first plan was, with her connivance, to reduce Tirelli one evening to a drunken stupor, a task they had already found to be by no means difficult. They would then bribe the turnkeys, release the prisoners, overpower the soldiers, and lead a mass escape into the moat. Turning their backs on Mantua they would cross the bridge San Giorgio making for the Po which marked the boundary of Lombardy no more than twenty-five miles distant. Thence they would scatter in the Apennines, and so reach Genoa and safety. Winter was coming on; the long nights would be ideal for the dangerous flight over open country. One of the turnkeys, Tommaso Frizzi, who was under notice to lose his job, could be safely used to make preliminary arrangements. Everything was ready; there wanted only money. Orsini calculated that the enterprise would cost 5,000 francs; that, he told Emma, was his minimum requirement.

To Orsini inside the jail, 5,000 francs seemed small enough a price for the delivery of so many valuable party members, of whom two besides himself were awaiting execution. To the party, which had just had such difficulty in scraping up a mere five hundred, it sounded like a fortune. Mazzini pettishly declared that he could do no more; Orsini's family must be approached. Emma agreed. Orsini's family had so far proved unhelpful, she felt convinced, only from fear of the Papal police. If they were asked discreetly, and had a safe channel of communication, surely they would respond. For that purpose it was necessary for somebody to go to Nice to interview the banker Abraham Colombo, and get him to advance the sum required. She approached Luigi Folli at Codogno, who positively refused to go. He was kept more or less under house arrest, he said; in his circumstances to attempt the journey would be madness. He sent a further 200 francs; he also made a final appeal to Sanguinetti, but in vain. Other appeals to other friends proving equally fruitless, he finally lost heart. They had done their best, and their best was not enough; there was nothing for it but to let fate take its course.

His sentiments of pious resignation were not, thought Emma, at all the kind of thing she could tell Orsini. She next tried Peter Cironi at Genoa. Cironi too considered it a hopeless task. Emma insisted: if Cironi would not do it, she declared, she would go herself; though it would be most embarrassing for her, a respectable matron, to undertake such a mission on behalf of a man to whom she was not related. Out of regard for his feeling towards her, and urged by his stern conscience as a loyal party member, Cironi eventually relented. On 24 October he went by steamer to Nice, called on Garibaldi, and persuaded him to use his influence. Together they visited Colombo, with the result they had foreseen. The banker clicked his tongue and shook his head. He agreed to forward a letter to Orsini's brother Leonidas in Imola; he did not expect a satisfactory reply, but if by any chance he got one, why, certainly he would at once inform General Garibaldi.[1] The weeks went by, no answer came from

[1] Luzio, *Felice Orsini e Emma Herwegh*, 87; Ghisalberti, 273.

Imola, and as a last resort Cironi opened a subscription list among the penniless refugees in Genoa. Though he had the energetic assistance of the exquisite warrior Giacomo Medici, and though Garibaldi was one of the first to contribute his "poor *obolo*",[1] it would be months before a respectable total was reached, and Emma had to tell Orsini that his figure of 5,000 francs was far too high. All the same her faith in her crystal was so keen, and her spirits so rebounding, that she never gave up hope. "Yet still he will be free," she kept repeating, until Cironi and her husband began to call her wrily "our dear Sibyl Emma".[2]

Meanwhile at Mantua Orsini was progressing with his part of the preparations. At the end of September he was moved from cell No. 3 to No. 9 where he had seven companions, lightly implicated, men of his own class, and cheerful, though badly racked by Mantuan prison fever. They included one of Calvi's cell-mates, and the elderly Count Ercole Rudio of Belluno who, with his daughter Luisa, had been arrested for their part in Calvi's operation in Cadore; his son Carlo, Orsini's former associate in the Valtelline affair, had managed to escape to Switzerland. There were also several Milanese compromised by the Hungarian Fissendi; among them Ambrogio Correnti, cousin of Dr. Piolti di Bianchi the leader of the rising of 6 February 1853. Correnti was an artist of considerable merit. On his release at the end of October he left with another prisoner a fine portrait carefully concealed behind a dullish landscape. It depicted Orsini wearing a winter overcoat which, though it had not yet arrived, was eagerly awaited and was the constant topic of their conversation.

On 5 October Orsini had openly asked Emma for the overcoat in question. In consequence of certain previous instructions *in simpatico*, a month or so later one of Mazzini's most responsible aides in London, Francesco Crispi, was amazed to find the philosopher in his bedroom, happily absorbed in opening the bone buttons of a greatcoat and filling the cavities with a blackish substance.[3] In the same letter of 5 October Orsini had also asked for a volume or two of chemistry and physics to assist

[1] Orsini, *Memorie politiche*, 263.
[2] Luzio, *Felice Orsini e Emma Herwegh*, 82.
[3] Luzio, *Biografico*, 208–9.

him in his studies. This second innocent request became in its turn the subject of a cryptic entry in Cironi's diary:

"26 December. The bookbinder H. Fürrer today left in the house of Sig^ra^ Emma Siegmund H. a second volume of the works of F. Arago. This book contains 700 francs in Austrian notes and two saws."[1]

Disappointed of the 5,000 francs required for bribery, Orsini had devised a less expensive scheme. There must be opium "of the best quality and in good quantity", enough for fourteen men at least. The banknotes, and a map of the countryside round Mantua, were to be bound into the cover of one of the volumes, so that they could not be detected even if the cloth covering were ripped away. As for the saws, they were to be of the finest steel, "precise, well-tempered saws, so delicate as to make as little sound as possible. It doesn't matter about a bow for them, as I can make that here; if they are placed along the edges of the boards right up against the spine there is no danger they will be discovered."[2]

Tirelli, a man of faulty education, found it very wearisome to keep the prisoners' food accounts in order, so it was arranged that the occupants of No. 9 should go to the jailor's room to do it for him. They induced the turnkeys to lay in great stocks of liquor bought in Mantua, and the approach of the festive season led to ever greater licence. The stove in No. 9 began to smoke badly enough to foul the atmosphere. Permission was sought, and granted, for the prisoners to take their meals occasionally in the jailor's room while the cell was being aired. On 2 December, the anniversary of the Emperor's accession, the eight conspirators and their guards sat down to a convivial banquet presided over by Tirelli and the blandly-smiling Giovanna which lasted long past midnight while they discussed (or so they afterwards maintained) the progress of the war in the Crimea. With Christmas and the New Year coming on it seemed likely that the celebrations would be frequently repeated.[3]

But time was passing, and Orsini still had not received his

[1] Ghisalberti, 274.

[2] For Orsini's secret correspondence with Emma Herwegh, see Luzio, *Felice Orsini e Emma Herwegh*, 35–62; Ghisalberti, 172–91; Orsini, *Memoirs and Adventures*, 151–64.

[3] Luzio, *Biografico*, 210–11.

winter comforts. Already once the moat had been thigh deep in snow. He dared not wait till spring; the decision of his case, he knew, had been speeded up on orders from Vienna. The "opportunities" he had secured cost money every time, and he was now penniless again. When the banknotes came, they would have to be changed into gold Napoleons by the turnkey Frizzi with whom he had come to an arrangement: that too involved delay. His communication with Emma was becoming every day more jeopardous; Fissendi had revealed everything, down to the lemon-juice method of correspondence. Scraps of Orsini's secret letters show an increasing desperation:

> 8 *December* 1855. "Things have come to a point where it would be folly not to try. I have the map and I am only waiting for what you are to send. . . . But quick, quick, quick, quick and then quick, and don't let this month pass: otherwise goodbye to all. The lives of two others due for the halter depend upon it; I will say no more in order not to compromise anyone."
>
> 23 *December* 1855. "I write and give my word for the last time for what we treat of. We are not speaking of huge sums, but only of what is essential; even 500 francs, even 200, even only one hundred which can be sent by post. . . . In any case write at once; if you delay another fifteen days even a hundred thousand francs would be no good.
>
> "It is disgraceful that there is no agent in Mantua. . . . It all shows the rottenness of the party. Everything is ready, and yet in spite of all that I have done, in three months a mere 500 francs have not been found.
>
> "I hope that 100 francs will be forthcoming. In short, send whatever you can, even if it is nothing but the overcoat. I will resort to robbery on the highway. Better to go than to remain. I put more trust in Madame than in all the others who only chatter and make promises, and I say that with all my heart."

Orsini's stinging accusations drove Cironi to renew his efforts to raise money quickly. On 22 December he contracted a personal loan of 800 francs for a six months' term with Count Giovanni Grilenzoni, an ardent Mazzinian at Turin. This loan, for which Emma and Mazzini divided the liability with him, was repaid in full the following February from the subscriptions collected by Giacomo Medici at Genoa. A further 200 francs were raised to make 1,000 francs in all, half the remainder being an outright gift from a mysterious Madame Giacomina Schwartzenbergh, the only non-Italian contributor.

On 26 December the bookbinder delivered the loaded volume of Arago. Because the overcoat, although despatched from London by Mazzini, had still not yet arrived, Emma bought another, personally put opium in the buttons, and stitched over them a covering of silk. The coat and book were sent off by parcel post from Zurich on the twenty-ninth, at the same time that a small balance for Orsini's maintenance was posted in an ordinary letter. Their delivery at Mantua was warmly acknowledged in a reply deliberately submitted by Orsini to Baron Sanchez and countersigned by him:

"Mantua, 7 January 1856

"Dear Madam,

"I have received quite safely the overcoat, the book, and the money, and I assure you I have not words sufficient to express my gratitude. The news of my children is most agreeable to me and I thank you for it.

"I beg you to convey my compliments to all your family; and I greet you, believe me, with friendship and esteem,

HERNAGH."

On 6 January Orsini organized a little party in celebration of Twelfth Night, to be attended by Tirelli and the turnkeys and all the soldiers of the guard. At four o'clock he abstracted the opium from the buttons and carefully measured out fifteen doses strong enough to put a man to sleep: to every glass he added a tot or two of rum. At six o'clock his guests arrived and each took his potion, Tirelli, already three parts drunk, jovially accepting two. The results were disappointing; one of the soldiers dropped his rifle, and was solicitously escorted by Orsini to a seat, while for a short time the turnkeys blundered round the room with their lanterns saying, "Oh, this is fine! I can no longer see."[1] By ten o'clock Tirelli could not stand, and collapsed on one of the mattresses in a vacant cell; but the others, who seemed to be totally unaffected, carried him out and gave him great quantities of rum and coffee which restored him to his senses.

[1] Orsini, *Memoirs and Adventures*, 159.

Next morning, when Tirelli awoke with bloodshot eyes and a throbbing head, everyone, himself included, merely supposed that he had had more to drink than usual. The President of the Court, Vincentini, ordered an inquiry into his conduct. Orsini, called in evidence, stood up strongly for Tirelli, supported by the other occupants of No. 9. Orsini could say, from his wide experience, that Tirelli was the best jailor he had ever known. So far from exploiting the prisoners, he was often out of pocket on the food accounts. The dinner parties and the other goings-on were no more than little acts of human kindness at a season of goodwill. As for Signora Tirelli, it was true she sometimes came to No. 9, but only to ask one or other of the inmates to mind her little daughter for a while. Their efforts were unavailing; Tirelli was dismissed from his post forthwith. He was to be replaced, they heard, by the present jailor at Mainolda, a square-headed German, incorruptible, precise, who had seen forty years of prison service. They decided to make another attempt in the few days remaining before Tirelli left. On 18 January Orsini received a box of chocolates with a double bottom and a further volume of Arago's works, containing morphine sent from London by Mazzini in three times the previous quantity of opium. "I gave the *bianco* on the twentieth in the doses indicated," he reported. "But nothing: the opium on the sixth had more effect. The *bianco* must have been stale."

Orsini reluctantly concluded that all chance of a mass escape was gone, and that he, whose plight was the most serious, must look to his own neck. Having tentatively arranged, as it turned out unsuccessfully, to provide his comrades in No. 9 with saws for their own use, he took fond leave of them, and applied to the President of the Court to return to a solitary cell. He suggested No. 12, the former torture chamber. No. 12 would be light enough for him to finish his book in peace, he said, as the window had only a single set of bars. The priest Tazzoli and Tito Speri of Brescia had in turn awaited execution there; he asked no better than to share their fate. Strangely enough, though the turnkeys recommended him for good behaviour, Vincentini would not hear of it. Instead, he ordered Orsini to be put in No. 4, the worst cell in the castle.

III

When, at the end of January 1856, the chain rattled on the door of No. 4 and the iron bolts shot into place behind him, Orsini counted himself as lost. So far as he could make out from the rather sinister optimism of President Vincentini, he had about three months more to live. Tirelli had gone, and with him all the haphazard opportunities of the last six months; everything was back as it had been under Casati. There were no more cosy sessions in the jailor's room. Tommaso Frizzi, the turnkey who had changed his banknotes, had been moved to another prison. He was completely isolated; not even the chaplain Monsignor Martini could any longer come to visit him.

For several days he sat quietly at his table working on his historical romance, *Di Spilberto e d'Altavilla.* He was perfectly resigned. He thought of asking to be shot instead of hanged, but decided not to; Calvi had sought no favours from the enemy. He made up his mind to cry "*Viva l'Italia!*" on the scaffold. Then one morning, reading his favourite Byron, he came upon the climax to *Mazeppa*:

At length I played them one as frank,
For time at last sets all things even,
And if we do but watch the hour,
There never yet was human power
Which could evade, if unforgiven,
The patient search, and vigil long
Of him who treasures up a wrong.

Revenge! Why should he wait upon the pleasure of the hangman, or at best go gnaw his heart out in the galleys? "I have not the patience or the resignation of Silvio Pellico, to content myself with taming a spider or a mouse. Curses on Austria! I will escape, and make them pay a hundredfold for the sufferings to which they have subjected me."[1] Though his attempts to drug the guards had taken money enough for eight months of normal maintenance, he still had, tucked away inside his mattress, five hundred francs in gold Napoleons. He was still in touch with Emma; and he still had his little saws. He

[1] Orsini, *Memorie politiche,* 252.

clambered up, he measured the bars, he clambered down again. "I clapped my hands with joy, as though the deed were already accomplished. I felt full of enthusiasm, and although enfeebled by confinement, I felt capable of attempting even the impossible. My country, my children, and Louisa, whom I seemed destined after all to see again, induced me to pronounce the words, *I will.*"[1]

Regaining some measure of composure, he made a minute examination of his cell. It was about six paces long, four wide, and very high, infested with lizards and scorpions. The window was a good six feet from the floor. It had two grids, a yard apart, each composed of twelve interlocking bars three-quarters of an inch thick: beyond them was a wire screen covered with canvas, so that, unlike No. 3, it was impossible to see out at all: on the inside were wooden shutters. The window was directly opposite the door; the guards on entering would immediately notice any alteration to the bars; and if, as they sometimes did, they tiptoed to the door and flung it open suddenly, they might easily catch him at his work.

First things first. He got out a reel of thread he had obtained to mend his clothes, tied four walnut shells to the end like a set of fishing hooks, pushed them between the bars and under the canvas with the handle of the broom, and let them down until he heard them rattling together at the bottom and knew that the ditch was dry. He then pulled them up and measured the thread on the edge of his table, which he reckoned to be a yard in length. The height of his window was about a hundred feet from the bottom of the moat.

On 1 February when a turnkey came to change his sheets Orsini was immersed in the works of Arago. "Let me finish these few pages," he said pettishly; "then I'll make my bed and do whatever you wish. Leave the clean ones here." As soon as the man had gone he hid the dirty sheets and towels under his mattress, and remade the bed. In the interval the guard was changed, and in a few minutes another turnkey entered.

"Have they changed your sheets, Signor Orsini?"

"Yes," he said absently without looking up. The laundry came from the common jail in Mantua where there were so many prisoners it would not be missed.

[1] Orsini, *Austrian Dungeons*, 105; Orsini, *Memoirs and Adventures*, 164–5.

Before going further another important matter had to be considered. The new jailor, Tirelli's successor, proved to be very different from the sort of German Orsini was accustomed to. Though scrupulous and infinitely cautious he was gullible, shaky and constitutionally querulous. He was an old man of seventy, a former corporal of Hussars, forever talking about the battle of Leipzig over forty years before. He had met no trouble at Mainolda; his only wish had been to spend his last years of service there in peaceable seclusion with his wife. On hearing of his transfer to Mantua he had begged and implored not to be forced into a task beyond his powers. His name was Funke. Under Funke all the liberties allowed by Tirelli had been withdrawn, except that the nightly examination of the windows had not yet been resumed. What was Funke's intention? Orsini tackled the most conscientious of the turnkeys, a married man with two children to support.

"Tell me, Giatti; when I was in No. 3 you always sounded the bars. Why don't you do so now?"

"Because we did not know you then as well as we do now."

"Very well; but remember that my case is desperate: you want to watch out I don't escape."

"Oh, but Signor Orsini is, well, he is an educated gentleman; he's not afraid to die. Besides, it's impossible——"

"Then what is that step-ladder for, outside the door?"

"That? Why that's to climb on, to examine the bars."

"Don't you ever use it?"

"Only with the Barabbases we can't trust."

"Well, my dear Giatti, since that's how you feel about me, let's take a glass of acquavite together—Yes—and call your friends." All the guards came crowding in, crying out, "Oh what a fine man! What a splendid gentleman!"

Orsini showed himself a man of precise and regular habit. Every evening he went early to bed, leaving his list of the day's expenses neatly made out on the stool beside him, so that when Funke paid his visit at half-past nine he would exclaim appreciatively, "What a fellow! He has everything ready for the morning, and he is always up at dawn." At the late-night visit at half-past one he was always sound asleep when the turnkeys held the lantern to his face. One night he woke up, blinking dazedly at the light.

"Oh, excuse us, Signor Orsini; we didn't mean to waken you."

"It's nothing, nothing: you have to do your duty."

"Sleep well, poor gentleman," they answered.

He thought it would be better to work at night since there were fewer interruptions, but the first few tentative scrapes of his file sounded in the midnight silence like the screeching of a sawmill. After dark an armed sentry was posted in the corridor; the door did not fit well, and Orsini could hear his every sound, his coughs, his mutterings, his footsteps pacing up and down. No, daylight was the better risk. For several days he stood underneath his window, his right ear towards the bars, his left towards the door, until his perceptions quickened and he could detect, or even anticipate, the slightest movement.

In order to reach the bars he had to balance precariously on the back of his chair, leaning his stomach against the wall, holding the little blade by both ends with one arm between the bars, sawing horizontally to reduce the surface to be cut. He had to stop frequently to cool the saw in water. Mantua, he found, boasted a plethora of belfries, and at this season of Lent the bells clanged out deafeningly every half an hour, forcing him to get down to listen for the guards. Before each regular visit he carefully patched the bars with a rust-coloured mixture of candle wax, brick dust and bread, put the chair back in its proper place, and was discovered at his table, or, if he had descended rather breathless, pacing the cell and humming to himself.

After four days he had severed the first of the bars when one of his two saws broke. He wrote to Emma for others, and cut two pieces of wood from the underside of his table which he bound together with tape from his jacket to form a handle. Holding it in both hands he got on faster, and at the same time relieved the telltale bleeding from his much macerated left elbow. Even so, reaching for the higher bars was a veritable torture; and as each segment was removed the remainder slipped slightly in their sockets, so that it was difficult to get them back in place before the warders' visits. Sleeping little and eating less, time and again he fell on his bed in despair.

At the end of February he was sharply roused when President Vincentini made his monthly round. "And how is Signor

Orsini?" he inquired. "Always studying—philosophy—literature—Capital! Capital!"

"I may as well keep myself employed, though it will all be useless in a few months' time."

"Ah well, we must be patient and resigned. Is there anything you want? Any complaints about the food, or service?" As soon as he had gone Orsini skipped a little dance around his cell, climbed back on his chair, and started sawing like mad.

In twenty-four days he cut through the inner grid in seven places, and was able to remove the four squares at the lower corner of the frame. With some difficulty he wriggled through to see what the outer bars were like. To his great encouragement the external masonry was somewhat worn. That verified, he rechecked the height of his window and the condition of the moat. He then started, much satisfied, to squeeze back feet first into the cell. When he got as far as his chest he stuck, and try as he would he could not budge an inch. For an endless time he hung there, truly caught in his own mesh, with the hour of the late night visit drawing nearer. He shook the bars, he raged like a wild beast in a cage, tearing himself freely on the jagged sawn-off edges of the steel. At last he calmed himself, tugged at his shirt with either hand to prevent it riding up, emptied his lungs of air, and managed to descend.

This experience, and the difficulty of replacing the bars every two hours of the day, persuaded him to tackle the outer grid by night. He chose a night of storm, not only to drown the noise, but because the operators of the semaphore to Verona worked directly opposite his window. On the dark, wet, windy night of 12–13 March he climbed out and had set contentedly to work when he saw lanterns moving in the Galletta Square and heard footsteps hurrying towards his cell. They had spotted him, then. He remained huddled where he was between the two sets of bars. The footsteps stopped at No. 3; he heard the door unchained and the occupant removed. Changing prisoners, so late at night? He clambered down, closed the shutters across his window, thrust the cut bars under his mattress and lay down on top of it. After a while he heard the new prisoner protesting as he was flung into No. 3. He recognized the voice. It was Carlo Redaelli, a young bank-clerk from Milan, one of the victims of the spy Bideschini, a loose-tongued scoundrel who, to save his own skin, had informed freely against all the others. What Redaelli was doing in the cell next to his, Orsini could not make out. But he heard the turnkeys carry out a thorough search, sounding the brick work and the bars. At dawn he made his window look as tidy as he could.

That afternoon, when the turnkey came to take a glass of wine with him, Orsini found out more. Redaelli, who was so unpopular that nobody would have him in his cell, had been in No. 12. Taking advantage of the storm, he had picked the lock and made his way on to the tiles, where he had been recaptured, clinging on by the cable of a lightning conductor. The rope he had laboriously constructed from his bedclothes, which in any case would not have reached one-third the distance, had been found forgotten in his cell.

"The fool!" Orsini murmured, most sincerely.

"He is mad and wicked," said the turnkey. "Does he want to ruin us all? He now has twenty-five pounds of iron on his feet. If he kicks up again, we shall put him in here and chain him to the wall."

"What, and make me change my cell again?"

"You would be better off in No. 3."

"That doesn't matter: I am used to this one."

"Now see what he has done," went on the turnkey; "we have orders to be much stricter; we are to sound the bars of everyone, no matter whom."

"Naturally," replied Orsini, filling up the turnkey's glass. "Well then, you had better start with mine."

"Oh, we shall never do it to our Signor Orsini, never fear; nor to any of the gentlemen in No. 9."

"Yes, but I am going to escape," Orsini said.

The turnkey looked startled. Then he began to laugh until the tears came to his eyes. "Signor Orsini is a caution, to be sure," he cried. Still chuckling, he took his glass, which Orsini had again refilled, and went away.

Orsini saw that time was running out. One day, climbing down too hastily from the outer grid, the chair slipped and he fell heavily, damaging his right leg. Fortunately there was no cut, and the doctor treated it as rheumatism, prescribing rest and "a little oil of almonds". As soon as he could walk Orsini finished cutting one bar at the bottom right-hand corner of the further grating, where it could not be noticed from the floor of the cell. He then made an excavating tool with the handle of his saw and two nails extracted from the shutters, and attacked the masonry. Once he had bored through the outer casing of cement the remainder crumbled easily, providing all the aperture he needed, and he quickly removed eight bricks and a quantity of soil which, with the severed bar, he concealed inside his mattress.

"Yes, all goes well . . . if the wings of Icarus do not fail I shall be free," he wrote to Emma on 16 March. "We shall meet again for certain . . . It seems that the circle of my life, as you foretold to me at Nice, is not yet entirely closed."

On 26 March it was time again for President Vincentini's visit. The second of his three months gone!

"Always studying! Is your work not finished yet?" Vincentini asked in faintly urgent tones.

"Not yet, *signore*, but it will be soon."

"Capital! Capital!" said Vincentini.

That night Orsini took from his mattress the spare pair of sheets and three towels, each two and a half yards long. He tore the sheets into four strips and the towels into two, and tied them together with careful sailor's knots. He thus made a rope 105 feet long, to one end of which he tied two bundles containing his overcoat, his better pair of trousers, a scarf, waistcoat, hat and shirt. He then removed the bars, tore a hole in the external canvas screen with his excavating tool, and began to pay out the rope. Two-thirds of the way down it stopped; sticking out his head he saw that the bundles were caught in the grille projecting over the window of the state archives on the first floor of the castle. He contrived to free them with the handle of the broom, but in so doing became for the first time acutely aware of the silent vertiginous depths below him. He recoiled aghast. Hearing the guards coming he jumped back into bed, leaving the bundles dangling outside the bars: not until dawn was he able to recover them.

He spent the next day in bed complaining of the injury to his leg in order to distract attention from the window. He ate nothing; he was consumed by a fever so intense that he could not even drink to assuage his burning thirst. The nights of the twenty-seventh and twenty-eighth were moonlit, and he let them pass, tossing restlessly on his mattress now chock-a-block with bricks and rubble and the knotted rope.

On the twenty-ninth he was very weak. He forced himself to eat a little, ordered a bottle of good wine, and bought some oranges to slake his thirst. His fever was replaced by an icy clarity and calm. He tested his rope against the bars, and worked out the best position for descending. After the nine-thirty visit he prepared his bundles as before, adding as ballast the manuscript of his romance, and, for light reading matter, Thiebaut's *Memories of the General Staff*. Once again the bundles caught in the bars of the state archives; once again he freed them; in the process they burst open and the books fell with sickening splashes into the mud of the moat below. He took no notice. He closed the shutters, and added the severed bars to the general clutter in his mattress: he then lay down and slept peacefully until roused by the sound of midnight tolling from the nearby belfry of Santa Barbara.

At 2 a.m. on Sunday 30 March, when turnkey Giatti and his mate Sartori made their final round, they found everything in order. Signor Orsini, whose leg had been troubling him, lay undressed between the sheets; he stirred drowsily in the lantern light, turning over to face the wall. As usual, he was tucked in under his cloak: beneath it, they did not doubt, lay as always the smart new overcoat of which he was so pathetically proud. His portmanteau was below the bed, where it had been for the last two months. His chair was in its proper place, and neatly folded on it were his normal clothes for the next day.

While they were busy searching Redaelli's cell, Orsini dressed, and climbed into the space between the bars. Sitting with his legs outside the sill, he took the rope firmly in his left hand, ducked forward with his head, and with his right hand clutched the far side of the bars. Turning to face the wall, his feet found the ledge of a former bricked-up window. He reached for an orange he had placed between the bars and dropped it inside his shirt. Then, gripping the rope between his legs he started gingerly to lower himself, keeping his right shoulder against the wall for fear of grazing his face and hands.

It seemed to take hours. The night was very dark and the sheets torn into flimsy strips were difficult to grasp; the frequent knots all slipped a little as they tightened to the strain, and he dared not try them too far by resting his weight upon them. At one point in the sheer depths below him the beacon of the semaphore, which every five minutes flashed its message to Verona, flickered across the wall. He pictured how he would look, if caught in its beam, to the yawning operators; the garish ghostly silhouette of a political prisoner, improbably suspended against the vertical wall, transfixed by the light like a butterfly pinned to a board. He tried to hurry past the place, but his agitation of the rope caused it to sway perilously in an ever-widening arc the further down he got. Panting, drenched with sweat, terrified that he would be dashed against the wall, he paused, and waited for the light to strike him. It flashed past just above his head. About twenty feet from the bottom there was a ridge around the castle wall, where its foundations began to broaden out. As he groped for it with his feet, the rope escaped from between his legs. Swinging helplessly by his aching arms he looked quickly down; the ground seemed near, much nearer than in fact it was, so he let go. He felt a burning pain in his weak right leg, and fell unconscious in the bottom of the moat.

He can only have been dazed for a few minutes, for when he came to he could still hear the turnkeys finishing their rounds inside the castle. His heart racing with apprehension, he set his teeth and tested his leg. He found that it would move a little; at least it was not broken, then. He felt for the orange in his shirt, and sucked its juice. After a time he struggled to his feet, changed into his clean clothes, and set off limping round the left face of the castle towards the front facing the bridge San Giorgio. At the angle of the two he found the sluice leading under the road from the moat to the reeds on the shore of the lake. He squeezed through the muddy vault, but just as he could see the shimmering verge which to him spelt freedom, he perceived that the end was blocked by an iron grating. Turning back into the moat he climbed on to the archway admitting to the sluice; then, inserting his two invaluable nails alternately into the soft mortar between the bricks, he started to ascend the counterscarp. He had almost reached the top when his bad leg gave way and he fell headlong to the bottom. That was that; his nails were still lodged in the mortar far out of reach above his head. Picking himself up he staggered back to the other corner of the moat adjacent to the city gate. He uncoiled a rope he had taken from the jailor's room, threw it over a stone conduit pipe which drained rain water from the road, and tried to climb it. His strength failed him, and he collapsed upon the ground. He saw all the ugliness of his position. Morning was coming; where he lay he was scarcely out of sight from the city gate, though mercifully the bedclothes hanging from his window were screened from view by a protruding buttress. At six o'clock the turnkeys would make their early visit to his cell.[1]

At five the city gate was opened. Two fishermen came out, going to tend their nets down by the water's edge. One of them paused by the moat to light his pipe. As he did so, he saw a smart-looking gentleman with a thick brown overcoat covered in mud, a dark felt hat, black striped trousers and ankle boots of reddish leather. In one hand he had a coil of rope; in the other he held up a leather purse, making its contents chinkle musically. He spoke in a cultivated voice. "Help me out, my dear fellow. I got drunk last night, and fell in here when I stopped to do a pee." So saying, he threw the rope. From force of habit the fisherman caught it, and called to his friend to lend a hand; but other people were approaching, and they made off across the bridge.

Time passed: no one would help the figure in the ditch. At a quarter to six Giuseppe Sugrotti came along.* Known to his friends as "Toffin", which means a high-class hunting dog, he was tall and sturdy, open, ruddy-faced, wearing fisherman's waders up to his thighs. He too was going, this brisk spring morning, to lift his snares and nets in the reeds at the far end of the bridge, to the right near the ditch called Stoppon. He too heard the appeal, now uttered as a hollow cry. Ungrudgingly he took the rope and tried to haul it up. Finding it beyond his strength he called to a group of peasants who were by this time crowding towards the city for their customary Sunday appearances at Mass and in the market place, and one of them ran to his assistance. When Orsini's head came level with the

* B. Mantua 1822, died there in poverty 1892.

[1] Orsini, *Austrian Dungeons*, 140 to end; Orsini, *Memoirs and Adventures*, 161–72; Orsini, *Memorie politiche*, 236–55.

edge of the moat, seeing that his hands were torn to a scarlet pulp and he was about to lose his grip, Toffin seized him by the armpits and dragged him bodily out.

As soon as he was able Orsini fumbled in his purse and gave a gold Napoleon to the peasant. "Be careful what you say. I am a political prisoner." He saw the man's mouth fall open, and watched him hurry through the gate into the city. He then turned to Toffin.

"I am Orsini, friend of Mazzini and Kossuth. Save me, my friend, and you will be no longer poor."

Toffin looked at the crowd that was gathering round them. "Follow me; we've got to cross the bridge." He hurried off along the road and dropped the rope into the water. He then waited for Orsini who was hobbling after him, limping, muddy, the blood dripping from his hands.

"All these people—this will never do. Here, get up on my back."

As Toffin swayed down the long straight causeway, Orsini astride his shoulders airily beat time with one arm and they roared out a local drinking song.

E morto el povar Piero
Che l'era el gran bon om

Such scenes were not uncommon on a Sunday morning. The crowd scuttled out of their way good-humouredly, and a picket of Austrian soldiers returning from guard duty joined wholeheartedly in the fun. Short of the guardroom at the end Toffin set down his burden and struck away from the causeway into the rushes on the right. Orsini followed, not without a morbid glance at the yellowish-black wooden pillar to the left of the bridge where Calvi had been hanged. After a brief rest Toffin took him up again and carried him for nearly half a mile, surefooted in the treacherous untrodden bog, to a place where none but waterfowl would ever find their way. There he rubbed the circulation back into Orsini's damaged leg, cut reeds for his protection from the biting wind, and went in search of necessaries.[1]

[1] Luzio, *Felice Orsini e Emma Herwegh*, 95–102; Luzio, *Biografico*, 234–5; Orsini, *Memorie politiche*, 255–7.

IV

When the conscientious warder Giatti finished his late night round at 2.30 a.m. on the Sunday morning, he returned the keys to the head jailor Funke, and joined his mate Sartori already asleep upon his bunk. Three hours later they were up again, and while Sartori watched the staircase leading to the guardroom, Giatti began his visit to the cells. On reaching the little corridor admitting to Nos. 3 and 4, he first called on Redaelli. That done, he dismissed the overnight sentry who was still standing at his post, drew back the bolts of No. 4 and entered. The bed, he saw, was empty, and the sheets thrown off as if in haste; he turned quickly to look behind the door, expecting to find the familiar bearded figure seated silently on the commode. Then he noticed the window, where the shutters hung wide open and the daylight, no longer impeded by the bars, streamed freely through with mocking radiance.

He stood for a moment clutching at his throat before he ran off to look for Funke, whom he found, anxiously matutinal as usual, already writing at his table. Funke sprang up aghast, but not excessively surprised; it was, he felt, the kind of trick he expected life to deal him. First Redaelli, and now this. Why could they not have let him die in peace in Mainolda? Together they hurried to No. 4, and from there clattered downstairs to the moat. People were passing to and fro across the bridge, but there was no sign of the fugitive, though Sartori, who had gone into the town, reported that a woman had told him of two countrymen who spoke of a fellow in the ditch offering them money to pull him out, which they said they had refused to do.

Baron Sanchez, who was the next to be informed, was so utterly astonished that at first he could not say a word. By half-past eight the description of the wanted man had been telegraphed in all directions, "a most dangerous and important prisoner from a political point of view". An enormous price was set upon his head; patrols were sent out right and left. So great in fact was the consternation that when the Chief of Police arrived from Verona by the evening train to open the inquiry, there was a great deal of confusion in the evidence submitted to him. In his report the eminent *sbirro* stated that Orsini had spent only six weeks with his companions in No. 9, whereas he was actually there four months. The inside grid had been severed in six places; in fact it was cut in seven. The height of the window was given as eleven *klafteri*, that is, about sixty-six feet; in reality it was a hundred. In the moat, besides tell-tale traces on the counterscarp, besides scraps of orange peel, the manuscript of a novel, and Orsini's discarded clothes much scraped and torn, were found two fragments of broken saw. These, confided to a committee of experts, produced breath-taking conclusions. It was not possible, the experts said, to cut through bars three-quarters of an inch thick with a saw as short as this; consequently Orsini must have been in possession of a saw of ordinary size. Even then, they added, it must have taken a considerable time. It followed, first, that Orsini had obtained a saw from outside the prison; and secondly, that his work would have been discovered, had not the practice of sounding the bars been allowed to fall into disuse.

There was a further complication about the rope of sheets. It would appear that the one used by Orsini was confused with that previously taken from Redaelli, which was less than a third of the necessary length. In consequence, the Commission wasted valuable time on ladders up against the castle wall, wondering whether a man in Orsini's state of health could possibly have swung himself across to a lightning conductor situated nine feet to his left. All in all, the Commission did not exclude the view that the cutting of the bars, the rope, and so on, might be a blind; that Orsini had bribed the sentinels, walked out through the gate, and was probably still at large in Mantua. More attention was therefore paid to pestering the inhabitants, such as the venerable Marchesa Teresa Valenti-Gonzaga, mother of Carlo Arrivabene, Orsini's exiled friend in London, than to searching the reeds or covering the roads on the far side of the bridge. As time went by the theory was kept alive by public rumours of an exotic foreign lady, going under the name O'Meara, who was supposed, out of love for Orsini and devotion to the cause, to have taken rooms in Mantua, charmed the guards, and conveyed the requisite instruments to her paramour concealed in a home-made *polenta*, or, alternatively, in some big fish.*

Suspicion became focused on the unfortunate turnkey, Tommaso Frizzi, who, already posted to another jail as being in concert with Orsini, was now found in possession of banknotes to a greater value than he could readily explain. In vain did he protest that they represented all his savings during twenty years of loyal service. To the jailor Funke, goaded by the smug evidence of his predecessor Casati that such a thing would not have happened in *his* time, Frizzi appeared as the embodiment of all the evils done him by the world. The case against him was elaborated by the infamous Redaelli who, bitterly envious of Orsini's success, and out of personal spite against Frizzi, volunteered a long-winded tale in the hope of mitigating his own plight: and by Frizzi's own wife, who frankly wanted to get rid of him in order to enjoy more comfortably the attentions of her lover.

In the end, Frizzi was sentenced to eight years hard labour.† President Vincentini was relieved of his position; Funke, after a few days in arrest, was allowed to go whimpering to retirement; and the two peasants who had boasted that they had refused to help Orsini out of the ditch were sent to prison for three years for having failed to denounce him instantly to the police. The cost of repairing the window of No. 4 was charged to the city of Mantua; the severed bars were sold, and were preserved as priceless relics by the public.[1]

* There is no evidence that O'Meara ever existed. Orsini was emphatic that Young Italy had no representative in Mantua, nor is there any longer doubt about how he obtained the money, opium and saws. In the folk-pageants representing the escape of Orsini, later witnessed by Luzio in the Arena Virgiliana at Mantua, the *Contessa Emma Herwegh di Brescia* was always depicted as Orsini's lover. It seems likely therefore that the fabulous O'Meara was a romantic exaggeration in the minds of the Mantuans of the part played by Emma.

† After the liberation of Venetia in 1866 he was restored to office on Garibaldi's recommendation, and died a jailor at Vicenza.

[1] Luzio, *Biografico*, 213–34, 243–57.

V

Orsini spent all Sunday in the reeds, listening to the rustle of the breezes and the harsh cries of birds, and letting the thin sunshine play upon his ruined limbs. From where he lay, a gunshot from his former prison across the lake, he could see gendarmes and warders scurrying about, posses of soldiers marching. Sooner than invite their attention by appearing on the bridge too often, Toffin arranged for Domenico Carlini, his close friend and neighbour and fellow fowler, to bring a razor to shave off Orsini's beard; and a basket containing bread, cheese and acquavite, and unguents for his leg. Carlini stayed talking an hour or so, telling how the Mantuans had held an unofficial *festa*, and the populace had crowded into the Galletta Square, craning their necks to catch a glimpse of the already famous aperture. He returned to Mantua about his normal dinner hour, when his appearance would occasion no surprise, taking with him the four gold Napoleons Orsini gave him to hire a conveyance to carry him to Brescia.

Toffin and Carlini decided to approach one Ephraim Bergatti, who owned a gig and was willing to undertake awkward journeys at a correspondingly awkward price. Prudently anticipating an early curfew on Mantua that night, Toffin paraded Ephraim Bergatti well before dusk outside the gate San Giorgio, and crossed the bridge without delay to the little village of Frassine, where they wined and dined till eight o'clock. They then drove to the water's edge, where Toffin half-led, half-carried Orsini to the bank. "What a deal of trouble to get hanged for," Toffin grumbled. Ephraim, who had been listening to the chatter at the inn, instantly demanded an extra ten Napoleons. "Barabbas that he is," cried Toffin, "you will have to pay it." For his own part, Toffin would not take a penny. It was just as well, for of the twenty-six Napoleons Orsini had brought with him from the castle, very few remained. Indeed, he left a canteen account behind him in San Giorgio which eventually had to be defrayed by two of his companions in No. 9.

Soon after nine they parted; Toffin ran beside the gig still clasping Orsini by the hand until the horse began to trot. When the gig reached the Brescia road at Marmirolo some four miles out of Mantua, Ephraim refused to take his passenger any further, and left him with a horse-dealer who he said was reliable. The horse-dealer, not feeling himself on the best of terms with the police, handed him over to a miller, and for the next week Orsini was shunted hurriedly about the village, eluding his pursuers on one occasion only because he lay hidden in a manger above an old mule which kicked out at every stranger.[1]

In the meantime, he got word to Luigi Folli at Codogno, and Folli, so timorous in lesser matters, sent his coachman Pietro Baggi, later a sergeant of Dragoons in the Italian army, to fetch him from Marmirolo. On the morning of Monday 7 April Orsini was on the bridge of Goito; by evening he was through Piacenza and beyond the Austrians' reach. On the way they passed many patrols, and once saw some poor devil arrested in his place. Regardless of expense, ten times in a hundred and fifty miles they changed their foaming horses. So furious was their flight that approaching Pizzighettone-sul-Adda, where Folli had come to meet them, the shaft of the carriage broke; the local gendarmes bound it up and politely wished the travellers godspeed. Two days later Orsini crossed the border of Piedmont. On 11 April he sent Emma an account of his escape, from Genoa, where he received attention to his leg, and was greeted with "extraordinary content" by Giacomo Medici and other friends.[2]

His glorious news preceded him. On 2 April Luigi Folli announced to Emma briefly;

"C, Monday [really, Sunday] at 4 a.m. Felice!—was free."[3]

Emma immediately informed Cironi, who in turn wrote to Mazzini. Mazzini put a notice in the *Italia e Popolo*, and told Matilda Biggs, who had been working hard to raise funds for her former colleague. Mazzini replied anxiously to Emma on

[1] Luzio, *Felice Orsini e Emma Herwegh*, 102–12; Orsini, *Memorie politiche*, 258–9.

[2] Luzio, *Biografico*, 235–42; Luzio, *Felice Orsini e Emma Herwegh*, 64–6.

[3] Luzio, *Felice Orsini e Emma Herwegh*, 80.

the seventeenth, "I was hoping for a further letter. Is he not only free, but in safety? Has he passed the frontier? I count on you and Peter for a word to reassure me when you *are able to send it.*"[1]

On 14 May, from his hermitage on the rocky island of Caprera, came the word of the great Garibaldi to Cironi:

> "*Amico,*
>
> "I have received your note, and I thank you warmly for it. I rejoice with you at the success of the attempt. To plan and carry out an affair like this required such force of will that it fully deserved to be crowned with a happy outcome, and so it has been. . . . Do not speak to me of gratitude: what I have done is nothing: it was a duty deeply felt but poorly executed."[2]

Orsini made Emma forward a scornful, taunting letter to the Imperial and Royal Court at Mantua, twisting a knife in the wounds of President Vincentini and Baron Sanchez. It was followed by a bitter indictment, published on 20 May in the *Italia e Popolo,* of Alexander Mauroner, editor of the so-called *Corriere Italiano* in Vienna, whose betrayal, coupled with that of Moses Formiggini, had led to his arrest at Hermannstadt.

Throughout Italy the uproar was immense. The government of the Papal States, in dread that their long-lost son might return to the district of his birth, subjected Orso and Leonidas Orsini at Imola to a rigorous midnight search. Luigi Folli also went through many scorching examinations at Codogno, though without result.* Old Marshal Radetzky, no less intrigued by the audacity of the escape than enraged at the stupidity of the police, sent his personal spies into Switzerland, who plied him with the wildest stories until at length his curiosity was satisfied by Orsini's own account, sent to Mazzini from Zurich, translated and edited by Emily Ashurst Hawkes, and published in the *Daily News* on 8 June.[3] So hot, indeed, was the pursuit that there was no safety for Orsini in Piedmont, and when he left Genoa for Zurich, Cironi thought it advisable to quote in

* Luigi Folli died in 1864 at the early age of thirty-four without his part in the affair becoming known. It is due to Luzio's researches that his great services to his friend have come to light.

[1] Orsini, *Memorie politiche*, 262.

[2] *Ibid.*, 263.

[3] Ghisalberti, 197–201.

the *Italia e Popolo* a report from a mythical English newspaper, *The Hope*, that he had arrived in London.

In the first flush of triumph, Orsini angrily reproached Orso and Leonidas for not having sent the paltry 5,000 francs required to save his life. Orso answered plaintively that they had never heard of any such request, and that if they had, they would gladly have given twice or three times the amount. Orsini's family piety was touched; he wrote to his uncle again, demanding "excuse and pardon".

> "Although he may be advanced in years, I trust that God will allow me to see him once again, to embrace him and to seek in person his excuse and pardon for all the injustices which have come into my mind and for all the evils he has undergone because of me. I will say no more: I beg his blessing and respectfully kiss his hand.
>
> His most affectionate Felice."[1]

Orso speedily sent enough money to set his nephew up in England. Orsini balanced his accounts. He found out exactly which of his friends had helped towards the thousand francs collected on his behalf. Emma was reimbursed for the overcoat, books and saws; Cironi for his profitless journey to Nice; and Mazzini was repaid his original two hundred francs. Then, disregarding an instruction from Mazzini to remain in Switzerland for further expeditions, Orsini prepared to leave for London.

Much to the relief of Cironi. Cironi felt that he had done more than his duty towards Orsini. Emma had promised, as they waited for Orsini to arrive by the lake steamer, that for reasons of delicacy she would not have him in her house, but of course she had done so; and now Cironi had to listen to him boasting, as if he enjoyed the pain he must be causing, how Emma let him kiss her, and, worse still, how Emma since his arrival had refused all marital contact with her husband. "Heaven save me from the praises of a man like F.O.", wrote the outraged Cironi in his diary. With the greatest willingness he gave Orsini his own passport to carry him through France and into England.[2]

On 21 May Emma saw him off from Zurich station. "When

[1] Ghisalberti, 196.
[2] *Ibid.*, 277.

you are in any danger, let me know, and I will come to save you," were her portentous parting words. At Dover, as Orsini hobbled up the steps, a policeman gently helped him by the arm; it was an unfamiliar, even weird experience.[1] England, he noticed, was still foggy; but one couldn't have everything. In London on the twenty-sixth he went straight round to Mazzini, with whom he remained in earnest conclave for five hours.

[1] Orsini, *Memoirs and Adventures*, 185.

CHAPTER FIVE
The Bombs of Orsini

I

THE fabulous news of Orsini's escape had flickered across the world. Repressive governments sombrely took note that the man who had raised four rebellions on the Italian confines, had stalked through the Austrian capital, and had thwarted death at Mantua, was at large again and threatening vengeance. To peoples longing to be reborn to freedom his solitary epic seemed somehow to symbolize the victory of right over injustice. In England all the newspapers copied his letter to the *Daily News*; even *The Times* laid aside its instinctive mistrust of his flamboyance, and gave him credit in a sober English way for his battle against odds. His friends, among them Colonel Ribotti, his comrade in old conspiracies before the '48, for whose delivery from King Bomba's jails he had bargained during his brief moment of power at Ancona, regarded him as a sort of marvel. In view of his odyssey in Hungary, the great patriot Louis Kossuth showed him particular favour. Time and again he was required to tell his story. Orsini was not accustomed to so much fame. His hot vanity took fire, and he bore himself with arrogance.

His first interview with his chief was bound to be embarrassing. After a scanty tribute to Orsini's exploits, Mazzini plunged into an enthusiastic account of his current enterprise, another rising in Italy involving the subversion of Piedmontese armed forces, in which he said he had need of Orsini's services. To Orsini, the man before him, once so gigantic, seemed to have shrunk in stature. He wondered how he could ever have committed his life so often and so long to the whims of this elderly, dreamy and opinionated scholar. He had emerged from Mantua with the idea that Mazzini had exerted himself more lightly than he should have done in his behalf—and how Orsini dealt with those who had failed him was shortly indicated in his icy repudiation of another old friend, the banker Achille Sanguinetti, who had refused him money.

Furthermore, on his way through Genoa after his escape Orsini had learnt much about the latest state of things in Italy. Mazzini's madcap insurrections from without, and their dreary toll upon the scaffold, were discredited. The man of the moment was Cavour. By despatching the army of Piedmont to fight with great bravery at the side of the allies in the Crimea, Cavour had secured at the Congress of Paris, if not the solid gains he had intended, at least the benevolent respect of France and England. There was a basic antagonism between Mazzini and Cavour, as personal as it was polemical. Mazzini aimed at the regeneration of Italy by her own moral efforts, the overthrow of all European thrones, and the establishment of new national republics united by his religion of humanity. He thought Cavour an unprincipled adventurer who had spilled Italian blood in the Crimea to aid a French tyrant to consolidate his power. Cavour, more earthy, aimed frankly at the enlargement of the Kingdom of Piedmont by opportune diplomacy and the force of foreign arms. He had taken King Victor Emmanuel to London and to Paris; he had come back with the promise of goodwill from England, of armed assistance from France against the Austrians as soon as Louis Napoleon the new Emperor had been able to set his own house in order. Cavour thought Mazzini a meddling revolutionary likely to enrage Austria to punitive measures, and to embarrass the all-important relations of his potential French ally with the Church. Twice Cavour had seen Piedmont go down fighting alone against the Austrians; next time he would be sure of French support, and he would permit no premature explosions.

The exiled patriots, whether in Genoa or London, had to choose between Mazzini and Cavour. To side with Cavour meant giving up republicanism, for many their most cherished principle, in favour of unity under a Piedmontese dictatorship. On the other hand Mazzini, for all his broad ideals, had shown himself trivial and dissentious in practice. Cavour's more realistic plans involved the certain expulsion of the Austrians from northern Italy, and ultimately, as Cardinal Antonelli and other luminaries of the restored Papacy fully realized, the stripping of temporal possessions from the Pope. Cavour had at his disposal his victorious army, well-filled coffers, and in his own person the craftiest diplomatist in Europe. Would it not be wise to settle for the liberation of the country, and leave the form of government till later? Upon that consideration, the Italian National Society was coming into being in Piedmont, formed of exiles from all provinces. Manin, hero of the Venetian republic, had blessed it from his lingering Paris deathbed. Cavour, aware of its uses, not only in his designs on central Italy but as an inspiriting counterpoise to Mazzinianism, was secretly encouraging it. Many former republicans whom Orsini much admired, such as Giacomo Medici, had joined the Italian National Society: it was said that before long Garibaldi himself would undertake its leadership.

Orsini therefore listened in dismay to Mazzini's intention of fomenting a rebellion in Piedmont. He expressed the folly, from the national viewpoint, of perpetuating discord, of deliberately angering Cavour. He explained that Mazzini, far away in England, had been misled about the state of mind in Italy. He made not the least impression. It was however obvious that Orsini could not participate in Mazzini's coming expedition: his leg occasioned him great pain, and he was subject to recurrences of jail fever. So the meeting ended inconclusively.

Orsini took rooms at 2 Cambridge Terrace, Paddington, a respectable apartment house just north of Hyde Park. Among the many friends who showered him with invitations was the Russian, Alexander Herzen, who at the moment occupied a prosaic brick villa in St. John's Wood, whence he issued his anti-Czarist newspaper, *The Bell*. In the course of a pleasant dinner party Orsini talked of the old days at Nice, and charmed the company with the never-wearying tale of his escape. It was therefore with surprise that two days later Herzen received from Orsini a note suggestive of a duel. He requested an interview. Was it true, Orsini asked in his most dangerous voice, was it true that in his absence Herzen and Saffi had been spreading the story that he was an Austrian spy? Herzen knew better than to make light of the matter. In the troublous Romagna the word "spy" was, and indeed still is in country districts, the ultimate epithet of abuse. He traced the story to its stem, to the tea-time gossip of Mrs. Milner-Gibson, wife of a liberal M.P., and a warm admirer of Mazzini.[1] But when Orsini went to tax Mazzini with it he had disappeared—gone, as it proved, to Genoa, to direct yet another futile invasion of the Carrara-Massa region—leaving only the message, "I count on you".[2]

Disgustedly, Orsini turned to his intimate concerns. One of his first actions on arrival in London had been to search for Miss Louisa, his Héloise, the muse who had empowered his arm to cut through the bars of Mantua. Miss Louisa, it transpired, had gone to Calcutta for some good reason of her own, possibly to marry some desiccated British army officer, and she had left no word for him.

If his romantic idyll had faded from his life, reality, in the shape of his wife and children, was very present. Assunta was still living at Nice with Ernestina and Ida, and his Uncle Orso was still supporting them through the banker Colombo, though the difficulties of the hemp business were making it an increasingly onerous burden. Orsini had softened in his attitude towards Assunta; he was almost ready to admit he had been hasty; but as for a reunion, "it is as possible as that a square and a circle should coincide".[3] Assunta had no heroic qualities, unlike the fiancée of his poor friend Colonel Calvi, who after his execution had taken the veil and gone to nurse Piedmontese soldiers in the Crimea, where she had died of cholera. Orsini counselled Assunta, through Emma Herwegh, to have no regrets, since he himself had none, and assured her he would never forget she was the mother of his children. He planned to bring the children to England, either sooner or later depending on Assunta's treatment of them; in which event she would become entitled to a fixed allowance. Whatever happened, he must obtain money quickly.

Before Mazzini went away he had suggested that Orsini should write a book of his experiences at Mantua. In a couple of weeks he dashed off two hundred pages in Italian, and through George Jacob Holyoake he sold the copyright to

[1] Herzen, III, 318–21.

[2] Orsini, *Memorie politiche*, 269.

[3] Luzio, *Felice Orsini e Emma Herwegh*, 69.

Routledge against an advance of £50 with a further £10 to follow on publication. It was very easy money, thought Orsini. For the purpose of translation he approached Miss Jessie Meriton White, to whom he had been given an introduction by Garibaldi on his way through Genoa.

Miss White was a red-headed young lady of twenty-three, the daughter of a Portsmouth yacht builder. Her mother was American, and she possessed the amazing self-dependence of American women which was even more noticeable in the nineteenth century than it is today. She had gone to Piedmont as companion to a wealthy English widow who at that time was engaged to Garibaldi. She was much taken with the General, and promised to nurse his wounded when the time came for him to fight for Italy again. Accordingly, on her return to England she studied medicine at University College, London, in a class otherwise entirely composed of men. "An excellent and brave young woman", Orsini found her. His feelings for her rapidly entered the speculative plane. If Héloise was not to come back from Calcutta, and if he were to bring his children over to England, they would need a mother as badly as he needed a replacement for his wife. "She does not seem English," he told Emma with approval; ". . . not beautiful, but worthy to be loved by an Italian with all his heart. I can say nothing: I feel much sympathy—perhaps she is the one who would live with me."[1]

His fond thoughts were rudely upset ten days later, when he received the printer's proofs of Jessie White's translation of his book. Almost all his political observations had been edited away, and the text had been misunderstood at crucial points. He wrote in dismay to his friend Count Carlo Arrivabene,* "You know how distractable women are, let alone literary ladies; well, this is one, and she has been most absent-minded."[2] In vain did Jessie White protest, probably with justice, that the omissions improved the book. Orsini knew better; he saw the hand of the Mazzinians in the ruthless excision of every syllable which struck them as offensive. Jessie, whom he had chosen especially because she had no connection with Mazzini, had

* Subsequently war correspondent to the *Daily News* during Garibaldi's Sicilian campaign.

[1] Luzio, *Felice Orsini e Emma Herwegh*, 69.

[2] Ghisalberti, 203.

fallen under the spell of that famous charm. Orsini found that "Pippo" already called her his *Cara Bianca*, and provided her with cigars. In these circumstances he was little mollified when the book, which appeared on 2 August 1856 under the title *The Austrian Dungeons in Italy*, was an instant success and sold 35,000 copies in its first year.

Mazzini! There was no escaping from the man or from his sickeningly silly clique, with their Jesuitical censorship and smarting calumnies. He approached the most respectable exile of his acquaintance, Panizzi at the British Museum, for an introduction to Cavour. But his republicanism, and the Mazzinian teachings of fifteen years, died hard. Besides, would Cavour accept him? His two escapades in Carrara-Massa had won him no favour with the Piedmontese. He feared rejection more than anything. Was it not rather his duty to combat, from within the party, Mazzini's disrupting tendencies, and to use his great notoriety in England to extend knowledge of his country's plight?

Not without pain he learnt by heart two lectures in English about his experiences, and with these, in the winter months of 1856–57 he travelled about the country. He was very well received. Although his audiences could not make out much of what he said, they were impressed by his good looks, by his fierce sincerity, by the "simplicity, sweetness, and soldierlike straightforwardness of his demeanour".[1] At Brighton, in October, "The ladies surrounded and shook hands with me; they wondered that I had not become old and half dead." In Newcastle, "The workmen took my hand in their horny palms and said, 'We hope you will succeed in your good cause.'"[2]

He persuaded the people of South Shields, led by their Mayor, to address a petition to Parliament in favour of non-intervention in the event of an Italian war with Austria. He secured a similar vote in Birmingham, and letters in the papers followed. His purpose, a very legitimate one, was to enforce parliamentary action on behalf of Italy. But Justin McCarthy of the *Morning Star*, who heard him speak at Liverpool, vainly warned him not to exaggerate all the hospitality and admiration accorded to him into excessive expectations. McCarthy was right. As time

[1] Justin McCarthy, *Reminiscences*, I, 135–8.

[2] Orsini, *Memoirs and Adventures*, 187.

went by, Orsini's appeals met with less response, and when the Indian Mutiny broke out his slim parliamentary backing crumbled before what was, as he himself admitted, quite naturally considered the more pressing issue. The failure deepened his bitterness.

Had Mazzini been in England, he might have been able to calm his old lieutenant and repair the breach. In his absence, the rupture was completed by Mazzini's circle of disciples, a narrow group revolving about the family of W. H. Ashurst, a solicitor and an ardent advocate of women's rights. Ashurst's striking youngest daughter Emily Hawkes, described by Swinburne as "a chosen sister", was the chief vestal; when asked what her religion was she used to say, Mazzinian. Her husband at that time (they were afterwards divorced) was in partnership at the Swan Brewery in Fulham with James Stansfeld, who was married to Ashurst's eldest daughter, Caroline. Stansfeld, formerly a lawyer, was a suave and cultured liberal M.P. A third daughter was Matilda Biggs, who had worked at Orsini's side in Nice. These Ashurst girls, pulling earnestly at their cigars, called Mazzini "Mazz", or occasionally, "the Angel".[1] The circle included Aurelio Saffi, Mazzini's former fellow triumvir, the husband of his friend Georgina Crauford; and there was also the talkative Mrs. Milner-Gibson. The somewhat cloying atmosphere was sharpened by Federigo Campanella, an Italian of Savonarola-like severity, who had taken part in every Mazzinian rising: and by his half-section in Genoa, Maurice Quadrio.

When he heard about Orsini's lectures, Stansfeld, who was collecting money for the expected rebellion in Genoa, suggested that Orsini should come in with them on a basis of half-profits. Orsini refused; he did not believe that funds subscribed by English sympathizers should be squandered on harmful undertakings; nor would he consent to have his speeches dictated by the party. Sure enough, his rival lecturers, headed by his once-intended sweetheart Jessie White, burst into paeans of praise for Mazzini, the "Prophet", the "New Mahomet", and, on one occasion, the "New Jesus Christ". Because of Jessie White's red hair, Orsini began referring to them as "the Red and Co.", a practice which afterwards brought one of his

[1] Rudman, *Italian Nationalism and English Letters*, 73.

correspondents into difficulties with a prosecuting counsel, who believed he had nosed out a Marxist plot.[1]

While he was lecturing at Blaydon Burn on Tyneside, Orsini received a letter from Mazzini, dated 14 October 1856, warning him against his heterodoxy. Orsini replied with some very disrespectful remarks about Emily Hawkes and her brother-in-law James Stansfeld. As luck would have it, in Mazzini's absence the letter went to Stansfeld, who responded with such heat that Orsini challenged him to a duel in Belgium. At this juncture Mazzini suddenly reappeared, and tried to persuade Orsini to withdraw by the promise of an important mission. Orsini answered that he was always ready for any likely venture on behalf of Italy, but that he would take no further part in half-baked affairs like those of Carrara-Massa or the Valtelline. Mazzini's last letter, of 17 November 1856, was virtually an excommunication.[2]

After due consideration, towards the close of his lecturing season, from Edinburgh on 31 March 1857, Orsini formally offered his services to Cavour and the Piedmontese:

> "My unalterable opinions are Republican. But my first thought is the salvation of our country. Without independence, liberty is a dream. Drive out the oppressor, drive out the foreigner. For the rest I have no right to oppose myself to the national will. I am no more than a private individual.
>
> "Convinced by sad experience that without large forces it is not possible to drive a powerfully organized enemy out of Italy; convinced that limited and paltry operations serve only to weaken and to give rise to recriminations, I am ready, as a duty deeply felt, to give my hand to any Italian government (except that of the Pope) which will put its means and its forces at the disposal of national independence."[3]

It was, Cavour admitted subsequently, a noble letter. Had he accepted the offer, he would have gained the services of a brilliant and devoted officer, and Orsini would have lived to fulfil a dazzling military career. Had Cavour made the least gesture of laying down conditions, the result might have been the same. But in fact he never answered the letter. He could not do so, he explained, without paying compliments to Orsini,

[1] Holyoake, *Sixty Years of an Agitator's Life*, II, 32.

[2] Orsini, *Memorie politiche*, 274.

[3] Ghisalberti, 221–2.

which at that moment he judged to be inexpedient. His silence was regarded by Orsini as the rejection he had so much feared. Trapped in the treadmill of Mazzinian futility, he grew desperate.

Meanwhile Orsini had finished his second book. By way of presenting to the British public a readable account of conditions in Italy, he had written an autobiographical study concealing none of his vicissitudes. He had obtained from Emma Herwegh copies of his secret correspondence from San Giorgio. He included as an appendix some state papers damaging to the Papal Government, which he had collected prior to his first arrest in the Romagna, and had since harboured carefully with friends during his wanderings. In conclusion he gave a short account of his hopes for the future of Italy, which necessarily involved some criticism of Mazzini. To avoid all risk of further "editing", he had a direct translation made by George Carbonel. *The Memoirs and Adventures of Felice Orsini* were published simultaneously in Edinburgh and London at the end of May 1857. The book, like its predecessor, was a great success.

In his eagerness he had exposed himself. In July, when Mazzini was once again away in Genoa, Federigo Campanella saw his opportunity to wreak the party's punishment upon the rebel. Campanella had fought with Orsini in many hazardous campaigns, and knew well how to hurt him most. Through the columns of the *Italia del Popolo*, he ridiculed as garrulous vanity Orsini's descriptions of his youth and family; he inferred that Orsini had killed his uncle's cook on purpose; he taunted him with Assunta's infidelity; he made fun of Emma Herwegh; he enlarged upon the Austrian theory of the escape from Mantua, saying that Orsini had bribed the guards and walked out through the door; that he was now luxuriating in his undeserved success, and would do nothing useful for the cause.

Campanella's cruel assault might have had less disastrous consequences if Orsini had been in full possession of his equanimity; but such was not the case. The horror of his fifteen months in prison had caused severe reaction. He was prey to fever, to splitting headaches, to pains shooting through his damaged limbs. The near-madness that had come upon him in Vienna returned at intervals. He had strange hallucinations, and fits of swimming in the head. He had been forced to take narcotics, and had developed a compelling taste for solitude.

Partly for this reason, though partly for another, in April 1857, at the end of his lecture tour, he had left his rooms in Cambridge Terrace and gone to live out of London in a lonely house, 2 Grafton Street, Aland Road, Kentish New Town, taking with him the reliable maid, Eliza Cheney, as his housekeeper.

He had very little money: he was worried about Assunta and the children. His attempts to win the solace of a woman's love, no less with Miss Louisa than with Jessie White, had ended in sad vacuity. In September Emma Herwegh, his one true friend, had broken off their correspondence because he would not admit the justice of her firm resolve to whitewash the reputation of her husband. In May he heard from Imola that his father Andrea had died, breaking yet another image of the past. Exiled for his love of Italy, proscribed by the Church, failed in his effort to win English help by parliamentary means, flouted by Piedmont, anathematized by the party he had served with uncommon loyalty—what should he do now, in face of this vicious attack upon his patriotism? He defended himself valiantly in the *Italia del Popolo*; but the attacks continued, and flowed in from other quarters, from Switzerland, from far-away Constantinople.

He tried to think clearly. What was his best course for his country? Cavour's monarchist ambitions were, he was certain, wrong in principle. Mazzini on the other hand was right in principle but wrong in practice—how wrong had just been demonstrated at the end of June, when he had at long last sprung his plot in Genoa. Garibaldi wisely had refused to participate in Mazzini's venture; but Maurice Quadrio had attempted a descent on Leghorn, while Carlo Pisacane, a high-born though reckless Neapolitan, had commandeered a ship at sea, released the convicts from the island settlement of Ponza, and made a landing on the coast of Naples. There had been the usual ineptitudes. Pisacane's expedition had been annihilated, not by King Bomba's troops, but by the local population who fell on them as thieves and pirates. In Genoa, Cavour had reacted with the utmost vigour.* Mazzini had been driven into hiding by a

* Partly from pique, but more from fear lest the affair should appear to the Emperor of France as Cavour's reply to his own design of setting Lucien Murat on the throne of Naples in imitation of his famous uncle, and so upset their delicate negotiations.

renewed sentence of death, and eventually escaped to England with the aid of yet another Englishwoman, who resourcefully hid him in a mattress. Jessie White had been clapped into jail. Orsini heard with grim amusement that the English minister was seeking her release on the unlikely grounds of her insanity, and also that she had fallen in love with Alberto Mario, a handsome Mazzinian journalist in a neighbouring cell. He wished Mario joy of her. The rising had produced the worst effect in England where Italian sympathizers, Orsini now knew to his sorrow, were not republican but constitutional in outlook, and were strongly in favour of Cavour.

In September, while staying at Glastonbury, probably with one of his new friends, a rich young Englishman called J. D. P. Hodge, Orsini hit on an idea. To the devil with both Mazzini and Cavour! He would found his own party of "true republicans", to operate from inside Italy. They would not show their hand in piecemeal risings, but when the time was ripe they would join with Piedmont or with any ally who would temporarily serve their purpose. He got into correspondence with one Ausonio Franchi, formerly a cleric, now a republican journalist living in Turin who had been waging a newspaper battle with Mazzini on grounds very like his own. Franchi was to found the new party in Turin. His paper, *La Ragione*, would be converted into a daily on funds provided from London by Orsini, and would compete with Mazzini's *Italia del Popolo* in Genoa. As for the party's bible, the counterblast to the many writings of the "New Mahomet", Orsini would recast his two English volumes into one, expressly oriented towards the youth of Italy, to be called *Memorie politiche*, and would send the manuscript to Franchi with full rights of publication. He omitted the offending family matters; he inserted many vigorous appeals; he added an appendix, "How to be a Conspirator", so hair-raising that Franchi did not dare to print it. His book, like his letters to Franchi, systematically abused Mazzini. "Here are the keys of the matter. It is necessary to destroy the Mazzinian party, because it is contrary to true liberty, because it tends to the despotism of its own leader, and to the establishment of a new religion."[1]

[1] Ghisalberti, 238. See also 234–47, and Orsini, *Memorie politiche*, 276–301, 312–13.

Yet when Orsini came to construct his thesis, he found he was webbed in by Mazzinian philosophy as if in a cocoon. He was convinced that the liberation of Italy was bound up with a republican revolution throughout Europe as a whole. He had not heard of Cavour's dealings with Louis Napoleon, and would not have trusted them if he had. Napoleon III was the arch reactionary, from whom all tyrants took their lead: he had a natural interest in preserving the existing state of things. Mazzini had said all this before him. How then could Orsini take the vital step ahead of Mazzini so necessary for his new party?

Only in one way. Orsini was a man of deeds and not of words: Mazzini had neither the flair nor the courage to compete with him in action. For several years, Mazzini's most cherished design had been the murder of the Emperor of the French. In 1854 an infernal machine, made in Belgium, was found on a railway line over which the Emperor was to travel the next day. In April 1855 Pianori, a wild Romagnuol, came from London to fire two shots at the Emperor as he was riding up the Champs Elysées, and went proudly to execution without saying from whom he took his orders. In the summer of 1857, at the time of Pisacane's expedition against Naples, the French police intercepted three of Mazzini's letters on their way from Genoa to London : with the result that a mild optician, Tibaldi of Piacenza, who lived in Paris but had been to London, was sent with two others to the penal settlement at Cayenne. Though Mazzinians afterwards disclaimed "the theory of the dagger", on 10 June 1857 Mazzini wrote to his henchman Campanella, "The execution of the attempt against Napoleon is a vital thing for the country: almost the whole matter is bound up with it."[1]

Orsini would succeed where Mazzini had failed. He, Felice Orsini, would destroy the Emperor of the French. But not with a furtive dagger or impersonal pistol: his crime would be a spectacular one: it would resound through Europe, set thrones tottering, and inaugurate the Orsinian campaign in Italy. He cared nothing for his life. If he lived, he could direct affairs. If he died, Franchi would rouse the party. His last testament, his *Memorie politiche*, would be stamped with a martyr's aureole.

[1] *Vita e Memorie di Felice Orsini*, II, 683.

Garibaldi would know how to exploit the moment. Mazzini would be outclassed, and Italy would be set free.

II

Orsini did not reach his drastic decision either suddenly or unaided. On arrival in London he had taken up his earlier habit of frequenting the Soho meeting places where the exiles gathered to exchange gossip and to hear the latest revolutionary doctrines bandied to and fro. Notable among these were Thomas Wyld's Reading Rooms in Leicester Square and di Giorgi's Café Suisse in Tichbourne Street, where he quickly made, or perhaps resumed, the acquaintance of Dr. Simon Francis Bernard.

Dr. Bernard was one of those Frenchmen who cherish, and fiercely uphold against all kindred brands, an indistinguishable shade of communism. He was a Phalansterist of the school of Fourier. A native of Carcassone, he had served as a surgeon on board a French man-of-war in two or more engagements before he was cashiered for fostering sedition, and became a demagogue in Paris, modelling himself upon the Jacobins of 1793. During Cavaignac's repression following the barricades of June 1848, on the very day when political clubs were forbidden he opened the *Bonne Nouvelle* where he harangued four or five thousand people nightly. There ensued a succession of clubs and prosecutions, with sentences mounting gradually from a fine of 100 francs to 2,000 francs and five years' imprisonment; at which point, in February 1849, soon after Louis Napoleon's election as President of the Republic, Bernard "le Clubiste" quitted France. In Belgium he was soon in trouble again; in 1851 he settled in London.

Understandably, in the course of his talkative career Bernard had become a specialist in elocution and impediments of speech. He took a consulting room at 40 Regent's Circus, as Piccadilly Circus was then called, and acted as visiting consultant to the Institute of Madam Dean, where he treated patients for the stammers. He also gave private language lessons at his rooms in Bayswater. He secured a partnership in Wyld's Reading Room, where he imparted the doctrine of militant communism and at the same time earned a valuable increase to his income. Aged about forty, physically he was a meagre figure, with crumpled shoulders and long arms and legs. He had a sallow complexion, squirrel-bright eyes, a receding forehead, a large nose, a drooping moustache to conceal his rabbit teeth, and long black hair falling to his shoulders *alla Nazzarene.* As he was slightly deaf, he had a mannerism of cupping his ear in his hand, like an old soldier. He was untidy in his dress; his collar and cuffs were usually soiled, and sometimes his black coat was stained with egg.

Apart from his political activities, Bernard seems to have been an upright citizen. "Those of us who knew him, liked him for his simplicity, genuineness, and courage," wrote George Jacob Holyoake. "Dr. Bernard had every virtue except prudence.—He took the town into his confidence. Partly it was England that misled him; he could not imagine that spies were in English streets." This dangerous misapprehension eventually brought him to a lamentable end. "A bewitching, angelic traitor was sent as a spy to beguile him" (presumably by the French police), "and to her, in fatal confidence, he spoke of his friends. When he found that they were seized one by one and shot, he realized his irremediable error, lost his reason, and so died."[1]

There was no end to Bernard's intellectual industry. Like Karl Marx, he was a denizen of the reading room at the British Museum. A keen amateur chemist, he dabbled in the new science of photography. When he heard of Orsini's lecture programme he at once became his agent, fixed his appearances, managed his finances, discussed his text, and travelled with him up and down the country. He arranged for the English edition of Orsini's *Memoirs,* and coached him in political theory for his attacks against Mazzini. Bernard had no admiration for Mazzini, and referred to him disrespectfully as the Grand Llama. He therefore listened sympathetically to Orsini's ravings against his former chief, and urged him to take his revenge by carrying out Mazzini's aims without his knowledge and before Mazzini himself could do so; in other words to steal his thunder.

It is likely that Bernard broached to Orsini the project of the

[1] Holyoake, *Sixty Years,* II, 34.

Emperor's assassination, and probably he did so towards the end of 1856, just after Orsini's violent quarrel with James Stansfeld. He persuaded his trustful friend, bemused and unstable as he then was, that Mazzini was right in regarding Louis Napoleon as the main obstacle to the dawning era of the brotherhood of peoples. The Emperor's death would give rise to a People's Government in France which would at once remove the French garrison from Rome, the prop of the Pope's theocracy, and march to aid Italy in driving out the Austrian oppressor. Orsini had never been a proponent of assassination; he was too much the soldier, wedded to military ethics. His handling of the critical situation at Ancona and Ascoli on behalf of the Republic had been remarkable for its avoidance of unnecessary bloodshed. He toyed with the appalling suggestion for a whole year before finally he accepted the role of Brutus. In reconstructing the developments in that year it is possible to trace the hesitations of his tormented mind.

In London on 16 October 1856, a Paris merchant, Outrequin, walked into the Café Suisse in Tichbourne Street, where he met Bernard for the first time. Thereafter for ten days they met frequently to talk (so they afterwards insisted), about silk. In March 1857 Outrequin, again in London, again met Bernard repeatedly at the Café Suisse. This time they spoke about a wealthy young gentleman called Hodge, whom Orsini had visited a month earlier at his home in Glastonbury. In due course Outrequin was taken to see Hodge; and not long afterwards Hodge, on a tour of the Continent, appeared at Outrequin's shop in Paris with a letter from Bernard recommending him to the merchant's care. From then on a regular business correspondence sprang up between Bernard and Outrequin.

Early in 1857, probably during the first half of April when he was lecturing at Liverpool, Orsini made a series of at least three visits to Birmingham to see Giuseppe Andrea Pieri, and on one occasion dined with him at his lodgings. Pieri, aged fifty, from Lucca in Tuscany, was something of an old trouper in the exile world, as much vagabond as patriot. At twenty-two he had been sent to prison for twelve months for stealing a watch and pawning it. He came out in time to take part in the rising of the Central Provinces of 1831. Two years later he was accused of stealing umbrellas. (He always denied this curious charge with extraordinary heat.) Whereupon he left Lucca for France as a political refugee, and plied the trade of capmaker. A girl who lived with him had been forced to leave him because he ran through all her savings, but in 1834 he married a Frenchwoman at Lyons. In 1843 he joined the Foreign Legion and during two years' service in North Africa became an officer. He fought on the barricades in Paris in February 1848, and was expelled from France by the Provisional Government. He returned to Tuscany, recruited forty Lombard exiles, and offered his services to Duke Leopold, who at that time was having such difficulty in maintaining his authority that he gave Pieri, with the rank of major, permission to raise a foreign regiment. When the Duke fled to Gaeta, Pieri joined the revolution; at the head of his nine hundred brigands he terrorized the region of Pistoia in the pretence of punishing royalists. On the Duke's return he again attempted to change sides, but was dismissed the service because of his exactions. He reappeared in Paris, but after the *coup d'état* was once more expelled in spite of a most abject appeal to the new Emperor. By this time Pieri had separated from his wife and family, who henceforth lived in poverty at the Barrière de l'Enfer on the southern outskirts of Paris; some say he had treated them badly, although Holyoake maintains that his wife was a domineering shrewish woman who goaded him into crime.

Except for a visit to Düsseldorf in 1855, Pieri had lived quietly in Birmingham as a teacher of languages since 1852. He was a thin, nervous man with a pointed black beard. His appearance was furtive, and his manner jerky; he had a quirkish humour and a cackling laugh. Orsini had apparently known him for some time, perhaps since his former sojourn in England in 1853, when he had made at any rate one visit to Birmingham. Pieri was clearly not the perfect tool for the momentous matter now on hand, but it must be remembered that Orsini was strictly limited in his choice to non-Mazzinian Italians. According to Rosina Hartmann, a German girl from Coblenz who was both maid and kept woman to Pieri, their conversations "turned on politics with the utmost violence; they spoke of the Emperor of the French, and Orsini said, 'If I could obtain that, I would return to Italy.'"[1]

[1] *Vita e Memorie*, II, 489.

In April 1857, when he came down from Liverpool, Orsini moved to the lonely house at Kentish New Town, with the faithful Eliza Cheney. In June a new figure came upon the scene, in the person of Antonio Gomez, who arrived at Pieri's apartment in Birmingham with a letter from Orsini, and applied for "work". Pieri looked him over, told him to go back to London and wait for orders, and gave him a letter for Bernard. Gomez, not yet thirty, was the son of an employé in the ministry of finance at Naples. He was a wild, cloddish-looking fellow, tall, with a thatch of light red crinkly hair, negroid complexion, a low forehead, longish face, and loose, disolute features. He made out that he had fought in Lombardy in the national war of 1848. From May 1852 until July 1855 he was in the Foreign Legion at Sidi-Bel-Abbes, but when it came to fighting he reported sick and bought himself a substitute. After his discharge he worked as a porter on the docks at Marseilles, where a cash-box entrusted to his care was found "forgotten" in his lodgings, and he was sent to prison for six months. Released in June 1856 he went to England and took a job as a waiter at the *Café Chantant* in Leicester Square. When he lost the job, he got in contact with Orsini—it is believed through the offices of one Carlotti, who acted as a kind of conspirator's employment agency.

There was a lull in the preparations during the summer of 1857. Orsini was, at first, still hopeful of the outcome of his letter to Cavour, and later he was taken up with the publication of his *Memoirs and Adventures*, his response to Campanella's attacks, the editing of his Italian *Memorie* and the foundation of his new party in Piedmont. It would seem as though, restored to some measure of bodily and mental health, he had decided against the project and resisted Bernard's insinuations that he must not take his enemies' insults lying down. On 24 September, having heard nothing from Cavour, he applied to the Piedmontese minister in London for a passport to visit that country on family business concerning his wife and daughters. He was accorded an interview on the twenty-sixth. His letters to Franchi indicate that he was confident of success. He planned to spend some days in Turin: then, since it had become impossible to raise sufficient funds for the new party in England owing to the distractions of the Indian Mutiny and to the adverse prejudices aroused by Pisacane's expedition, he intended to go to New York for the same purpose. Early October found him lecturing again, in Edinburgh, trying to earn money for Assunta, of which it is clear from his letters to his Uncle Orso and his brother Leonidas she was gravely in need.

The day of decision was 15 October 1857, when Orsini received his reply from the Piedmontese government. They did not consider it prudent to issue him a passport; however, if he wished to go direct by sea to Nice to see his family, instructions would be given for that city to admit him.[1] Their answer, not unreasonable considering his antecedents, determined Orsini's course. He would go on with the creation of his Party, but there would be a resounding deed to mark its birthday. He sent off to Franchi the manuscript of his *Memorie* with instructions to have it printed quickly. He told him he would not, after all, be going to Piedmont, though he maintained for another month his intention of going to America, doubtless as a blind. He sent 500 francs to the banker Colombo at Nice for Assunta's needs. He sent his uncle a Power of Attorney to settle his affairs.

Events now began to move quickly. On that very day, 15 October, Bernard and Orsini conferred in London: they then met Gomez in the street. Orsini took Gomez home with him to Kentish New Town, and asked whether he would take part in a grand rebellion on behalf of Italy: Gomez readily agreed, but shortly afterwards was observed coming out of a police station. It seemed that something Bernard had indiscreetly mentioned in the street had come to the ears of the police, and Gomez had been called in for questioning. Gomez had been told nothing about the Emperor of the French; nevertheless, Orsini did not trust him far. He placed him on a retaining salary of 14 shillings a week and sent him to Pieri in Birmingham for observation.

The next day, 16 October, at the Café Suisse in Tichbourne Street, Bernard spoke to Giuseppe di Giorgi, brother of the proprietor, who was about to take employment at the sister establishment in Brussels, also called the Café Suisse. Bernard talked to Giuseppe di Giorgi about appliances for gas lighting, and asked whether he knew anyone in that line of business. di Giorgi mentioned a certain M. Bremachre of Brussels.

[1] Ghisalberti, 242.

Bernard said he would like to meet M. Bremachre; he had, or he shortly would have, some new gas appliances.

On the same day a significant interview took place in Birmingham. A reputable metal engineer, Mr. Joseph Taylor, received a visit from a burly Englishman, a Mr. Thomas Allsop, who brought what appeared to be a wooden model of a new type of military grenade, and asked him to cast six metal copies of it in two different sizes, three of each. Allsop also left a specimen of a percussion cap, a number of which were to be screwed into the cover of each grenade. He stressed that though the grenades were only models, they were to be constructed rapidly and with great precision. Taylor supposed that Mr. Allsop, who seemed an elderly and responsible businessman, must have some contract with the War Office.

There is a certain degree of argument about the origin of these mechanisms. The commonly accepted view is that Orsini, on his way through Brussels as Tito Celsi in 1854, saw in a glass case in a museum a reconstruction of the bomb recently laid on the railway line over which Louis Napoleon was to travel: that he worked out a specification, paid a woodworker to make a model, and gave the whole to Bernard who in turn passed it on to Allsop, who not being a foreigner could have it manufactured without suspicion.[1] Other authorities, notably Luzio and Montazio, maintain that although Orsini himself adhered to this version, he was trying to protect Bernard, as was in other respects undoubtedly the case.[2] The idea, they say, was Bernard's, who, through di Giorgi, Outrequin and others, was in constant contact with the Continent. A further source reports that one of the Brussels conspirators, a certain Fourdrin, was in London all the time.[3] It has also been stated that an aged canon at Sarzana, fond of making chemical experiments, originally designed the bomb, and urged Mazzini, then triumvir at Rome, to use it against Pio Nono: and that the canon, while he continued to sing as lustily as ever in the cathedral choir, always regretted that Mazzini never adopted his suggestion.[4]

Whatever the truth about the invention, there is no doubt

[1] *Vita e Memorie*, II, 505.
[2] Luzio, *Biografico*, 286–7.
[3] Claude Gével, *Deux Carbonari: Orsini et Napoléon III.*
[4] Caddeo, *L'Attentato di Orsini*, 120.

that Orsini, an expert in firearms of every kind, carried out important modifications, or that the finished product, fired upon impact instead of by a fuse, was of a type hitherto unknown, and of a power then considered stupefying. The smaller kind was as large as a medium-sized Easter egg, divided across the middle into two hollow half-spheres. The lower half, considerably heavier than the upper, was perforated with holes the size of a penholder, into which the nipples screwed so that each one pointed directly into the powder cavity, and whichever way up the bomb was thrown they were bound to come forcibly in contact with the ground. The thinner upper shell was segmented so as to shatter into some 150 tiny fragments. The two halves were held together by a single heavy screw, and fitted so closely that M. Devisme, the Paris armourer who ultimately had to dismantle one of the projectiles, feared at first that it was all one piece and that he would have to cut it with a saw. There was a filler plug at the upper end. The whole was of cast steel, slightly bronzed to dull the gleam; it weighed about 3 lb. when loaded, and had a capacity of 130 cubic centimetres.*

At the end of October 1857 Orsini was once more lecturing in Liverpool and Birmingham. On the twenty-ninth he and Pieri purchased two revolvers, in handsome cases of varnished yellow wood with copper arabesques, complete with all accessories—powder, bullets, bullet-moulds, screwdrivers, a little box for grease, another for oil, and a disarmer—from Mr. Hollis, the Birmingham gunsmith, for which Orsini paid. On 2 November Orsini, in a letter to Franchi, asked him to make sure that Pieri's name had not been forgotten from the list of "true republicans" to be mentioned in the *Memorie*.

On 4 November Bernard, accompanied by "another person who spoke better English"[1] (it may have been either Hodge or Allsop) went to Mr. Herring's pharmacy at 40 Aldersgate Street, London, and bought eight pounds of brandy and ten pounds of pure nitric acid. Bernard later explained that his purchases were for making daguerrotypes, but expert witnesses adduced that these ingredients, when combined with a pound

* There was considerable disagreement about the shape, size and number of the bombs, and about the number of nipples. The reasons for this are discussed in the appendix.

[1] *Vita e Memorie*, II, 633.

of mercury he obtained elsewhere, would yield two pounds of fulminate of mercury and nothing else. On the occasion of one of Orsini's later visits to Pieri it was observed that his hands were burned and stained—he said, from making chemical experiments. At about this time, too, the Milanese firm of Grassi-Velini, who had offices in Southampton Street between Covent Garden and the Strand, and were developing Dr. Grassi's discoveries as a means of greatly increasing the power of gaslight, were approached by Bernard and granted him use of an empty hut on their experimental grounds in Putney. Early one morning the peace of Putney was shattered by an explosion and the hut was found to have disappeared. The inhabitants of Putney complained to the police.[1]

Meanwhile something was learnt that added urgency to the preparations. It was perhaps the date of the Emperor's return to Paris from his annual visit to his hunting box at Compiègne. During November, Allsop wrote several letters to Taylor the Birmingham engineer demanding the early delivery of the grenades, and on the seventeenth required that they be brought to him not later than the following Monday at Ginger's Hotel, near Westminster Bridge, a familiar haunt of his.

Thomas Allsop, who, as an English barrister was soon to declare, "is, I say with grief and shame, an Englishman",[2] was a very queer man indeed. Though over sixty, he looked younger; he was tall, heavily built with a slight stoop, and clean shaven. He had very wide grey eyes, his face was ruddy, and his fair hair was thinning slightly: he spoke rapidly in a low voice, and he was rather deaf. The son of a Derbyshire gentleman farmer he had entered his uncle's silk-mercer's business, only to experience, at the age of thirty, "the hopeless ruin of my prospects".[3] Nothing abashed, he had joined the Stock Exchange and amassed a modest competence in railway speculation. In 1852–53 he had visited the Californian gold mines.

His oddity lay in his intellectual progress. When he was nine, hanging lazily on a gate at his father's farm, he decided that everything in the country scene about him was unreal.

[1] Montazio, *Felice Orsini*, 89.
[2] *Annual Register*, 1858, 310–29.
[3] Allsop, *Recollections of S. T. Coleridge*, 243.

Naturally, he became an avid follower of Coleridge, and when he grew up he made the acquaintance of the sage. Coleridge, who was not at all averse to Mrs. Allsop's lavish hospitality, called Allsop his "favourite disciple", and their children respectively "the fairy prattler" and "the meek boy".[1] Others joined the circle at various times, notably Charles Lamb, Robert Owen, Hazlitt, Barry Cornwall, Cobbett, Mazzini and the Emperor of Brazil. At Coleridge's death Allsop published, in 1836, his *Recollections* of him, largely designed to prove that Coleridge rejected the doctrine of original sin, for Allsop was a violent anti-clericalist—indeed, once when advertising for a house he stipulated that there must be neither church nor clergyman within five miles. His socialistic views advanced beyond those of Owen to embrace the French version of centralized state communism. He was a keen Chartist; when Feargus O'Connor was elected Member of Parliament for Nottingham, Allsop provided him with the necessary property qualification, £300 a year in land; and the night before the abortive Chartist demonstration of 10 April 1848, urged him to "firm, calm, resolute action".[2]

Of later years Allsop had avoided a fixed home and roamed about between Reigate in Surrey, Kent and Devonshire. In London he was usually to be found, tastefully dressed in a dark brown frock-coat, drab trousers and black billycock hat, if not at Ginger's Hotel, then at the Jamaica Coffee House, Cornhill, or possibly at the White Swan Hotel in Covent Garden. He had met Orsini at Nice in 1851, knew Bernard well, and there are signs that he knew the engineer Taylor more intimately than was ever realized, though as things turned out Taylor was not likely to admit it.

On 23 November Allsop descended wrathfully upon Taylor's works in Birmingham and demanded his grenades. He expressed dismay when he saw them, for Taylor had not carried out the exact specification for the percussion caps. However, Allsop said he would take the shells without the caps to the inventor, and if the inventor was satisfied would pay in full; and in fact a few days afterwards he sent Taylor a postal order for £2 6*s.* 6*d.* which, with an earlier deposit of 30 shillings,

[1] Allsop, *Recollections of S. T. Coleridge*, 212.
[2] D.N.B.

completed the transaction. On the same day in another part of Birmingham Pieri bought a third revolver from the gunsmith Hollis, and had it sent to his rooms at 106 Bath Street.

The conspirators were deeply disturbed at Taylor's departure from his instructions. It was considered essential to retain some of the bombs for trial in England, and to get them replaced as soon as possible in Belgium. There was no time to lose. On 26 November Orsini took the final steps preparatory to his departure. First, he wrote letters introducing Hodge to his three best friends in Italy, Garibaldi, Colonel Ribotti and Luigi Folli. Hodge, he informed them, was an excellent, wealthy young Englishman devoted to Italy who wished to meet the leaders of the national movement personally: he had already done a great deal for the cause, and was above all a convinced anti-Mazzinian; he would bring them good news, and what he told them they should keep to themselves.[1] Next, Orsini called at the Belgian legation with a passport in the name of Thomas Allsop, and asked for a visa for Brussels. When the Vice-Consul objected that the owner of the passport must appear in person he went away, and returned with a large, venerable Englishman, "a veritable John Bull", who signed the necessary papers while grumbling mightily at having been dragged from his office for a lot of red tape.[2] Finally, Orsini went to the Bank of England with £435 in gold which he changed into notes, twenty to the value of £20, three tens and one five. When he was later asked where the money came from, he condescendingly replied that it was the proceeds of his lectures, and that Kossuth for example had compiled £18,000 in that way. He was certainly not telling the truth: his lectures seldom did more than balance the expenses, and any little profit he might make was immediately needed for Assunta. He was presumably protecting his donors, who no doubt included Allsop, Hodge and perhaps others.

Orsini left England on 28 November. He carried on his person a paper parcel containing two pounds of fulminate of mercury, enough to destroy a palace, a sandy-coloured crystalline powder done up in a piece of linen. Fulminate of mercury is a highly unstable explosive : if allowed to dry out it is liable to

[1] Ghisalberti, 249–51.
[2] *The Times*, 15 March 1858.

go off at room temperature. He therefore had to moisten it from time to time during the journey, an operation which must have demanded some ingenuity since at that date there were no lavatory facilities on the trains. In spite of this difficulty he reached Brussels safely on the twenty-ninth, and deposited his formidable luggage at the Hôtel de l'Europe, 1 Place Royale.

On 3 December at the Café Suisse in Tichbourne Street, Bernard approached Giuseppe di Giorgi, who was now about to leave for the Brussels branch, and asked him to carry over some samples of his new gas appliances and give them to an English friend of his from Liège. di Giorgi duly crossed the Channel with five half-spheres of hollow metal in his suitcase. declared them as gas fixtures at Ostend, and paid a small duty on them. He reached the Café Suisse, 6 Place de la Monnaie, Brussels, late in the evening and went straight to dinner, leaving his bag with his coat on a table in the hall. After dinner he opened the bag to look for a handkerchief, took out the metal contraptions, and laid them on the mantelpiece, where they were examined with curiosity by several of the guests, and where they still reposed a day or two later when Bernard arrived instead of the Englishman from Liège. Bernard told di Giorgi that the appliances were valuable inventions and that he must put them in his bedroom.

It is to be assumed that these five half-shells represented two complete bombs, and half of a third which was to be used as a pattern for the extra ones to be made in Belgium. In a few days Bernard called again and took them all away wrapped up in a piece of paper. He subsequently returned them, together with four additional halves of the same general type though rather larger, which he said had been manufactured in the country. He then talked some more about meeting M. Bremachre, the gas expert.

Bernard told di Giorgi that his English friend was going to Paris and would take the samples with him. His friend had also bought a horse; was there anyone to take the horse to Paris? After some discussion with the manager, the stableboy, Casimir Zeighers, was told off for the task. On 11 December Bernard introduced his English friend, Mr. Thomas Allsop, to di Giorgi. di Giorgi instantly recognized him as Orsini from the Café Suisse in London; he did not however feel it was his place to comment on it. Bernard told di Giorgi to give the gas appliances to Zeighers, and Orsini told Zeighers to meet him at his hotel at half-past five that evening. Zeighers did so. He and Orsini left the Hôtel de l'Europe for the station in a cab, accompanied by the hotel commissionaire. Zeighers brought with him a bag containing a currycomb and brush, the horse's grooming apparatus, and also eight half-shells; that is to say, four complete bomb cases, two original, two made in Belgium; somehow or another the odd half-shell was left behind at the Café Suisse in Brussels. Orsini was wearing the explosive as a deadly stomacher.

At the station Zeighers took charge of the horse. It was a noble beast; Orsini had acquired it from a Belgian *Guide*, so that in addition to good looks it possessed the advantage of a military upbringing, and was not gun-shy. Orsini bought tickets for the seven o'clock train to Paris. Zeighers put the horse aboard a horse-box with the bag, and found himself a third-class seat. Orsini entered a first-class compartment further up the train. They arrived in Paris at six next morning. Orsini saw the horse and bag unloaded, and gave Zeighers a card bearing the address Hôtel de Lille et d'Albion, 211 rue St. Honoré, to which he had been recommended by the proprietor of his hotel in Brussels. He then took a cab, leaving Zeighers to manage the horse, and declare the contents of the horse's toilet kit to the French customs, which he did without the slightest trouble. At the hotel, Zeighers stabled the horse: as his patron did not seem to be about he emptied the contents of his bag on to a sofa in the foyer and told a waiter they belonged to the English gentleman. His job completed, he then went off to see his "sister". Orsini, coming in later, gave a start of surprise when he saw the bombshells spread out on the velvet couch with the horse brush and currycomb, and curtly ordered them to be taken to his room. In the evening Zeighers returned to the hotel and saw Orsini, who in an excellent humour gave him his return fare and a gold Napoleon for a tip. Zeighers went back to the Café Suisse in Brussels, where he told Bernard everything had gone off smoothly. Bernard said that he already knew it.

In London on 15 December, Bernard again bought the ingredients of fulminate of mercury at Mr. Herring's pharmacy. According to George Jacob Holyoake, when required for use it was dried out by Orsini's heroic housekeeper Eliza Cheney in front of her kitchen stove at 2 Grafton Street, Kentish New Town. Holyoake had been called in to examine the remaining bombs. The spiritual successor to Francis Place, he was typical of that class of English nineteenth-century working men who were the natural pioneers of the Labour Party and the T.U.C. but, since those bodies did not then exist, were forced to combine their earnest pursuit of self-enlightenment—the study of Mill's *Political Economy*, the formation of Cooperative Societies, and candidacy for Parliament—with more nefarious occupations.

Holyoake was the last person to be imprisoned (six months) for uttering blasphemy at a public meeting. In Chartist days he sheltered a desperado who had a plan for blowing up the whole of London by pouring explosive down the sewers, and tried out his mixture, fortunately unsuccessfully, in Holyoake's cellar while Holyoake was having tea in the parlour above. Holyoake was editor of *The Reasoner*, and his office at 147 Fleet Street was a meeting place for radical dissent of every nation. *The Reasoner* was deliberately perverse; "when others decorated for war, it remained drab: when they illuminated for peace, it put up defiant mottoes".[1] On the occasion of Louis Napoleon's visit to London in 1855 it displayed an enormous placard of Mazzini, and the Emperor put his head out of his carriage window to look at it. Holyoake's friend Edward Truelove, who had served a four months' term for publishing Robert Owen's *Physiology in Relation to Morals*, was held to blame for this; "the course of Truelove never did run smooth," sighed Holyoake.[2] For his own part, he always kept beneath his desk a warm overcoat, a brandy flask, and biscuits, to tide him over in the case of sudden arrest. He was Thomas Allsop's closest friend; he had known Bernard since his arrival in 1851; he had first met Orsini in June 1856, when Orsini came to 147 Fleet Street with the manuscript of *Austrian Dungeons*, and was successfully referred to Routledge.

Holyoake met Allsop and Bernard by appointment at Ginger's Hotel, Westminster. The bombs were lying on the couch between them; when other people came into the coffee-room, Bernard vaguely pushed them out of sight. Holyoake had some

[1] McCabe, *G. J. Holyoake*, I, 243.
[2] *Ibid.*, 247.

knowledge of machine work; he was asked, without being given details, whether they looked efficient for their obvious purpose. After a discussion he was given two to try.

The bombs were quite heavy. Thinking that any force employed in removing the nipples might cause them to explode, he put one bomb in each side pocket of his coat and walked home carefully. His wife was very tidy-minded. To leave them lying about the house would be to court disaster, while to lock them in a cupboard would arouse her curiosity and probably her anger. Reluctantly he had to tell her what they were; she accepted the situation calmly.

Next morning Holyoake packed them into an attaché case. He was due to lecture at Sheffield, and Sheffield, a distant city with plenty of noise, seemed as good a place as any to dispose of them. In the train he found that the attaché case required constant supervision; he dared not get out to buy refreshments at the stations. He contrived to unload the bombs into his coat pockets as before, but even so, he still had worries; once, just as he was dozing off, a workman dumped a weighty toolbag down beside him.

His landlady at Sheffield struck him as likely to be inquisitive, so he took the bombs with him to his lecture. Next day he waited until the landlady had made his bed, then put one bomb under the mattress and set out with the other. After a long search, he at length discovered a disused quarry near the centre of the town. He looked cautiously about him, lobbed the bomb, and flung himself flat before it struck the bottom. "The sound was very great, and reverberated around." He sauntered off as unconcernedly as he could. He collected the remaining bomb, and sent a note to his employers in London, couched in the whimsical jargon they always used for similar correspondence. "My two companions behaved as well as could be expected. One has said nothing; perhaps through not having an opportunity. The other being put upon his mettle, went off in high dudgeon. He was heard of immediately after, but has not since been seen."

Holyoake returned to London, where Bernard gave him a third bomb and sent him down to Allsop at a house he had taken called "The Den", at Teignmouth, Devonshire, to test the reaction on a softer surface. They chose a suitable lane, and while the tall Allsop stood on guard, Holyoake from behind a wall tossed one of the bombs into the roadway. It settled in the mud with a dull squelch. At that moment, Holyoake saw Allsop waving vigorously in warning. He ran out, tenderly lifted the bomb, and dropped it back into his pocket. Then, in case the oncoming rambler should have thought his actions strange, he asked him "if he knew of a good place for football hereabouts". After that they found a hard, flat place, where, to Holyoake's relief and Allsop's glee, both the bombs went off like thunder. Holyoake reported to Bernard in London, "Leniency of treatment was quite thrown away upon our two companions. . . . The harder treatment had to be tried; and I am glad to say it proved entirely successful. But nothing otherwise would do."[1]

On New Year's Day 1858, Allsop, now back in Kent, wrote to Bernard. By a common, but for him convenient accident, he dated his letter 1 January 1857.

> "My dear Doctor,
>
> "Many thanks for the two slips which you propose sending to the friends of Italy. I hope that some answers have been received in London. I am glad to learn that any difference of opinion is limited to one point. . . . The abominable miscreant of the 2nd December seems to have reached his culminating point. . . . He must be killed, and with him the system which he seems to be necessary to keep up. I shall be glad to hear of Orsini's progress."[2]

The "two slips for the friends of Italy" referred to the two revolvers bought in Birmingham by Pieri and Orsini. Next day, 2 January, Bernard did them up into a parcel and took it to an acquaintance of his in the employment of the S.E. Railway, whose offices were in Regent Street not far from his consulting rooms. After some dubious references to the coming state of things in France, he sent it off to the merchant Outrequin at his shop, 277 rue St. Denis, Paris. The "difference of opinion" concerned the method of execution of the plot, based upon doubts about the efficacy of the bombs. As a result of Holyoake's tests the question seems to have been resolved. Both types of weapon would be used.

[1] Holyoake, *Sixty Years*, II, 19–25.
[2] *Annual Register*, 1858, 310–29.

Orsini had now been in Paris for three weeks, since 12 December. At first, at the Hôtel de Lille et d'Albion, his thoughts were of a maudlin kind. He asked the porter where the Place de la Révolution was, and when told that it was now called the Place de la Concorde, he remarked, "It was there that Louis XVI and Marie Antoinette were beheaded, . . . but executions now take place on the Place de la Roquette."[1] After three days he told the porter that, as his visit would be prolonged, he would like to move into an apartment. The porter suggested 10 rue Mont Thabor, just round the corner from the rue St. Honoré on the way to the Place Vendôme. Orsini moved there the same day, complete with bombs and explosive, and settled in under the wing of an excellent couple, M. and Mme Morand.

M. Morand went round to fetch Orsini's horse and lodged it in the next door stable. Thereafter Orsini frequently rode out in the Bois de Boulogne, where he mingled gracefully with the stylish throng of ladies and gentlemen of the Second Empire in their elegant *équipages*. Often the Emperor would be there, on horseback or driving in his tilbury, doffing his hat and pausing to converse in an egalitarian way with strangers, particularly those who were singled out with special commendation by M. Pietri his chief of police. One day Orsini rode back thoughtfully down the Champs Elysées, past the place of Pianori's attempt, and when he reached 10 rue Mont Thabor he said to Morand, "I saw the Emperor; I approached him; he has no fear—no, the Emperor has no fear. Seeing the simple courage of this sovereign confident of the people's loyalty, do you not think it would be shameful to abuse it in order to murder him?"[2]

He was rescued from his gloomy hesitations by young Hodge, who came and took him round to Outrequin at 277 rue St. Denis with a letter from Bernard, requesting the same courtesies for Thomas Allsop that Outrequin had already shown to Hodge. Orsini took to going there every day for letters forwarded by Bernard who was dealing with his mail at Grafton Street in London. At the news of Holyoake's satisfactory experiments his doubts evaporated. Accustomed to carry out the commands of others, it was

[1] *Vita e Memorie*, II, 480–1.
[2] Luzio, *Biografico*, 334–5.

with relief that he found himself once more under orders. Obsessed with his desire to score off Mazzini, and with the means of executing Bernard's plan, he fell victim to what, too late, he saw to have been "a fatal mental error". The Emperor, the embodiment of the overweening power that held Italy in thrall, must be immolated: France would rise in revolution, and Italy would be set free. Darkly brooding, Orsini mixed with the crowd which cheered the Emperor on his way back from a fitting with his tailor. When the Opera was illuminated for a royal performance, Orsini bought a ticket for the pit. On 5 January, heralded by letters from Bernard, the pistols despatched from London arrived at Outrequin's. Orsini called to see them; he returned next day and carried one away.

The time was drawing near. From Birmingham, on 6 January Pieri and Gomez, who had now safely finished his probation, went to London where they dined with Bernard at Orsini's house in Grafton Street. Bernard gave Gomez a passport in the name of Swiney, a gentleman's servant. Gomez noticed on the mantelpiece a curious half-sphere of metal, which Pieri dropped into his bag before they left. They landed at Calais in the early hours, and took the train to Lille, where Pieri ordered Gomez to wait for him while he went on to Brussels. There he sought out, for old times' sake, Rosina Hartmann, his former drudge and mistress, who was now working in Brussels as a lady's maid. In his desire for her he grew loquacious. He boasted that he was on his way to Paris for a desperate undertaking which, if it failed, would cost him his life; with a leer he drew his finger across his throat and made a horrible gulping sound. Next, Pieri went to the Café Suisse; on showing a note from Bernard he collected from di Giorgio the odd half-shell forgotten by Orsini. He fitted it to the half he had brought with him, and so made up a complete fifth sphere which he exhibited to another acquaintance in the café, a Birmingham girl who had lately married a Frenchman. At seven o'clock he left with his booty to return to Lille, where he picked up Gomez, and they resumed their journey to Paris.

On Friday 8 January they booked in at the Hôtel de France et Champagne in the rue Montmartre, where Orsini came and took coffee with them. Later that day he received them, and also Hodge and Outrequin, in his rooms at 10 rue Mont

Thabor. As a result of this meeting Orsini hurried round to Devisme, a leading armourer on the Boulevard des Italiens, to buy a further pistol; in his haste he did not notice that it was defective, and he had to take it back next day for attention to the hammer. Two pistols already had come from London, and Pieri had a third. The extra one was needed because Pieri had brought word from Bernard that a fourth confederate was on his way.

Carlo di Rudio, only twenty-five, was the youngest of the conspirators and by far the most unfortunate. His paternal grandfather had been préfet at Belluno in Venetia under the First Empire, and his uncle had been one of those many Italians who died in Russia under Prince Eugène. His father thus grew up to hate the Austrian overlords with Carbonarist vehemence; but he eloped with a girl of the opposite faction, a daughter of the Governor of Belluno, who in consequence was disinherited by her Austrophile family and had to rear her children in an atmosphere of polite distress. Young Carlo secured a cadetship at the military academy in Milan, but ran away at the age of fifteen rather than serve the Austrians when the national war of '48 broke out. He took part in the defence first of Rome and then of Venice. He served under Calvi in Cadore, and eluded the warrant issued against him from Mantua by the terrible Captain Kraus. He sailed for America, was shipwrecked off the coast of Spain, survived, and scraped a living in Barcelona and Marseilles. He went to England at the end of 1855, where he plied the inevitable trade of language teacher—unprofitably, because his education was so indifferent that he could hardly write his native tongue. He found his way to Nottingham, seduced Eliza Booth, a fifteen-year-old confectioner's assistant, and married her to save her mother's shame. They moved to London with their tiny baby and lived in a slum apartment in Bateman Street Buildings. Their neighbours, far from affluent, lent them money and vowed they had never seen a family more wretched. For weeks on end Rudio went out to look for work in nothing but thin trousers and a ragged shirt. His parents believed him dead; he did not undeceive them.

In April 1856 at a restaurant in Panton Street just off the Haymarket, Rudio received six knife wounds from a berserk patriot who afterwards died in Pisacane's expedition. Three

Orsini preparing the bombs
From a print in the Civica Raccolta Stampe Bertorelli, Milan

others attacked at the same time were panders to the French police, and Rudio was suspected, unjustly, of having betrayed Calvi to the Austrians as the price of his own freedom.[1] After a lingering recovery he was approached by the agent Carlotti on behalf of Orsini, in the autumn of 1857 when the loyalty of Gomez was in question. He wrote eagerly to Orsini, whom he wrongly supposed to be in Birmingham; his letter was answered by Pieri, who told him to wait till a gentleman came to see him. On 29 December Rudio, in increasing desperation, wrote that he was "always ready for your orders, at whatever time, in whatever place, for whatever purpose they may be",[2] but that if nothing happened soon he would be forced to join some rival enterprise.

On 2 January the promised gentleman, Bernard, cashed one of Orsini's £20 notes and called at Bateman Street Buildings. Rudio was out, but Bernard spoke kindly to Rudio's child-wife, and gave her half a sovereign. It was arranged that whenever he rang the bell twice, Rudio should go down to him: this happened immediately Rudio returned. Bernard warned him that he would be leaving England, and gave him fourteen shillings. Thereafter Bernard came frequently, always after dark. On 7 January he cashed another note. On the eighth, while Rudio was out, Bernard gave his wife ten shillings and told her to redeem her husband's clothes from the pawnbroker; he also produced a carpet bag to put them in. Later that evening he gave Rudio his ticket to Paris, a further fourteen shillings, and a passport in the name of da Silva, a Portuguese salesman travelling in beer. He then told him to report to Allsop at 10 rue Mont Thabor; as a means of identification he was to take with him a pair of gold spectacles from the house in Grafton Street. Bernard promised Rudio to give his wife twelve shillings every Monday, and told her to come to him at the Café Suisse if she needed anything. He appears on the whole to have kept his promise well, though later on when his own skin came in danger he sent her out of London to her mother's house in Nottingham, with orders to use her maiden name of Booth.

Rudio arrived in Paris on Sunday, 10 January. He called on Outrequin and on Orsini, but neither was at home. They were,

[1] Luzio, *Biografico*, 342–5; Holyoake, *Sixty Years*, II, 41.
[2] *Vita e Memorie*, II, 559.

as it happened, talking together outside Pieri's hotel, the Hôtel de France et Champagne in the rue Montmartre, what time Pieri collected from Mme Outrequin, the remaining pistol sent by Bernard. Next morning Rudio went again to Mont Thabor, and as he entered caught his first sight of Gomez cleaning his master's leather in the servant's room: he went on up to see Orsini. Orsini had no need of Bernard's spectacles; had Rudio not been with him in the Valtelline fiasco? He remembered too the father Count Ercole di Rudio, and the handsome sister Luisa, who had been locked up with him in Mantua for their part in Calvi's rising. He instantly recognized the small body, short neck, olive skin, and vivid eyes; the brief moustache, and the black hair falling to the shoulders; but how pinched and wasted the youth had grown! Rudio, he recalled, was well-intending; but he was careless and boastful, given to self-pity; he would have to be watched.

Pieri then arrived, and Orsini jovially introduced Rudio as "the fellow we have been waiting for".[1] Gomez entered with a tray, and when the landlord M. Morand happened to look in he found them all behaving in a manner he approved. The English merchant Mr. Allsop (Orsini) and his German friend Pierri (Pieri had not taken much trouble with his passport) were at table. Allsop's valet Swiney (Gomez) was waiting on them, and da Silva (Rudio) the visiting Portuguese stood obsequiously before them, trying to sell his beer. But when Morand later unexpectedly returned, the scene had strangely altered. Rudio was seated, leaning across the table; Orsini and Pieri were arguing hotly, and Gomez lounged against the fireplace listening. To cover the situation Orsini resourcefully broke off, and said to Rudio, "You see if we don't sell your beer."[2]

Such were the trammels of the plot. Here were the four Italian assassins, on Monday, 11 January 1858, three days before the attack, assembled in Paris ready for the deed. They had, between them, five bombs of unprecedented power, four pistols, and in the case of Pieri, a poniard for good measure: they were armed, as *The Times* said, "not so much for a murder as for a field day".[3] To assist them they had Outrequin the

[1] *Vita e Memorie*, II, 419.
[2] *Ibid.*, 479, 392.
[3] *The Times*, Leader, Sat., 23 January 1858.

merchant, their Parisian go-between; and the eager Hodge, flitting indeterminably between Paris and Piedmont, rousing the leaders of the Italian cause. In England, Thomas Allsop, his share of the work complete, waited in ill-concealed impatience; Holyoake, though less fully informed, was none the less expectant. In England, too, lurked the French doctor, Bernard, the chief of those

> *Some six or seven, who did hide their faces*
> *Even from darkness.*

There may have been one other. If so, he, or she, was so carefully protected by the rest that all trace is lost to history.

Up to this point Gomez and Rudio had no clear notion why they had been brought to Paris. They were in it frankly for gain, and neither of them was trusted. At 6.30 that evening Rudio was summoned by Orsini. He unlocked his chest of drawers and revealed to Rudio what looked like a clutch of monstrous bird's eggs, spiny and fantastic and yet hideously real. He gave Rudio one to handle. Rudio strove for calm; "since I knew a little maths and physics I realized that I had better not drop it"[1]—though in fact the bombs were not yet filled.

Perhaps because of his queasy showing on this occasion, next day, the twelfth, Rudio was sent to replace Gomez in Pieri's twin-bedded room at the Hôtel de France et Champagne. Thenceforth he was seldom out of Pieri's sight, and was subjected to an alternation of promises and threats. He was in a hopeless plight. He was now a party to the plot: he had been kept short of money so that he could not run away: besides where could he go? He could not go back to England where once already vengeance had been wreaked on him as a suspected traitor. Gomez in his turn was moved to a small hotel found for him by M. Morand, the concierge of 10 rue Mont Thabor, just round the corner in the rue St. Honoré where he would be better placed to carry out his menial services. After several abortive visits noticeable for his increasing agitation Gomez succeeded in collecting from the armourer Devisme the pistol which had been brought back for repair. He was still largely in ignorance, "this obscure soldier, unexpectedly saddled with a

[1] *Vita e Memorie*, II, 419.

frightful undertaking which he had not been able to meditate and scarcely able to understand".[1] On the evening of the twelfth Orsini rather sardonically took Rudio and Gomez to the Théâtre des Ambigus on the Boulevards, to see a piece called *La Berline de l'Émigré*, about the dire fate of a servant who betrayed his master.

On Wednesday the thirteenth, the papers announced a gala evening on the following day at the Opera in the rue Lepelletier, a farewell benefit performance for the famous Italian baritone Massol. Massol was to appear in the first act of Rossini's *William Tell* and one act of Auber's *Muta di Portici*. He would be followed by the incomparable Italian actress, Mme Adelaide Ristori, making her début of the season, in a recitation of Alfieri's *Mary Stuart*. The proceedings would close with a ballet depicting the murder of Gustave III of Sweden, led by the sylph-like Rosati, another Italian. Possibly by royal arrangement the chosen programme accented sharply the tragic aspects of tyrannicide. The Emperor and his Consort were to attend.

Orsini went round to warn the others that their moment had arrived. He then returned to his lodgings and dried out the fulminate of mercury, standing before the fire with a thermometer in one hand and his gold watch in the other. Later, he primed the bombs, filling each one two-thirds full. Gomez, who had a powerful wrist, helped him to tighten the nipples and screw up the locking pins. That evening they all four met at the Place Vendôme and went to the Barrière des Martyrs (now the Place Pigalle), presumably to loosen up their arms and test their aim.

The fourteenth was a day of hasty final preparations for Orsini, and of sickening apprehensions for the rest. At ten o'clock he hurried round to Outrequin and anxiously demanded news of Bernard; he was most annoyed when told there was none, although what news he was expecting no one knows. He drove out to the rue de Miroménil beyond the Madeleine, again on an unknown quest. He then joined Pieri and Rudio at their hotel, where Gomez, seemingly impressed by the gravity of the occasion, soon arrived riding Orsini's horse. During dinner their final plans were laid. In the afternoon Pieri took Rudio by omnibus to the Barrière de l'Enfer in the southern suburbs and

[1] *Vita e Memorie*, II, 551.

left him in a *bistro* while he made a vain attempt to see his wife. After that they went all over the city, Rudio waiting dutifully in various vintner's shops and cafés while Pieri tried to find his son.

At about 4.30 they returned to their hotel, and heard that Orsini had just called. When he came back they took him to their room. At dusk Orsini and Pieri hurried away in a cab, and Rudio followed them on foot to Mont Thabor, where Gomez served them all with mulled claret Orsini had sent him out to buy. They drank it solemnly for some little time, before they noticed that Gomez had disappeared. They were certain he had gone to the police. Suddenly he returned and said he had been to buy a pair of gloves. "Enough of this nonsense!" said Orsini firmly. He distributed the bombs; Gomez and Rudio had a large one each, Pieri a small one, and Orsini the two remaining small ones; Pieri had already provided Gomez and Rudio with their pistols; Orsini gave Rudio three hundred francs in case they were separated after the assassination.

At seven they all went out, Gomez last, his bomb slung in a red handkerchief. They turned left out of rue Mont Thabor, through the Place Vendôme, up the rue de la Paix; at the top they turned right, crossed the Boulevard des Italiens, and mixed with the crowd already assembling in the rue Lepelletier. It was only a fifteen-minute walk, so they were early; the Emperor was not due until 8.30, and he was invariably late. The entrance to the Opera was about a hundred yards down the rue Lepelletier, on the right. A little beyond the lighted peristyle one of the city roadmen was scattering sand at the mouth of the private carriageway which the royal coach would enter. Pieri and Rudio at once made for this passage, but after a noisy altercation were ejected. Pieri then became aware of the unusual brilliance of the illuminations; the Emperor was particularly fond of elaborate ornamental gaslight. As Pieri was the only one of the four with a police record in Paris, he moved away from the others and skulked in the shadows further up the street, near the corner of rue Rossini.

His prudence went unrewarded. At about 8.15 Inspector Hébert of the Paris Sûreté was strolling in plain clothes along the rue Lepelletier. It was his day off, and he was going to the opera. At the corner of rue Rossini he spotted a swarthy figure who was curiously familiar. He stopped the man, and asked him if he were not the Italian, Pieri, whom he had arrested some years before, in 1852, and who had been sentenced to expulsion? The man's manner was excited, and his explanations positively incoherent, so Hébert led him off to the nearest police station, where a cursory frisking yielded an exceptional trove—an armed fulminating grenade, a fully-loaded revolver of the latest English pattern, a fearsome dagger, and a considerable sum of French and English money.[1]

Orsini had seen Pieri walk back past him in company with a stranger, but failed to interpret the lightning wink Pieri shot at him as he passed. Pieri was so full of quirks. Orsini fell to stationing his remaining minions along the pavement facing the Opera, first Gomez, then Rudio, then himself, close enough to keep them under observation, yet not so close as to form a group. Gomez and Rudio stood behind the rows of spectators who were to form their shield; Orsini stood boldly out in the front rank, directly opposite the private passageway. Half-past eight sounded. In a few minutes there was a stirring in the crowd, like a rustling of leaves before a storm. First distantly from the Boulevards, mounting to a roar in the rue Lepelletier, came the sounds of a throaty clamour, and the jingling of bridles.

III

On that afternoon of Thursday, 14 January 1858, Napoleon III, the Emperor of the French, was driving through Paris in his carriage with Duke Ernest of Saxe-Coburg who was paying him a state visit. He was anxious to impress the Duke, the brother of the Prince Consort who, the Emperor regretfully knew, did not altogether like him. The previous evening there had been a banquet at the Tuileries; that morning they had gone shooting out at Fontainebleu; this evening they were going to the Opera. Now, taking advantage of the unusually mild and sunny weather, he was showing the Duke his many improvements in the Capital—the restoration of Nôtre Dame, the new galleries at the Louvre, the magnificent metal structure

[1] Caddeo, 137.

at Les Halles, the church of St Clothilde, a triumph of the neo-Gothic style. They bowled along towards the newly laid-out Bois de Boulogne by the broad strategic arteries Baron Haussmann was driving through the centre of the city. Some people thought that these new avenues destroyed the ancient charm of "the picturesque old rookery"[1] that was Paris. All the same the public crowded out on Sunday afternoons to gaze at the long rows of lamp posts and freshly planted saplings, or to peer into the trenches where the gas and water mains were being laid.

Louis Napoleon, the old Emperor's nephew, the adventurer of Strasbourg and Boulogne, the prisoner of Ham, had come far since that December day six years ago when he seized power. The terrible cost of the *coup d'état*—215 killed in Paris alone, and 27,000 arrests of whom half had gone to prison or exile—did not disturb his conscience. He was the first modern dictator, resting his authority directly upon a carefully controlled expression of the people's will. Among his first cares had been the restoration of their votes to the three million citizens deprived by the Republic, and three crashing plebiscites had confirmed his actions.

His results had shown a dividend. The Second Empire was at the height of its achievement and prestige. In the Crimea he had avenged 1812 upon the Russians, and France had been master of the Peace of Paris—the "Capitulation of Paris"[2] as Lord Derby called it. He had reversed his uncle's disastrous error of offending England. He had received Queen Victoria in August 1855, at the time of the stupendous Paris Exhibition, and had charmed her utterly. They had stood side by side in torch light at Napoleon's tomb. He had sent a special courier to England to fetch her little dog from Osborne. He had had the legs of an antique table sawn down to suit her height. He had done his best to please Prince Albert by singing long duets with him in German, and he had taken young Bertie, Prince of Wales, for carriage drives. "*Most* agreeable", Queen Victoria had found him. Above all, "the *dear* Empress" was about to have a baby.[3]

[1] Fisher, *Bonapartism*, 91.
[2] Thompson, 165.
[3] *Ibid.*, 161–2.

The "*dear* Empress", Eugénie, with her auburn hair and bright blue eyes was the most gorgeous first lady France had known since Marie Antoinette, whose relics she hoarded and whose fate she expected to share. The Emperor did not love Eugénie—no one did; she was too cool, severely Catholic, possessive, stupidly reactionary in her ideas, and talkative. She was not Royal. Her father had been the Spanish Comte de Montijo; her mother, part French, part Scottish, left widowed, had brought her two daughters to court to seek their fortunes.

But Eugénie had drive. She had first seen Louis Napoleon in 1836 when she was ten, as he was sipping champagne and munching biscuits in the Conciergerie at Paris, on his way to New York after the Strasbourg episode. Thirteen years later she had told his cousin Prince Napoleon, then Ambassador at Madrid, that Louis must rise like his uncle from Consulate to Empire. Louis noticed her at a review in 1850 and invited her to St. Cloud. She resisted his intentions, though like Miss Howard, Comtesse de Beauregard, she contributed her pittance towards the cost of Empire: and she brought him to the point of marriage two months after his enthronement.

It was the task of General Fleury, the royal Master of Ceremonies, to model the court on that of the First Empire. The lack of noble blood was compensated by a rigid etiquette combined with ostentatious luxury. Visitors were presented to the royal pair on a velvet-covered dais. Eighty persons would sit down to elaborate dinners to the strains of a military band. The extravagance of the costumes, mostly designed by M. Worth, late of Swan and Edgar, now first couturier of Paris, beggared description. Eugénie was always queen of the ball. By her command, the ladies' shoulders and arms were always bare. In her simple white dress of *tulle d'illusion* starred with sequins she outshone even Princess Jusopopoff, who could wear a million francs in diamonds and a gown of embroidered satin studded with pearls as big as peas.[1] By way of variation there was an occasional *bal masqué*, where, however, dominoes were forbidden, to prevent foul play. There were frequent cosy evenings, devoted to charades written by serious authors, or to Eugénie's favourite game of blind-man's-buff, or to "carpet dances", when the Emperor stood passively turning the handle

[1] Luzio, *Biografico*, 354. The correct name is probably Yusupov.

Napoleon III and Eugénie
From a popular print of the time

of his treasured hurdy-gurdy. Whatever the occupation, the Emperor's mood was paramount in every mind, the "depressed parrot", a sinister, sickly, half-extinguished looking roué, with a cosmopolitan accent, purring voice and spine-tingling reputation, who yet spoke as a kindly, broad-minded, well-travelled man, with a "surprising sweetness of nature and deep experience".[1]

The atmosphere of court, hollow but glamorous, embraced the nation. All France was swept up on a wave of material prosperity. Money was easy: loans were nationally financed out of Orleanist expropriations. Speculation was rife on the Bourse, in railways, war loan, gas and coalmines; in 1857 three transatlantic steamship services were opened. Women stole from their husbands to invest; gambling from the provinces started a boom in electric telegraph. "Morny is in it," was the cry—dandified Morny, bastard brother of the Emperor, President of the Legislative Assembly, lolling back in his chair and gripping the reins of absolute power.[2]

For there was no freedom. The fine-sounding elective bodies were permitted no initiative; the Emperor's candidates were everywhere returned; the editors of the so-called "opposition" journals were appointed by the crown. Spies abounded, and there were prosecutions for defeatist talk about the price of corn, vine mildew, or the cholera epidemic. Free expression was largely limited to student demonstrations at the funerals of respected democrats, and to the copies of *Les Châtiments* smuggled in from Jersey in plaster replicas of the Emperor.

Yes, the Emperor may well have thought as he sat up in his carriage on that sunny January afternoon, his rule was still despotic. But it would not be for long. In accordance with the Legend, he was advancing from a system of order to one of liberty. Soon he would be able to grant concessions, a political amnesty, and parliamentary opposition to his decrees. Then, too, would be the time to go to the rescue of Poland and Italy, especially Italy. Italy must be free, and Austria, his only remaining rival save for insignificant Prussia, must be humbled.

The difficulty was that the old-fashioned policy of his Foreign Minister Count Walewski, the offspring of his uncle and the famous Pole, forbade the creation of a powerful kingdom south

[1] Christopher Sykes, *History Today*, January 1953, 54.

[2] René Arnaud, *The Second Republic and Napoleon III*, 123–54.

of the Alps. He frequently deceived Walewski, but he must not go too far. Worse still was his dependence on the Church. It was the Church that had forced him to destroy the Republic of Rome, and since the Pope's restoration the Church had flouted all demands for more liberal government. Now, Pio Nono had been named godfather to the Prince Imperial, and Cardinal Antonelli, asked when the French garrison would be withdrawn from Rome, had answered, "When I withdraw my garrison from Paris."[1]

Still, one of these days he, Napoleon III, would be strong enough to defy his clergy, his ministers, his generals, and the greater part of his people, and make Italy a kingdom. All important Italians except Mazzini knew what was in his mind. Napoleon himself had promised Cavour in no uncertain terms that the present peace with Austria would not last long. Napoleon knew that the Austrian Ambassador had no illusions. He also knew that Cavour was doing all he could through friends of Italy close to the royal ear, Princess Mathilde, Dr. Conneau and Prince Napoleon, and had sent his own niece, the Contessa di Castiglione, to woo the imperial favour. She, a not unwilling sacrifice, a voluptuous girl whose house was filled with casts of her own hands and legs, had gone into action at a masquerade dressed as a gipsy fortune teller in very short skirts, before the glum eyes of her husband who had lately witnessed the same tactics applied to King Victor Emmanuel. In the present case she was less successful. The Emperor of the French received her enthusiastically, took her to Compiègne, and showered her with gems worth as much as 15,000 francs apiece. But when she wept and implored the salvation of Italy, he could only tell her that the time had not yet come.[2]

Meanwhile, he had to put up with the recurrent nuisance of Mazzinian outrages, which strengthened the hand of those opposed to the Italian venture. Crossing the Pont Neuf, as they passed before the statue of Henri IV, the Emperor said to the Duke of Saxe-Coburg, "I fear only the dagger, like that of Ravaillac; in all other cases the criminal hopes to save himself by flight, and that thought paralyses his arm."[3]

[1] Trevelyan, *Garibaldi and the Thousand*, 76.
[2] Rheinhardt, *Napoleon and Eugénie*, 178–80.
[3] La Gorce, *Second Empire*, II, 219.

They drove back to the Tuileries, where the Emperor attended to his papers, dined, and got ready for the Opera. The procession was formed up in the courtyard; first a carriage for the members of the Household, next a troop of Lancers of the Imperial Guard; then the heavy, closed-in state berlin, with mounted officers to left and right; another carriage for Mathilde; and last, another troop of Lancers headed by the Commandant of Paris. In full tenue, with medals, the Emperor followed Eugénie to the coach; General Roguet the Aide-de-Camp occupied the fly-seat opposite. They were a little late as usual.

The imperial cavalcade rode on. The carriage of the Royal Household deposited its occupants outside the theatre. To a roll of drums the escort of Lancers wheeled into review order, as the coachman of the imperial berlin reined in his horses to enter the private carriageway.

General Fleury, Master of Ceremonies, waited with the Duke of Saxe-Coburg at the foot of the plush staircase in the foyer of the Opera, under the gleaming portraits of past prima donnas. Statuesque, around them stood Sergents de Ville in their tricorne hats and tasselled swords of state. The Directors of the Opera were there with their symbolic candle, ready to bow the Emperor backwards to his box. The Emperor was late as usual. Only with the utmost difficulty had he been persuaded to have an escort.

When, with relief, General Fleury heard the cheering of the crowds, he turned to his companion.

"Don't worry. The policing of the streets is perfect."

As he spoke, the world burst open. The heavy candelabra tottered crazily, and crashed. The glass of the peristyle rained down.[1]

The Cavaliere Debrauz di Saldapenna, Paris correspondent of the Austrian *Gazetta di Milano e Venezia*, stood talking with a friend outside the Café Riche, in the rue Lepelletier close to the Opera. It was a beautiful clear evening with the lightest snap of frost. He watched the notables arriving in their capes, their diamonds and furs. A flurry of Italians gibbered excitedly

[1] La Gorce, II, 220.

at the side doors; homesick for *La Scala*, he ironically supposed. He was particularly attracted by the magnificent illuminations. Above the peristyle a pyramid of light, composed of a thousand gas jets, soared up towards the royal monogram and the crown imperial surmounting all. Suddenly, as he watched, to a sound like thunder, it all went out, the lesser lamps along the street as well, and all was darkness.[1]

At a sign from Orsini, Gomez had loosed his bomb. One of the spectators saw it go, and thought it was a bouquet for the Emperor. It landed wide, amongst the Lancers in front of the coach, where it spread immense destruction. Before the lights went out, the face of the coachman was observed, a frightened mask, as he hurriedly whipped up his horses.

Almost simultaneously, Orsini muttered to Rudio, "*a te*". A second explosion like a cannon shot rang out. This one was closer. By its vivid glare the coachman was seen to clap his hands to his head and slump down on his box. One of his horses reared and fell motionless in its traces. The coach ground to a standstill, the silken tassel in its centre-panel window swinging aimlessly. For a moment there was a stricken silence in the darkness. Then came shrieks of pain and cries of terror, the clattering of skidding hooves, the whinnying of maddened animals, the showering of shattered glass. The second group of Lancers following the procession moved forward to defile about the Emperor's coach. Inspector Hébert, racing up from the guardroom where he had left Pieri, dashed forward to wrestle with the door of the wrecked conveyance. Some of those who had been prostrated by the blast began to stagger to their feet.

A third flash, a third roar, this time immediately beneath the coach itself, knocked them all flat again. Hébert fell, severely wounded in the leg and shoulders, his cloak literally torn from his back. The remaining carriage-horse went down, and fragments splintered from the underside of the battered vehicle. A scurrying stampede began; excited crowds pouring down from the Boulevard collided with the fugitives. There were hoarse shouts, uncertain orders. Wavering lights appeared in the entrance to the Opera. A police officer came forward, stepped over Hébert's body, and wrenched open the carriage door. As

[1] Luzio, *Biografico*, 348.

The Attempt of 14 January 1858
From a reconstruction in *L'Illustration*, 23 January 1858

he lowered the footboard, even amidst the carnage a rousing cheer went up. First General Roguet descended shakily, then the Emperor, who turned and graciously held out his hand to Eugénie.

The great fear now was daggers. The officers pressed round. Eugénie passed a lawn handkerchief across her brow: she is alleged to have murmured something about, "the risks of our trade".[1] The Emperor enquired after Princess Mathilde in the coach behind, and then said peevishly, "But my dear fellow, how *can* she get out if you don't let down the footboard?"[2] He wanted to go back to see about the wounded, but Eugénie dragged him away saying, "Don't be a fool! There's been enough *bêtise* as it is."[3] They picked their way fastidiously across the few yards to the Opera.

At the muffled sounds of the explosions the orchestra had stopped playing the overture to *William Tell*, and there had been a moment's panic. As they entered their box with the Duke of Saxe-Coburg, a sea of jewels, white arms, ribands and shirt-fronts were upturned towards the royal pair. Both were pale. The Emperor had a slight scratch on the side of his prominent nose, and his hat had been shot clean through. The corner of Eugénie's left eye was inflamed by a splinter of flying glass; there was a gasp when it was seen that her white dress was stained with blood—not hers, but General Roguet's, who had been wounded in the neck. The conductor struck up *Partant pour la Syrie*, an insipid melody written by the Emperor's mother Queen Hortense, which had become a secondary national anthem on a par with "Rule Britannia".

It was noticed that the Emperor's mind was not on the performance. Some put it down to fear. He examined pieces of metal that were passed to him, and the Empress was observed to drop one in her bag. Morny, Walewski, Persigny, Billault—almost all the ministers were in the theatre, and during the interval they all went up to tender their felicitations. To Pietri, chief of police, hastily summoned from a dinner party, the Emperor indignantly remarked, "Your police have covered

[1] René Arnaud, 154.

[2] Maurice Soulié, "L'affaire Orsini", *La Révue Hebdomadaire*, August 1925.

[3] Hübner, *Neuf Ans de Souvenirs*, II, 91.

themselves with glory."[1] Later, he slipped away to a nearby pharmacy, where he removed from his coat a glittering cross, and gently pinned it on the breast of a dying Lancer of the Escort.[2]

The return to the Tuileries at midnight was a triumphal progress. All Paris had turned out, all lights were ablaze, and Eugénie fluttered her handkerchief through the window to the delirious crowd. At the palace an anxious gathering, hustled from Prince Napoleon's soirée, was waiting to receive them. Before they went up to face the long session of congratulation, the Emperor and Empress crept along the corridor to the Prince Imperial's nursery, next to the Emperor's study, where they gazed at the sleeping infant. Then, in floods of warm tears, for the first time in months, they fell into each other's arms.[3]

It took some time to estimate the damage. Next morning reporters flocked to the rue Lepelletier, which had been cordoned off. Sand had been scattered to sop up the blood. The façade was a ruin; the heavy awning over the entrance had been punctured like a drum; the walls all round were pitted; the ground was littered with fragments of twisted metal, and broken glass crunched underfoot. The windows of the houses opposite were smashed in, frames and all; plate glass at some distance from the Opera had been neatly drilled with holes.

The royal coach had been taken to the courtyard of the Tuileries, where it was on view to a host of curious witnesses. According to *Le Droit*, "all the underpart and front of the carriage had the appearance of being blown to pieces".[4] How the Emperor had escaped destruction remained a mystery. Devisme, the armourer, and his experts afterwards testified that Orsini, in his anxiety to obtain the maximum explosive force, had filled the bombs too full, and had thus produced a fragmentation that was too minute.[5] The explosions seemed to have gone off laterally; most of the wounds were in the lower

[1] René Arnaud, 154–5.

[2] Boulenger, *L'Attentat d'Orsini*, Ch. 2.

[3] Luzio, *Biografico*, 353; d'Auvergne, *Napoleon III*, 152–9; Caddeo, 142.

[4] *The Times*, Monday, 18 January 1858.

[5] *Vita e Memorie*, II, 470–1; Caddeo, 123.

portions of the body, with the result that women, protected by their far-flung crinolines, were relatively immune.[1]

Out of twenty-eight Lancers, thirteen men and almost all the horses had been wounded; and thirty-one agents of the police—a significantly heavy figure. Dr. Tardieu gave evidence that the casualties brought to his attention totalled 156, many of them hit in several places, and that others had gone privately to pharmacies and hospitals. Of these 156 eight had later died, including an American merchant and a young boy aged thirteen. None of them, said Dr. Tardieu, had been killed outright. The injuries were characterized by small, deep, bloody wounds; in many cases inextractable slithers had penetrated to the bone, where they might set up fatal abscesses or prolonged neuralgic pains. Three persons had been blinded.[2]

When Gomez had thrown his bomb, he slipped into the Ristorante Broggi, a fashionable supper place opposite the Opera often patronized by stars such as Mario the Italian tenor, to avoid the effects of those that were to follow. There he was soon joined by some fifty shouting people, in various conditions of distress. For the first time he realized what he had done. His nerve completely shattered, he sat weeping and moaning with his head between his hands, crying out, "My master! Oh, my master!"[3]

Rudio, as he launched the second bomb, flung himself flat behind the onlookers to escape its blast. He likewise then took refuge in a tavern. When all was over, he walked down the rue Lepelletier to the Boulevard, and so back to the Hôtel de France et Champagne in the rue Montmartre, where he arrived about ten o'clock. Without pausing to take a candle, he went straight up to the room he shared with Pieri, but came down again to demand his bill for early the next morning. The police, who were making a routine check, entered the lobby and questioned him. He gave them the passport of the Portuguese beer-merchant da Silva, which they kept for scrutiny.

Orsini, who had taken no precaution for his safety, was struck on the right temple by a fragment of the third grenade; dazed

[1] *Illustrated London News*, 23 January 1858.
[2] *Vita e Memorie*, II, 472–3.
[3] *Ibid.* 549.

and unsighted by the blood, he waited for Pieri's final attack, which never came. He then stumbled off up the rue Lepelletier, turned left into the rue Rossini, and thence into the broader rue Lafitte, where he joined a group of people seeking attention to their injuries at the pharmacy of M. Vautrin. His course was marked by his discarded weapons. At the corner of rues Lepelletier and Rossini the bell-boy of a neighbouring hotel picked up, at the end of a seven-foot trail of blood, a heavy object in a black cloth bag, which he at first thought to toss back into the gutter. Fortunately he investigated further, and then took it to the police. Further up the rue Rossini, near the corner of rue Lafitte, a *brigadier* of the City Guard later found a loaded revolver with a blood-stained butt. These articles were locked in the medical cabinet at the Opera overnight. Having obtained a first dressing for his wound, Orsini left the pharmacy, and inquired from an inhabitant of the rue Lafitte the best way to his rooms in the rue Mont Thabor. The man helped him to a cab rank, and he got home at nine o'clock. In reply to the alarmed exclamations of the Morands, he said he did not know what had occurred, except that the French had tried to murder him. He went to his room, where the Morands brought a basin of warm water and bathed his face. The wound began to bleed again and a doctor was summoned. The doctor realized that his patient was not English, but thought nothing of it one way or the other.

The Sûreté were on their mettle. They could not deny the justice of the Emperor's rebuke. So long ago as June they had received, from Jersey, a description of the bombs and their intended purpose. Sir Richard Maine, Chief Commissioner of the London police, insisted later that he had given the Préfecture full notice of the movements of Orsini and Pieri, and their plans. Furthermore, Rosina Hartmann had told her mistress about Pieri's indiscreet confidences in Brussels, with the result that on 10 January the French Ambassador informed the Paris police of Pieri's departure by train with another man to kill the Emperor. Yet to all these warnings, delivered in good time, the secret police had paid not the least regard. Pieri had been restrained from his final assault only by his chance encounter with Inspector Hébert: while according to Eugénie, Orsini "had always appeared opposed to political assassination, and that is why he was allowed to enter France without police surveillance".[1]

When the sound of the first explosion reached Pieri at the police station he declared theatrically, "Do what you like with me—the blow is struck!"[2] But as subsequent news of the failure filtered in he became disconsolate. After two hours of crazy prattling he admitted the Hôtel de France et Champagne as his address. In his room the police found the rest of his paraphernalia, and Rudio lying half-dressed upon his bed. The hotel books disclosed that Pieri had registered under his Christian name of Andrea, and also that "da Silva" had replaced one "Swiney" a day or so before.

Meanwhile, in the rue Lepelletier the police were systematically examining all persons found in the vicinity. At length a waiter in the Ristorante Broggi drew their attention to the uncouth, loutish fellow who still sat sobbing in a corner. He told them in broken English that he was Peter Bryan Swiney, the valet of an English visitor. A loaded revolver was discovered on a table near him. The police hurried to his hotel in the rue St. Honoré where, now in full cry, they routed a dishevelled *gamine* from his bed, who gave her name as Mlle Ménager. The management revealed that Swiney had been brought to them on 12 January, the day he had vacated the Hôtel de France et Champagne in favour of da Silva, by M. Morand, concierge at 10 rue Mont Thabor.

At Mont Thabor they found Orsini sleeping peacefully on a blood-soaked pillow. Their search yielded the English passport and calling cards of Thomas Allsop, and about 8,000 francs. The superintendent questioned him in English. He said he came from Kent.

"And how far is that from London?"

"Oh, about thirty kilometres."

The superintendent clapped him on the shoulder. "If you are English, then I am a Turk. An Englishman would have answered 'twenty miles'!"[3]

Thus, before daybreak, thanks more to the inertia of the criminals than to their own astuteness, the Sûreté had notably

[1] Luzio, *Biografico*, 315.
[2] *The Times*, 19 January 1858.
[3] Caddeo, 150.

retrieved their reputation. Next morning in an adjacent stable they apprehended Orsini's only trustworthy confederate, the horse. In London at the Café Suisse, the little French doctor Simon Bernard, apprised of the affair, opened his eyes wide in astonishment. "But Orsini must be mad," he said.[1]

IV

A shiver of horror ran through France. A rumour spread among the ladies of the court that the day before the attack Orsini and Pieri had tried to gain access to a Grand Ball at the Tuileries in order to execute their plan—an arrant falsehood, since there was no ball at the Tuileries on the night in question. A distinguished Italian cellist, called to play before the Royal Family, had his instrument ripped open in a search for infernal machines.[2]

In this atmosphere of alarm, Eugénie made the most of her unaccustomed popularity. At a reception of the Corps Diplomatique two days after the attempt she described to Baron Hübner, the Austrian Ambassador, how before her carriage door was opened the coach had been surrounded by figures armed with daggers. By the time she told the story to her maids-in-waiting, the malefactors had become transmogrified into a lowly but loyal citizen who had insisted on smothering her hand in kisses. Dancing a quadrille with Hübner, she boasted that even if the Emperor had succumbed she would have saved the dynasty, standing with the infant Prince Imperial in her arms at the head of her heroic army. On 1 February she was formally proclaimed Regent in the event of the Emperor's sudden death. "She rejoices naively in her triumph," Hübner noted.[3]

Other persons less naive, far more reactionary than the Emperor, the ministers, whose wealth and position were intimately involved with his, made use of the opportunity to silence all opposition in the forthcoming Paris elections. Two Parisian periodicals, *Le Spectateur* and *La Révue de Paris*, were

[1] Caddeo, 151; Luzio, *Biografico*, 322.
[2] Holyoake, *Sixty Years*, I, 91.
[3] Hübner, *Neuf Ans*, II, 96.

suppressed. On 1 February a Law of Public Safety, commonly known as the Law against Suspects, was passed almost without question. Under its provisions 2,000 arrests were made, and some four hundred people were deported. General Espinasse, a braggart who had dissolved the Assembly of the Roman Republic, and had taken a foremost part in the execution of the *coup d'état*, became Minister of the Interior. He based his policy upon the slogan: "It is time for the good to be reassured and for the wicked to tremble."[1]

France was divided into five military commands. This measure, though partly designed to prevent any one of the generals from gaining absolute control, did nothing to disguise the brutal fact that the stability of the Empire rested upon the army. There was an outbreak of Gallic chauvinism and an indignant rattling of sabres. Stiff demands, which could not be ignored, were sent to Switzerland and Belgium for the tightening of their restrictions against aliens and for the chastisement of their journals. Orders in a similar vein, amounting practically to an ultimatum, were despatched to Piedmont and were in great part carried out, although King Victor Emmanuel refused with dignity those clauses which were incompatible with the age-old independence of his royal house.

The principal odium fell upon England, the "nest of vipers" whence had come in recent years so many would-be regicides. "Is hospitality to be given to assassins?" asked the Foreign Minister Walewski of his Ambassador.[2] The Emperor's chief adviser, Morny, who had returned from the Czar's coronation with a sumptuous Russian bride, and had consequently developed a strong anti-British bias, organized a sort of "military plebiscite" in *Le Moniteur*, where the Colonels of the various regiments were invited to express their feelings about that "laboratoire de crime".[3] "And if your Majesty wants soldiers to get at these wild beasts even in the recesses of their den," ran one of these bellicose missives, "we humbly beseech you to choose the 82nd Regiment as part of the vanguard of that army."[4]

[1] La Gorce, II, 232.
[2] René Arnaud, 154–69.
[3] Wellesley, *Conversations with Napoleon III*, 132.
[4] *Annual Register*, 1858, 221.

Lord Palmerston's government bowed before the storm. On 14 February Dr. Bernard was arrested in his lodgings at 10 Barke Place, Bayswater, and there then began a wordy duel before the Bow Street magistrate between Mr. Bodkin for the Crown and Mr. Sleigh for the defence. A reward of £200 was offered for the apprehension of Allsop, a warrant was issued for Hodge, and a Conspiracy Bill was introduced in Parliament to put an end to such occurrences in future. But these sensible measures of appeasement were upset by an irruption of public opinion, deeply resentful of the tone used by the French colonels. To the surprise of Palmerston, and to the even greater astonishment of his successor, Lord Derby, the Conspiracy Bill was defeated. "C'est la guerre! C'est la guerre!" cried the French Ambassador as he strode to the Foreign Office sword in hand[1]; and Lord Derby, going gloomily to Buckingham Palace to take up his unexpected duty, felt that "peace was a question not of months or of days, but of hours".[2] To Hübner, "France seemed as if drunk with anger and hatred of England".[3] In Eugénie's presence, General Espinasse let out some oaths so overheated that he thought an apology was called for. "*Mais non*," said the Empress demurely; "*mais non. Répétez*."[4]

"If only they are not Italians," prayed Cavour the day after the outrage.[5] The common view of the diplomatic world as expressed by Hübner was that "this horrible crime would lead Napoleon III back into the paths of political sanity, and would make him break, finally and for ever, the bonds formed in his youth with the Carbonari".[6] He hoped that the Emperor's coolness towards him, so noticeable before the attempt, would vanish, and ventured to suggest "that the time has come to establish an intimate accord with Austria" against Piedmont.[7]

These expectations would doubtless have matured with a more orthodox monarch, but Louis Napoleon was seldom

[1] Caddeo, 167.
[2] René Arnaud, 154–69.
[3] Hübner, II, III.
[4] *Ibid.*
[5] Caddeo, 167.
[6] Hübner, II, III.
[7] Caddeo, 165.

orthodox. It was not, as Queen Victoria supposed, an "almost mad state of fear"[1] that had made him so pale and thoughtful in his box at the Opera, that made him continue to seem "disconcerted and sad"[2] or "low and discouraged"[3] to Hübner and his English colleague Lord Cowley. It was that the memory of his youthful battles in Italy, of his brother's death, his many promises and equally many failures to carry them out, rose up in his conscience like the ghost of Banquo. Just when he had been about to redeem his pledges to Italy, and to derive popularity from a successful small war against Austria, his designs had been shattered by the bombs of Italian fanatics. The hand of the Catholics had been strengthened against him; and he had to see his secret negotiations with Piedmont, his laborious alliance with England, ruined by the excesses of his ministers.

Though he appeared to conform to the tide of repression, Louis Napoleon was determined to save what he could of his policy. To calm the panic, the day after the attempt he drove round Paris in an open carriage without escort. He visited the wounded in hospital, and on the Sunday rode out as usual in his phaeton. When the Austrian Ambassador, who had not been in the Opera on the fatal night, hastened to tender his congratulations, the Emperor pointedly refused to see him. Two days later he wrote to reassure his friend the Queen of England:

> "In the first flush of excitement the French are bent on finding accomplices everywhere, and I find it hard to resist all the demands for extreme measures which I am asked to take. But this event will not make me deviate from my habitual calm."[4]

To Piedmont he was even more explicit. When he heard of Victor Emmanuel's proud reply to Walewski's threats, he told the Ambassador, "That is what I call courage. Your King is a brave man."[5] And to Cavour's Mission Extraordinary of Congratulation he said, "I love Italy, and I shall never be allied with Austria against you. . . . If in 1849 I had occupied the

[1] Benson (ed.), *Letters of Queen Victoria*, III, 347.
[2] Hübner, 96.
[3] Wellesley, 133.
[4] Luzio, *Biografico*, 316.
[5] Trevelyan, *Garibaldi and the Thousand*, 73.

position I occupy today, I would have come to the help of Charles Albert."[1] He ordered them to invite Cavour to enter into correspondence direct with him. As Hübner afterwards admitted sadly, "In a word, the attempt, on the contrary, made Napoleon determined to renew his pact with the Revolution."[2]

Then there was Orsini, so much superior to the general run of Italian cut-throats. Napoleon understood his motives well enough. Besides their shared dream of Italian independence, they had much else in common. Both were romantics, both adventurers; the Emperor had selfishly succeeded whereas Orsini with no thought of gain had repeatedly and heroically failed. Professionally speaking, the epic of Mantua made the escape from Ham seem cheap. He dreaded the thought that he personally would have to sign the warrant for Orsini's execution. There was only one way out. There was still one way in which perhaps he could preserve his Italian policy, save Orsini, and reduce the uproar against England. He sent Pietri, his chief of police, to interview Orsini.

Pierre Marie Pietri, a Corsican by birth, an Italian in sympathy, and surely the gentlest head of state security that there has ever been, found the patriot languishing in his cell in the prison of Mazas, the picture of dejection. Orsini, the most dreaded conspirator in Europe, had bungled the affair, had failed in his métier, and had emerged as the common murderer of eight innocent victims. On that account his life was forfeit, as indeed he had always expected that it would be. Moreover, even if he had succeeded, the upsurge of furious loyalty in France had made it abundantly plain that he would not have achieved the hoped-for revolution. And Pietri now explained to him, truthfully he could not doubt, that the Emperor, so far from being Italy's main enemy in France, was almost her only friend—that St. George had pursued an illusory dragon. How could he atone for his "fatal mental error"?[3]

By doing Pietri's bidding, Orsini requested his best clothes from the prison governor, and prepared to cut a handsome figure at his trial. On 21 January, by whose advice we can only conjecture, he put his case in the hands of Jules Favre, the

[1] Labadini, 99.
[2] Hübner, II, 112.
[3] Kossuth, *Souvenirs de mon Exil*, 41–2; La Gorce, II, 353.

most brilliant advocate of the day. Favre, a former minister of the Second Republic, was a strong opponent of Louis Napoleon's dictatorship and of the *coup d'état*. But there was no personal animosity between them, and once when Eugénie in a jealous mood had consulted Favre about a separation, he had dissuaded her despite the possible advantage to his party. He was one of those Liberals upon whom the Emperor could rely to rescue him from his present reactionary advisers, and he was a friend of Italy who had hotly opposed the French intervention against the Republic of Rome.[1]

Favre did not accept Orsini's brief without violent agitation. The man's dastardly crime revolted him; on the other hand he could not but admire his dogged and courageous patriotism, and felt that his name did not deserve the loathing heaped upon it.[2] He realized that Orsini desired not pardon for himself but freedom for his country, and persuaded him that he could still promote that end if he addressed a letter to the Emperor which should be at once an appeal and an apologia.

The two-day trial began on 25 February before the Assize Court of the Seine. The stuffy court-room of the ancient Palais de Justice had been stretched to its limit to accommodate two hundred passholders, including a heavy representation of the Diplomatic Corps, reporters, and a sizeable detachment of the Royal Household. Even so, before dawn, two hours before the doors were due to open, dense crowds descended on the Ile de la Cité in the heart of Paris.

The proceedings were at first something of a disappointment. Characteristically, the prisoners were charged with the attempt to kill the Emperor, not with the actual murder of eight citizens. Dressed all in sombre black, all save Rudio who sported a tricoloured tie, they were a meagre lot, pinched and pale from confinement and their obvious terror. Only Orsini, the most clearly guilty of them, aroused any sympathy by the dignity of his bearing. The public prosecutor had no difficulty in establishing the uncontestable facts, and his procession of witnesses on crutches, maimed and blinded by the explosions, sent a dismal thrill through the spectators.

Gomez and Rudio both confirmed the confessions they had

[1] Rheinhardt, 185–8; Paléologue, *The Tragic Empress*, 245.

[2] Jules Favre, *Discours du Batonnat*, iii.

originally deposed, and blamed all upon Orsini. Gomez' counsel based his plea on his menial status, and took for his text, "My master said, follow me; so I followed him."[1] Rudio pleaded his youth, the misery of his wife and child, his ignorance of the purpose of his visit to Paris, and earned from the President the crushing rebuke, "You, then, who belong to an honourable family, sinking from step to step have become a hired assassin for 336 francs, plus twelve shillings a week to give your wife."[2] Pieri increased the almost visible contempt by his simian grimaces, his nervous cackle, his virulence against his associates, his cock-and-bull story which invited the judicial observation that, in his case, "lying is not a wicked action, but a manner of speech".[3] His counsel, who had been appointed by the court, begged sympathy for his own unhappy lot, and made the lamest of defences: "Pieri denies the plot, and I support his denial; but I cannot support it heavily."[4]

When Orsini stood up there was some sense of returning drama. On his arrest he had, as was his habit in such predicaments, denied the whole. Then, incensed at his betrayal by his confederates, he had reciprocated, indicating the responsibility of each. Just recently, as though he had suddenly come under a new and decisive influence, he had retracted his confession. What would he do now? Ignoring the questions that were put to him he started, "without baseness and without imposture", into a justification of his past career, his hatred of Austrian oppression, his respect for France until that day in 1849 when French soldiers, who were welcomed as the friends of the Roman Republic, treacherously destroyed it. "O *Signori*, we were judicially murdered!"[5] At this point the President felt bound to intervene. Orsini went on to describe his quarrel with Mazzini, and his growing conviction that the Emperor, who alone had power to do so, would never move on behalf of Italy. "Once convinced that this was the great obstacle to our independence, I frankly confess that I resolved to kill him."[6]

[1] *Vita e Memorie*, II, 412–13.
[2] *Ibid.*, 424.
[3] *Ibid.*, 566.
[4] *Ibid.*, 541.
[5] *Ibid.*, 426.
[6] *The Times*, Sat., 27 February 1858.

His speech, so lofty and unhesitating, produced a maximum impression. It was as though he, an impartial advocate, were pleading not for himself but for his country at the bar of history. Up to a point he seemed willing to cooperate with his accusers. He listened keenly to the evidence, and his interjections were apparently inspired by his anxiety to have everything correct in detail. He freely admitted his own part in the affair, the carriage of the explosive, the preparation of the bombs, and volunteered statements to clarify his movements. But he maintained his recent refusal to indict his comrades. He would have preferred to act alone had it been possible. He forgave them for betraying him, he offered his head as a sacrifice for his country, but "let me not be judged by the declarations of these men"; the jury would understand that they had spoken under the influence of fear, and that fear was a wretched counsellor. He must have known that his sudden reticence could help them little, for the judge merely read out his earlier confession, wherein he had stated scornfully that they were not children, and knew very well what they had been at. Either he too, driven by fear and by his own theatrical temperament, was seeking to curry sympathy, as the public prosecutor declared with some asperity: or else, as only a handful of people could have guessed, he was developing some mysterious and externally dictated policy.

The climax came when Jules Favre rose to defend Orsini. It was at once clear to all that the trial took on a new significance. What would the great democrat say in his attack upon the throne? How far would he dare go? In his bombastic appeals to loyalty, the public prosecutor had revealed a wary apprehension. As the royal pair had alighted safely from their coach, he had said, "It seemed that from their eyes emanated a providential ray, to heal and to console."[1] "Yes, a man might fall beneath the dagger of an assassin, but what can never fall is his reign, his government, his dynasty."[2]

Favre began quietly. He paid tribute to his learned friend, the public prosecutor. He protested his own loyalty, his abhorrence of the crime. He made scarcely any reference to the facts. His, like Mark Antony's, was a funeral oration. "Behold me now at

[1] *Vita e Memorie*, II, 512.

[2] *The Times*, Mon., 1 March 1858.

my post. I am not here to glorify Orsini, nor to justify him, any more than to save him. I wish only to cast on his immortal soul some rays of the light of truth—of that truth which I trust will protect his memory against the execration of posterity. I do not come here to pretend to excuse, but simply to offer some explanations."[1]

In terms of honeyed eloquence he went on to recapitulate the tormented existence of this man, this boy who had drunk in hatred of the foreign oppressor at his mother's breast. "Must not an Italian feel his chains?"[2] With satanic skill he recalled Orsini's father who had served the great Napoleon to the last, who in 1831 attacked the Papal power at the side of "illustrious accomplices" (he did not need to name them) "whose names are known to history".[3] He shrewdly compared the plight of Italy with that of France since 1815, where governments imposed by force of foreign arms had been overthrown by conspiracies to which no dishonour was imputed and which had in fact been sanctified. "There, gentlemen, you have before you a man who has tried to do for Italy what some have done for France!"[4]

"You will see once more, gentlemen, in this document which I must now read to you, having obtained permission to do so from him to whom it was addressed,* the whole thought of Orsini's life revealed." The great advocate paused, and fluttered ostentatiously among his papers. Then to a hushed court he began to read.

"To Napoleon III, Emperor of the French . . ."

It was a fine letter, measured, defiant and respectful. It recaptured like a falling echo the proud phrases used earlier by Orsini in his speech. It wrung the hearts of its hearers, according to Eugénie, like a patriotic sigh. It renounced all pardon for himself, and cried only for help from mighty France for his unhappy country. It ended with a threat, a threat already ex-

* The permission had been requested by Orsini, without doubt by the advice of Favre, if not at the wish of the Emperor himself, in a second letter to the Emperor dated 16 February 1858, five days after the first and ten days before the trial (Luzio, *Biografico*, 317).

[1] *The Times*, Mon., 1 March 1858.

[2] *Ibid.*

[3] Jules Favre, 156–7.

[4] Caddeo, 205.

pressed by Cavour in nearly identical words,[1] and with a promise.

> "Remember that so long as Italy is not independent, the peace of Europe and of Your Majesty is but an empty dream.
>
> "May Your Majesty not reject the words of a patriot on the steps of the scaffold! Set my country free, and the blessings of twenty-five million people will follow you everywhere and for ever."[2]

"So," went on the great advocate in a low voice, "I have now done, . . . and God, . . . who views the sufferings of this man—his anguish, and the ardent passions which have filled his heart—will, perhaps, render to his sensitive and noble spirit the forgiveness which, in their weakness, men will not be able to extend."[3]

He had exacted the utmost price for the life which had been given to him to spend. Pandemonium was let loose. The President, his velvet cap awry, battered his gavel in vain for order. Why had he not been warned? The Emperor had committed contempt of court. M. Chaix d'Est Ange, the public prosecutor, plucked at his gown in anger. If he were expected to represent the Crown, why had the Crown not informed him of this unheard-of intervention? And why had that old fox, the President, permitted the letter to be read?

The remaining proceedings were a pure formality. The jury took only a hundred and fifty minutes to reach a verdict on the 173 charges submitted to their decision. They generously rejected the subsidiary counts relating to the attempt on Eugénie and found extenuating circumstances in the case of Gomez. While the court debated sentence, Orsini alone appeared totally unmoved. "Why should I be distressed?" he said to Gomez' counsel who, exuberant at his success in an impossible defence, asked him how he kept so calm. "Today or tomorrow—what does it matter when one dies?"[4] The court returned. Gomez was led away to begin a life sentence in the terrible penal colony of Cayenne. The other three would die the death of parricides. They listened standing, pale and mute; only Rudio

[1] Thayer, *Cavour*, I, 538.
[2] Ghisalberti, 254–5.
[3] *The Times*, 1 March 1858.
[4] Caddeo, 227.

begged the Emperor to apply "the most gentle prerogative of the Crown". They were hustled back to the Conciergerie, where they were put in strait-jackets. Next day they were removed to the condemned cells of the prison of La Roquette.

V

"Set my country free!" The Emperor's *coup de théâtre* had brilliantly succeeded. The trial had been nothing less than the canonization of the leading criminal. "Orsini is the hero of this sad drama," Hübner wrote. "All the great ladies, Russian and Polish, who pressed against the benches of the assize court rage about him. They admire his beauty, his courage, his resignation. The Empress too is in raptures over this murderer in kid gloves."[1] The Emperor pressed home his point. To General Espinasse who, as Minister of the Interior, suggested that only a truncated account of the proceedings should be given in the press, he insisted on the greatest possible publicity, and the full reproduction of the now famous letter in *Le Moniteur*.

Hübner was exasperated about the letter. The ministers from whom he demanded an explanation were hard put to it to excuse the conduct of their royal master. They spoke of the Emperor's over-scrupulous love of justice. They blamed the folly of Pietri in showing him the letter, the indiscretion of President Delangle in allowing Favre to "*faire de la politique en plein tribunal*".[2] Hübner was not convinced. Both Pietri and Delangle were men of experience and ability. There was something suspicious about that letter. Certainly it agreed in every word with what Orsini had said in his own defence. On the other hand it expressly mentioned what the Emperor had lately secretly required of Russia, the neutralization of Germany in the event of war between France and Austria; and it ended by repeating in more colourful language the argument advanced to him by Cavour. The Emperor and his would-be assassin were evidently so much of one mind about the future of Italy, that there was room for doubt about its authorship.

[1] Hübner, II, 117.
[2] *Ibid.*, 119.

Meanwhile the Emperor saw every chance, not only of gaining his mandate to intervene in Italy, but of saving Orsini's life. His object was to combat the jingoism of the colonels by spreading the royal plea for mercy through the Court, the Diplomatic Corps, the fashionable and intellectual salons, down to the real arbiters of the Second Empire, the common people. In that regard, Eugénie, as figurehead of the clerical party, was a valuable conquest. Hübner watched her progress with anxiety. "The Empress has had her head completely turned," he wrote on 28 February; "she spends all her time weeping, and appealing to the clemency of her husband to spare the life of this wretch." And again on 2 March, "It is no longer a secret that the Empress is moving heaven and earth to save Orsini."[1]

Next day Lord Cowley, less perceptive than his Austrian colleague, reported to the Foreign Office, "Fancy the Emperor telling me yesterday that he could not help feeling the greatest sympathy for Orsini. I should not be in the least surprised if he pardoned him. . . . The Empress is upon her knees to him to do so. . . . His Majesty has evidently been tickled (I can use no other expression) by Orsini's letter. . . . There never was a man more easily caught by flattery of this kind."[2]

By 4 March Lord Cowley had been startled beyond measure. The Emperor had approached him on the personal plane. "Did I think it possible, not as British Ambassador but as a friend, to commute the sentence of death on Orsini? . . . He is regularly bitten by this miscreant."[3] On 7 March *The Times* reported in its "Foreign Intelligence" column rumours of a commutation in honour of the Prince Imperial's birthday on the sixteenth.

A movement was afoot in the Italian colony of Paris, supported by Princess Mathilde, La Castiglione, Prince Napoleon, Dr. Conneau, and others high in royal favour, to arrange by means of Countess Walewski, the Florentine wife of the Foreign Minister, an occasion when Orsini's wife Assunta with her two children, perhaps accompanied by the wives of Rudio and Pieri, might publicly intercede before the Empress. Assunta and the children were brought up from Nice, and

[1] Hübner, II, 119–20.
[2] Wellesley, 134.
[3] *Ibid.*

Eugénie personally proposed the time and place. But in the event Assunta refused to demean her husband and herself in such a manner, or to expose the children to the hostile crowds. Whereupon Dr. Bernard intervened from his cell in Newgate to suggest that Mme Ristori, the Italian *tragédienne* of the fatal night, should take Assunta's place in presenting the children to the *Espagnole*. "Above all, you must act through women," Dr. Bernard said.[1]

It was no use. The people of Paris, never very pliant to the Emperor's will, refused to forget as their superiors had too easily done that the matter had involved deliberate and wholesale harm to a great number of their fellow citizens. As Eugénie elegantly explained long afterwards, "People were still not used to bombs. . . . The dagger or revolver which strikes a single person, even the most exalted, does not arouse the same feeling of mistrust with the mob. . . . That was why public opinion was against the pardon."[2]

The popular approach had failed. The issue became a private struggle between the Emperor and his ministers. On 11 March the appeals against the capital sentences, filed as a matter of course, were as a matter of course rejected. On the twelfth Baron Hübner, more mystified than ever, found the Foreign Minister exhibiting every symptom of a constitutional convulsion. "The secret history of this business, if it is ever written, will be very strange. When I came back yesterday to Walewski's house, I found him pale, defeated, almost in a state of utter prostration. He told me that the Empress was *comme fascinée*. She begs her husband to pardon Orsini, and they have the utmost difficulty in preventing her from running to the Conciergerie to see him."[3] It was, therefore, in an atmosphere of tension that the Privy Council met to discuss the question of revoking the executions due to take place at dawn the following day.

Pietri, at the Emperor's bidding, had canvassed all the members of the Council, but their lukewarm promises melted away in the Audience Chamber. They begged the Emperor to remember the effect of a pardon upon public opinion and upon Austria, and that it would be a direct invitation for the crime to

[1] Luzio, *Biografico*, 314.
[2] *Ibid.*, 316.
[3] Hübner, II, 125.

be repeated. Morny, Fleury, Espinasse, all the political flower of the Second Empire were violently opposed to what Walewski called the "morbid sentimentality" of the royal family. They threatened to resign en bloc. Worse, Morlot, the Cardinal Archbishop of Paris, who carried in his hand the vital Catholic vote, expressed himself most earnestly against the Emperor's proposition.

At last Morlot, a supple cleric, suggested a compromise. If the Emperor were determined to exercise his princely quality of grace, why must he fasten upon Orsini, the head of the conspiracy and most obdurate of culprits? Why not pardon Rudio, the least guilty of the three? He pointed to Rudio's noble birth, his youth, his fallen circumstances, his terrified subjection to the others. He recalled Rudio's confession, and his abject prayer for mercy: the pathetic plea that his waif of a wife, with a half-starved baby at her breast, had laid before the Empress: the heartbroken appeal of his aged parents, who had learnt of his continued existence only to hear of his condemnation. Here was a case where the claims of humanity could be satisfied with credit to the Crown. And there was another consideration: if Rudio were spared, his wife would be able to give her damning testimony against Bernard at his forthcoming trial in London. With alacrity born of relief, the Council wholeheartedly agreed.

Only then, when he had brought his carefully-fashioned vessel of statecraft to the brink of shipwreck, and his throne was threatened, did the Emperor give up hope. Very well, Orsini had to die. But at least he should die content, in the knowledge that the cause he valued far above his life was safe; that the dream which had driven his honourable soul to crime was, by very reason of the failure of that crime, to be fulfilled. Looking back on it across a span of fifty years, Eugénie averred, "I think I can say it was on this day that the Emperor resolved, in his innermost conscience, on the Italian war."[1]

Yet Louis Napoleon had his price for everything. The attempts against the dynasty must cease: the hatchet of 1849 must be for ever buried. Orsini's letter, valiant as it was, had contained nothing to dissuade other suicidal patriots from following his example: indeed, he had refused to ask for pardon because "I will not humiliate myself before him who destroyed

[1] Paléologue, 160.

in the bud the liberty of my unhappy country."[1] We may assume that the day before the Privy Council meeting, when he sensed his coming defeat, the Emperor once more sent Pietri, his faithful and most confidential servant, to explain these matters to Orsini. On 11 March, two days before his death, Orsini wrote a third and last letter to his intended victim:

"Sire,

"Your Majesty's permission that my letter of 11 February should be read in public session, while it is a clear testimony to Your generosity, has shown me that the hopes expressed in favour of my country find an echo in Your heart: and for me, although near to death, it is no small consolation to see that Your Majesty can be moved by true Italian sentiments.

"In a few hours I shall be no more: before I breathe my last, I wish it to be known . . . that assassination in whatever guise does not enter into my principles, although by a fatal mental error I allowed myself to be induced to organize the attempt of 14 January. No, political assassination never was my system, and I have discountenanced it as much in my writings as in my public deeds, even at the peril of my life. . . .

"May my compatriots put far from their counsels all trust in assassination, and learn from the words of a dying patriot that their redemption must consist in their self-denial and unity, and in the practice of true virtue. . . .

"As for the victims of 14 January, I offer my blood in expiation, and I adjure those Italians who one day will be free to compensate all who have suffered harm.

"Your Majesty will permit me to conclude by entreating him to spare, not my life, but those of the two accomplices with me condemned to death.

"With the deepest respect, I am,
"Your Imperial Majesty's
"FELICE ORSINI."[2]

Cavour's diplomacy, and not the dagger of Mazzini, was to lead the way to Italy's salvation. This letter of Orsini, like its predecessor, was widely published at the Emperor's order. Together, they reconciled the tragic adversaries upon the ground of their common aspiration. A week later, Pietri, that most susceptible chief of police, resigned his office.

[1] Ghisalberti, 254.
[2] *Ibid.*, 257–8.

"Viva l'Italia! Viva la Francia!"
From a print in the Civica Raccolta Stampe Bertorelli, Milan

VI

The Paris correspondent of *The Times* reported:

"The prisoners had been brought to the condemned prison known as the Nouveau Bicètre—one of two new prisons at the end of the rue de la Roquette. The Place de la Roquette, a small square between the jails, is now the site of the guillotine. The rue de la Roquette runs from the Place de la Roquette to join the Boulevard at the Barrière d'Aunay, near the cemetery of Père la Chaise. You feel long before you emerge on to the Boulevard that you are approaching the receptacle of the dead; more than half the upper part of the rue de la Roquette is filled with the shops of dealers in tombstones, coffins, and funeral garlands; further on rise gloomily the two large prisons, and from the prisons to the cemetery is little more than a step."

When he was put in a strait-jacket after his conviction, Pieri burst out that he wished Orsini had twelve separate heads, so that they could be cut off one by one. He then fell to worrying over his umbrella, no doubt a symbol of his guilty past, which he wished to be ready waiting for him when he was released. As the days passed, Abbé Hugon, chaplain of La Roquette, could not endure his railing, and Abbé Nottelet of the Conciergerie had to be summoned to attend him.

Orsini's first thought, in the prison of Mazas, was to obtain books from the *Bibliothèque de faveur*, in order to read how Brutus and Cato had faced their deaths. He sent no message to Assunta, who was lingering in the Hôtel du Louvre. He answered the sad greeting he received from Emma Herwegh, who was confined by the birth of her youngest son, through his counsel, Favre. The only personal contact he allowed himself was with his faithful housekeeper, Eliza Cheney, who travelled from London to visit him, and was shocked to see his black hair turned to white.[1]

In la Roquette, on 10 March he made his will. He bequeathed his furniture in London to Eliza Cheney. His clothes were to be sent to her from Paris. He also left her his gold watch, his most valuable possession. Years later, within the memory of his

[1] *Vita e Memorie*, II, 639.

still-living grandson, Eliza went to Imola to return it to his daughter Ernestina. He instructed his executors to buy a second watch for Jules Favre as a souvenir. His daughters he commended, with strict instructions for their upbringing, to the care of his uncle and his brother, and also of his friends, particularly Hodge.

On Saturday, 13 March, the day about to dawn was bitterly cold; the pavements wet and slippery from fallen snow. "The sky was covered with clouds of a slate colour, and under that dismal canopy dark grey mists, transparent like funeral crape, were drifting about. Near the prison, the streets changed into a vague and swaying mass. There was an occasional flash of bayonets in the gaslight. Now and then a butcher's or a market gardener's cart, with its red lamp in front, rolled heavily along, and with difficulty made its way through the crowd. Many of the spectators had brought their breakfasts; they had loaves under their arms, and their pipes were in their mouths."[1]

At five o'clock the cavalry clattered up to drums and bugle calls, the men wrapped in cloaks of blue and white, their helmets gleaming. They quickly herded the throng out of the Place de la Roquette. As it grew lighter, infantry arrived to cordon the approaches. The military force deployed was over five thousand, a brigadier's command.

At six o'clock Pieri was informed by the governor of the prison that his last hour had come. Asked what he wished to eat, he demanded bread, and rum with coffee. He devoured the meal greedily, with chattering teeth. He drained his beaker, and demanded more rum, this time with wine, which was however soberly refused him. Orsini was roused from an untroubled sleep. He requested merely a glass of spirits to steady him against the cold, and with it gravely drank his jailor's health. For a few minutes Pieri and Orsini knelt with their confessors in the chapel. After that, they were taken to the *chambre de la toilette* to prepare for execution.

In the *chambre de la toilette* the prisoners stood back to back, while the executioners attended to their attire. As soon as his strait-jacket was taken off, Pieri began gesticulating wildly. He jumped when the scissors touched his neck to trim his hair. The white shirt of the parricide was slipped over his shoulders: as

[1] *The Times*, Mon., 15 March 1858.

the black veil went on his head, he cried, "They're making me look like an old whore": and, when his footgear was removed, "It's a good job I washed my feet well yesterday." He turned, and saw Orsini similarly arrayed. "Hullo, old fellow!" he exclaimed. Orsini in a deprecating tone replied, "Be calm! Be calm! my friend."[1]

At seven o'clock the prison doors swung open, as if of their own accord. To the mournful notes of the prison bell the procession started across the fifteen paces to the scaffold: Pieri in front, between Abbé Nottelet and the executioner of Paris; followed by Orsini, between Abbé Hugon and the executioner of Rouen. Nottelet whispered something to Pieri. "Oh, I'm not afraid, I'm not afraid," he muttered. In a trembling voice he then began to sing the old Hymn of the Girondins, *Mourir pour la Patrie.*

In the "dismal glimmering of a winter's morning", the drab cortège filed on to where the dark red guillotine reared greyly, a ladder without steps, the coffins ready to one side, the basket at its front. They mounted the fifteen frost-dewed stairs with watchful tread. An aged usher read the warrant. Orsini was seen to peer beneath his veil, looking about him for the crowd. The droning stopped. The crucifixes were extended to Pieri and Orsini. Pieri resumed his thin lament. In a trice he was fastened to the plank, lowered to the horizontal, his neck secured in the lunette, his song silenced by the crashing knife.

Orsini watched unmoved. He raised his veil, tossed back his hair, advanced across rivulets of blood to the front edge of the scaffold. Spectators posted in the trees made signals; the unseen multitude took off their hats. Putting his trust in all that there was left to trust, the many times perjured word of the man he had tried to kill, he cried out in a loud voice which reached to a great distance, "*Viva l'Italia! Viva la Francia!*" At five past seven his head creaked in the basket.

"The morning was becoming clearer every moment. The troops began to move as if about to leave the ground. The guillotine was lowered, and taken off; the crowds gradually thinned; some few groups still lingered about the spot; but the cold was bitter, and the snow began to fall, and in a few hours the place was deserted."

[1] *Vita e Memorie*, II, 589–91; Caddeo, 235–8; Luzio, *Biografico*, 367–8.

Epilogue

ORSINI and Pieri very justly paid with their lives for their crime. What became of their accomplices?

The servile Gomez, after years of suffering in Cayenne, returned to Naples a forgotten and impoverished old man. Shortly before his death, his memoirs were published in *La Stampa* at Turin, in August 1908.

Rudio's life continued as adventurously as it had begun. When the news of his reprieve was brought to him on the morning of the fatal day, he fell into a fit, believing that the executioners had come for him. He was hurried away in convict's weeds to hear the reading of the commutation, and barely had time to express his thanks in a quivering hand to the Emperor for his clemency. After three years in Guiana he managed to escape in a small boat, some say with royal connivance, to the British Colony of Berbice, and thence in 1861 to England. By plaguing Mazzini, Holyoake and others, he raised enough money for his transatlantic fare. In 1864 he sailed for America, where he distinguished himself in the Federal army during the latter stages of the Civil War, and attained the rank of major. In 1908, soon after Gomez, he published his reminiscences, containing a sensational account of the conspiracy with which he vainly tried to dupe the scholars. He died at San Francisco a year before the outbreak of the First World War.

Outrequin, Holyoake, Hodge, Allsop and Bernard had all been skilfully protected by Orsini at his trial, under cover of his revelations concerning those who were already hopelessly incriminated. Outrequin was let off with a caution. Holyoake's name was never called in question until he himself revealed the part that he had played. The French government demanded Hodge's extradition from Piedmont, but the British government, whose consent was necessary, refused to give it. Hodge returned to England, honoured his debt to Orsini by providing for Ernestina, and in 1860 lent Holyoake £1,000 towards the fund for Garibaldi's Legion, styling it a contribution from "a member of the old firm of 14 January".[1] Allsop eluded the reward that had been offered for his arrest by going to Santa Fé. He was quite unrepentant, and suggested further cataclysms. On 1 March 1858 he wrote to Holyoake "the essential difference is that little Vicky has never had the opportunity to play the tyrant. . . . I need not say that if it were possible that she should ape his [Louis Napoleon's] rascality, she would be exposed to his fate."[2] In July, when the uproar had subsided, he offered, through Holyoake, to surrender, provided that the amount of the reward could be used for his defence. The Home Secretary, Mr. Spencer Walpole, withdrew the case. Allsop returned to England in September, and lived on till 1880. In 1888 his son, Robert Owen Allsop, was on Holyoake's electoral committee.

On 12 April 1858, Dr. Bernard's six-day trial began at the Old Bailey in an atmosphere of patriotic fervour. Lord Derby's government, no more comfortable than its predecessor under the menaces of the French, had altered the charge from one of mere conspiracy to one of murder in the person of a sergeant of the Paris Civil Guard. The Attorney General amply proved his case, and the Judge went so far as to say plainly to the jury, "I think it will be your duty to find a verdict of Guilty."[3] Nevertheless, Mr. Edwin James, the florid counsel for the defence, shamelessly ignored the facts, and based his plea upon national prestige. In this he was abetted by the excesses of the French police, who expended £30,000 upon the trial, introduced a scurrying of spies into an English courtroom, and engaged in dark practices concerning the appearance of their vital witness, the miserable Eliza Rudio. Mr. Edwin James was enabled to say, in the course of his peroration:

> "Will you destroy that asylum which exiles have enjoyed, and which, I trust, they will ever continue to enjoy? No, gentlemen, you will not. . . . Let me implore you to discharge your duty

[1] McCabe, *G. J. Holyoake*, I, 256.
[2] *Ibid.*, 252.
[3] *Annual Register*, 1858, 310–29.

> unintimidated by the French army, and by the threats of French invasion. Tell the French Emperor that he cannot intimidate an English jury. . . . Tell him that though sixty thousand French bayonets glittered before you, though the roar of French cannon thundered in your ear, you will return . . ."[1]

The jury, regardless of the Judge's clear directive, returned a verdict of Not Guilty.

Eugénie's indignation notwithstanding, the Emperor hastened to patch the feud with England. On the day that Bernard was discharged, the Duc de Malakoff, the hero of the Crimea, whose name was very dear to English hearts, arrived to take over the duties of Ambassador from his pugnacious forerunner. On 4 August Napoleon and Eugénie received Victoria and Albert at the opening of the new port of Cherbourg. The decorative streamers were embroidered with the royal monograms entwined to make up the word NEVA, a device considered tastefully reminiscent of the old days of alliance.

Orsini living had "overturned Palmerston's ministry, reduced France to a state of siege, terrified Belgium and Switzerland into gagging their press, and put the stability of liberalism in Piedmont to the test".[2] Orsini dead was yet more powerful. Napoleon and Eugénie could not forget Orsini. After their deaths, the originals of his three letters were found carefully treasured among their Farnborough archives. They encouraged the fund subscribed at Paris under the lead of Mario, the great Italian tenor, to assist Assunta and the children. They tried to have the law whereby Orsini's property was forfeit mitigated in Assunta's favour.* Orsini's elder daughter, the late Signora Ernestina Spadoni (the younger, Ida, did not long outlive him), writing to Luzio from Imola on 20 July 1913, testified to Eugénie's consideration:

> "Besides receiving us at the time of the impending execution of poor Papa, the gracious lady showed the greatest kindness to us

* Not with any great success, however. As Assunta complained in her preface to the two-volume *Vita e Memorie di Felice Orsini* (Florence, 1863–4), the widow of "the first martyr of our independence" was left destitute. In 1891 her daughter Ernestina made a claim for restitution on behalf of her five children, but the republican government of France bureaucratically replied that her rights had lapsed.

[1] *Annual Register*, 1858, 310–29.

[2] Thayer, I, 514.

orphans, and to Mama. I remember as if it were today the beautiful toys she sent us during our stay in Paris by the hand of a lady-in-waiting. Afterwards, she even felt impelled to provide outfits of stricter mourning for us three: all of this has never left my memory and my heart, and I know that so great a sympathy certainly did not approve the sad fate meted out to my unfortunate father."[1]

Orsini's great-grandson, Signor Cesare Milano, adds that the Emperor paid, in whole or in part, the cost of Ernestina's excellent education at a convent.

This time the Emperor kept his promise to help Italy. Cavour, whose dispraisal of Orsini was severe, was unusually slow to take him up. He said that "the Emperor's attitude towards Orsini makes our task a hundred times more difficult",[2] and that Favre's reading of the letter at the trial "has put Orsini on a pedestal from which it is no longer possible to pull him down".[3] When, therefore, Cavour was ordered by the Emperor to print Orsini's two letters in the *Gazetta Piemontese*, he did so incredulously on 31 March, protesting that it was tantamount to a direct attack on Austria by both countries.

The reins were in more impulsive hands than his. On 22 March Lord Cowley reported to the Foreign Office, "the Emperor is warming up for Italy again".[4] In April Jules Favre was elected to the Legislative Assembly, and became one of the leaders of the opposition to the Emperor; in opposition, that is to say, about everything except the Italian question. In early May the Emperor told General MacMahon to prepare for war with Austria. At the end of May his personal friend Dr. Conneau arrived in Turin to summon Cavour to a secret meeting.

On 20 July 1858, six months after Orsini's attempt, the Prime Minister of Piedmont met the Emperor of France at Plombières. "Partly indoors, and partly in the Emperor's phaeton among the wooded valleys of the Vosges",[5] it was arranged that Cavour should provoke a rising in the much-incited Carrara-Massa region; the Austrians would intervene,

[1] Luzio, *Biografico*, 314–15.
[2] La Gorce, II, 350.
[3] Caddeo, 243–4.
[4] Wellesley, 136.
[5] Trevelyan, *Garibaldi and the Thousand*, 76-7.

and the Emperor would drive them from the whole of northern Italy. The Pope would be stripped of his temporal dominions, but to allay Catholic opinion he would be invested, with French military support, as President of a federation of the Central Provinces. King Bomba of Naples would be left to the reprisals of his people.

In December, Cavour placed Garibaldi in command of all voluntary elements in Piedmont. Occupied Lombardy was full of rumours: enterprising tobacconists did well with a new brand of Cavourian cigars: in Milan, Verdi was surprised by the augmented acclamations of the public, until he realized his name stood for *Victor Emmanuele Re D'Italia.* In his New Year message, the Emperor gave the Austrian, Baron Hübner, a brusque diplomatic warning. In early spring, to seal the pact of Plombières, the sixteen-year-old Piedmontese princess Clotilde was married to the Emperor's middle-aged, gross, but well-meaning cousin Prince Napoleon. Inevitably, there were last-minute hesitations; but in the end Cavour joyfully declined an Austrian ultimatum, and on 29 April 1859 Napoleon III crossed the Alps at the head of 200,000 men.[1]

Mercurial and elusive as he was, he could not carry his design to its conclusion. After two costly victories at Magenta and Solferino, on 9 July he met the Austrian envoys at Villafranca. The news from home was bad: Cavour's slick progress in the central provinces had roused the anger of the Catholics: there was also word of Prussians massing on the Rhine. Besides, he doubted if his force was strong enough to go much further, while the heat and dust and slaughter offended his impressionable feelings. He secured Lombardy for Piedmont, and returned to France, leaving Venetia still in the hands of Austria, and the rest of Italy as it had been before.

He had pleased no one. In Piedmont he was accursed. Cavour resigned in a tantrum; and as the recently saluted Liberator rode homewards in disgrace through Milan and Turin, he saw that portraits of Orsini now replaced his in the windows of the lithographers. His ministers, no less than the Church, were horrified at the prospect of an enlarged Piedmont south of the Alps; and the people scoffed at his half-inglorious campaign. Prussia ceased her military concentrations, but only for the

[1] Bolton King, II, 48 *et seq.*

moment. All historians of the Second Empire are agreed that the Italian war was the first step towards its ruin.

Yet the events which the Emperor had set in motion could not be halted by his discomfiture. Italy's day had come at last. The way was open for Garibaldi to repeat Pisacane's ill-fated expedition, this time with the aid of, not in defiance of Cavour, and the whole of southern Italy was added to King Victor Emmanuel's crown. By March 1860 the accretion of the Papal States and the remaining central provinces to Piedmont was an accomplished fact; the Emperor could do no more than cynically accept Savoy and Nice as the price of his approval. In 1866, after Sadowa, Austria gave up Venetia, and the Kingdom of Italy was complete.

APPENDIX

The Trial of Orsini and his Accomplices

IT must be said at once that the trial was full and fair, the amount of publicity allowed exceptional, and the penalties, considering all things, moderate. But though justice was substantially done, certain aspects of the evidence were never clarified.

1. *The Bombs*

At the time, it was taken for granted that of the six bombs manufactured in Birmingham by Taylor the engineer, five found their way to Paris, and the sixth was unaccounted for. As it has since become known that Holyoake exploded three of them in England, this assumption is obviously incorrect. Moreover, even allowing for the understandable evasiveness of the witnesses, there was a manifest conflict of evidence about the size, shape and number of the bombshells, and the number of detonators they possessed, at various stages in their journey.*

* A study of the evidence given at Orsini's and at Bernard's trials reveals the following contradictions (*Vita e Memorie,* II, 467–92, 601–53):

(*a*) Number of Bombs
Taylor originally made six complete bombs: that is, twelve half-cases. Giuseppe di Giorgi said he took five of these halves to Brussels, where he received two more from Bernard, but later forgot one in the Café Suisse. He must therefore have given Zeighers the groom six halves to take to Paris. Zeighers however remembered taking eight or ten halves. Orsini insisted that Zeighers brought him nine halves, comprising four whole bombs and the top half of the fifth.

(*b*) Size of Bombs
An expert witness defined the bombs recovered by the police as $7\frac{1}{2}$ inches

At his trial, Bernard declared that the bombs taken to Brussels by di Giorgi were not those used in Paris.[1] While Holyoake observed many years later, "Some time ago sections of the shells used in Paris were drawn and published. They certainly were not of bombs which passed through my hands."[2] This statement seems to confirm Bernard's contention.

---

long and $5\frac{3}{4}$ inches wide. Jules Fourmarien, a waiter at the Café Suisse in Brussels, said that the bombs he examined there were 5 inches long. Susanna Meckenheim, the woman to whom Pieri showed the fifth bomb at the Café Suisse in Brussels, said that it was a little heavier than those exhibited by the police. di Giorgi said that the extra bomb given to him by Bernard in Brussels was rather larger than the English ones. Debarge, the coachman at 10 rue Mont Thabor, saw Gomez leave there carrying in his handkerchief a weighty object, considerably larger than those produced in court. Taylor stated firmly that he made only two sizes of bomb in Birmingham. Fourmarien was certain that he saw three sizes in Brussels.

(*c*) Shape of Bombs

di Giorgi said that they were round, like an orange cut in two. Susanna Meckenheim said that the one she saw was like an orange. The coachman said that Gomez' bomb was as big as two oranges. On the other hand, Luigi Righenzi, proprietor of the Café Suisse at Brussels, maintained that the bomb he saw was shaped like a pear. Fourmarien also insisted that they were oval. The expert witness, too, stated that the bombs recovered by the police were oval.

(*d*) Was the bomb collected by Pieri from the Café Suisse in Brussels a whole or a half?

di Giorgi stated that he left "one" behind at the Café Suisse. The proprietor, who found the package, said that it contained a whole; and Meckenheim, the husband of Susanna, testified that di Giorgi handed over to Pieri two half-grenades. But Orsini was definite that it was a lower half only, matching the odd top half brought to him in Paris by Zeighers.

(*e*) Position of Detonators

Righenzi said that the holes were in the lower half of the grenade. Fourmarien said that they were at one end, and about as big as penholders.

(*f*) Number of Holes for Detonators

Taylor stated precisely that each bomb made by him had twenty-five holes. According to Holyoake (*Life of Dr. Bernard*), Righenzi said that there were twenty-four; and other witnesses spoke, some of seven, some of fifteen holes.

All this suggests that the bombs brought from England by di Giorgi were supplemented by a number of others, with minor variations, acquired in Belgium.

---

[1] *Annual Register*, 1858, 310–29.

[2] Holyoake, *Sixty Years*, II, 25. Holyoake was probably referring to a sketch in the *Illustrated London News* of 27 February 1858.

On the whole, therefore, the account given in the text seems the most probable, and in addition explains Orsini's hurried departure for Brussels on 28 November. Of the five complete bombs taken to the rue Lepelletier, three were of English make of which two were recovered by the police and identified by Taylor. The two larger ones thrown by Gomez and Rudio were obtained in Belgium, to replace those left in England to be tested by Holyoake.

2. *The Missing Accomplice*

From the moment of his arrest until his execution, Orsini, who admitted so much else, denied that he had thrown a bomb. He maintained that of the two in his possession when he started for the Opera, one was subsequently found in the rue Rossini, and that he gave the other at the last moment to an Italian he refused to name, whom he met by appointment in the rue Lepelletier, and who threw it in his stead.[1]

His confederates denied that this could have occurred without their knowledge, and the police, after an exhaustive examination of all aliens in Paris, could find no trace of the alleged additional participant. The court refused to accept Orsini's story. They decided that since nobody had actually seen him throw a bomb, he was trying to escape the public odium attaching to the deed.[2] They were very likely right. It was consistent with Orsini's habitual method of defence (he was, after all, himself a lawyer) to deny whatever could not be directly proved. Moreover, he who had so carefully shielded his associates in England,[3] who had disguised his source of revenue,[4] and had tried to cover over Bernard's guilt in the purchase and manufacture of the explosive,[5] would surely not have gratuitously implicated an extra accomplice whose existence would never otherwise have been suspected.

After a lapse of fifty years, Rudio brought the matter up

[1] *Vita e Memorie*, II, 433, 435–8.

[2] *Ibid.*, 516–17, 565.

[3] *Ibid.*, 428, 430–1.

[4] *Ibid.*, 443; Ghisalberti, 223.

[5] *Ibid.*, II, 432. Orsini further maintained that Bernard genuinely believed the bomb cases he handled were samples of a new gas fitting (p. 429).

again in his reminiscences.[1] Retracting his former denial, he identified the missing accomplice as Francesco Crispi, who by that time was a prominent figure in the new political life of Italy. Crispi had indeed been in Paris on 14 January 1858, but he was questioned that same evening by the police who found him guiltless. He was, furthermore, a keen Mazzinian who would have had no dealings with Orsini. As a final implausibility, Rudio depicted Crispi in the moustaches which he favoured in his later years, whereas at the period in question he had worn a magnificent full beard. Rudio's belated accusation, like many other of his recollections, was a pure invention. It was supported only by Orsini's half-brother, Cesare Orsini; as he was a notorious *blagueur*, and had been in South America at the time of the attempt, his corroboration does not command great weight.

Nevertheless, the legend of the unknown assistant has persisted. Alessandro Luzio, Orsini's excellent and scholarly biographer, has speculated upon it at some length, though a more recent authority, Rinaldo Caddeo, is inclined to disbelieve it.[2] It is not to the purpose to enlarge upon the subject here, except to point out two strains of evidence which have not so far been explored. The young Englishman, J. D. P. Hodge of Glastonbury, an ardent disciple of Orsini, was with him in Paris as late as 8 January, less than a week before the attempt.[3] We then lose sight of him until he was afterwards located in Piedmont.[4] As has been mentioned previously (p. 283 above), he styled himself "a member of the old firm of 14 January". Secondly, Mme Outrequin, the wife of the Parisian go-between, stated that early in January at her husband's shop, "A lady came to see me; this was a lady whom I did not know."[5] The lady asked for some solidified pitch which had been enclosed with the two revolvers sent from London by Bernard. Jean Kim, the city road-mender who had been scattering sand outside the Opera on the night of the attempt, likewise testified that shortly before he expelled Pieri and Rudio from the royal carriageway, "I

[1] *Resto del Carlino*, 9 August 1908.
[2] Luzio, *Biografico*, 295–308; Caddeo, 152–63.
[3] *Vita e Memorie*, II, 479 (evidence of M. Morand).
[4] *Illustrated London News*, 20 March 1858.
[5] *Vita e Memorie*, II, 612.

turned out a lady dressed in black."[1] Whether these two women were one and the same, and if so what part she played in the affair, there is no means of telling.

3. *Movements of the Conspirators before the Attempt*

Mme Brion, of the Hôtel de France et Champagne, said that the conspirators left her establishment at about five o'clock. Mme Morand said they arrived at 10 rue Mont Thabor at about 6.30, and left again a little after seven. Debarge, the coachman, said he saw them leave between 6.15 and 6.45. Kim, the road-mender, thought it was about seven o'clock when he turned Pieri and Rudio out of the royal carriageway. All disinterested witnesses, therefore, agreed that the four men set out for the Opera at seven, if not before.[2]

The conspirators, however, insisted separately that they had started an hour later. Rudio said that Gomez did not return from buying his gloves till after eight;[3] Orsini, that they all left for the Opera at about eight:[4] Pieri, that they arrived at Mont Thabor at 7.45 and left as the clock struck eight.[5]

Why were they so anxious to "lose" an hour? Pieri and Rudio broke in excitedly when the road-mender mentioned the lady dressed in black.[6] Orsini did his utmost to confuse Mme Brion and Mme Morand by continually interrupting them on matters of unimportant detail.[7] It seems possible that a clue to the problem of the missing accomplice may be hidden here.

4. *Ineffectual Planning*

Orsini was normally a man of great resource and daring. His shiftless direction of the attempt remains utterly perplexing. Although he had so frequently reviled Mazzini for providing him with inferior associates, he himself relied upon the meanest tools. They all looked to Orsini for their orders: their orders were ill-concerted, fortuitous and vague. In consequence, Pieri was detained before he had an opportunity to throw his

[1] *Vita e Memorie*, II, 477.
[2] *Ibid.*, 478–9.
[3] *Ibid.*, 421.
[4] *Ibid.*, 432.
[5] *Ibid.*, 457–8.
[6] *Ibid.*, 478.
[7] *Ibid.*, 475–7.

bomb: Gomez, his nerve broken, was arrested in a restaurant within a few yards of the scene of the crime: Rudio invited suspicion at his hotel by demanding his bill for the following morning: Orsini, wounded in the head through his own lack of forethought, went aimlessly home to bed. Except for providing a horse which was never allowed to prove its mettle, Orsini seems not to have taken the least thought for their escape, though he had ample time to do so. It must be remembered that he was temporarily unbalanced. Did he think they would be able to lie low in Paris until the revolution started? Or did he never intend that they should get away?

Works Consulted

Works marked with an asterisk are of particular relevance.

BIOGRAPHICAL SOURCES

"ANCIEN PROSCRIT" (pseud.). *La Verité sur Orsini*, 4 parts. Paris, n.d.

Annual Register. London, 1858

BOULENGER, Marcel. *L'Attentat d'Orsini*. Hachette, Paris, 1927

BYRON, Lord. *Mazeppa*, edn. of 1820

CADDEO, Rinaldo. *L'Attentato di Orsini*(1858).* Mondadori, Verona, 1932

D'AMBES, Baron. *Intimate Memoirs of Napoleon III*, 2 vols., Tr. A. R. Allison. London, 1912

FORSTER, John. *Works and Life of Walter Savage Landor*, 2 vols., London, 1876

Gentleman's Magazine. Vol. IV (N.S.). London, February 1858

GEVEL, Claude. *Deux Carbonari: Orsini et Napoleon III*. Emile-Paul, Paris, 1934

GHISALBERTI, Alberto M. (ed.). *Lettere di Felice Orsini*.* Regio Istituto per la Storia del Risorgimento, Vol. VIII, Series 2. Rome, 1936

HERZEN, Alexander. *My Past and Thoughts*,* 6 vols., Tr. Constance, Garnett, London, 1924–7

HOLYOAKE, G. J. *Bygones Worth Remembering*, 2 vols., London, 1905

—— ("LANCET", pseud.). *Life of Dr. Bernard*. London, 1858

—— *Sixty Years of an Agitator's Life*,* 2 vols., London, 1893

HÜBNER, Comte de. *Neuf Ans de Souvenirs, 1851–1859*,* 2 vols., Ed. Comte A. de Hübner, Paris, 1904

Illustrated London News. London, January–June 1858

KING, Mrs. Hamilton. *The Execution of Felice Orsini*. London, 1862?

KOSSUTH, Count Louis. *Souvenirs et Écrits de mon Exil. Période de la Guerre d'Italie*. Paris, 1880

LUZIO, Alessandro. *Felice Orsini. Saggio Biografico*.* Cogliati, Milan, 1914

LUZIO, Alessandro (ed.). *Felice Orsini e Emma Herwegh, Nuovi Documenti*.* Le Monnier, Florence, 1937

MCCABE, Joseph. *Life and Letters of George Jacob Holyoake*,* 2 vols. London, 1908

MCCARTHY, Justin. *Portraits of the Sixties*. London, 1903

—— *Reminiscences*, 2 vols., London, 1899

MASTRI, Paolo. *Felice Orsini*. Commemorative pamphlet. Savigno di Romagna, 1909

—— *Felice Orsini nel Forte di San Leo*. Imola, 1908

MONTAZIO, Enrico. *Felice Orsini.* Turin, 1862

ORSINI, Felice. *Geografia Militare della Penisole Italiana.* Pomba, Turin, 1852

—— *The Austrian Dungeons in Italy.** Tr. Jessie Meriton White (Mario). London, 1856

—— *Memoirs and Adventures.** Tr. George Carbonel. Edinburgh and London, 1857

—— *Memorie.** Colombo, Rome, 1948

—— *Memorie e Documenti intorno al Governo della Republica Romana.* Caisson, Nice, 1850

—— (ed. anon.). *Vita e Memorie di Felice Orsini,** 2 vols. Florence, 1863–4

ORSINI, Luigi. *Il Mio Sentiero.* Imola, n.d.

PALÉOLOGUE, Maurice. *The Tragic Empress. Intimate Conversations with the Empress Eugénie, 1901–1911.* Tr. Hamish Miles, London, 1928

RUDMAN, Harry W. *Italian Nationalism and English Letters.* London, 1940

SANTI, Angelo. "Felice Orsini in the Meldolese Records." *Il Pensiero Mazziniano.* July–August 1951

SOULIÉ, Maurice. "L'Affaire Orsini." *La Révue Hebdomadaire.* Paris, August 22, 29, 1925

*The Times.** London, 14 January–15 March 1858

VENOSTA, Felice. *Felice Orsini.* Milan, 1865

WELLESLEY, Sir Victor, and SENCOURT, Robert. *Conversations with Napoleon III.* London, 1934

INCIDENTAL CHARACTERS

ALLSOP, Thomas (ed.). *Letters, Conversations and Recollections of S. T. Coleridge,* 3rd edn., London, 1864

BLISS, Trudy (ed.). *Jane Welsh Carlyle. Letters.* London, 1949

CRISPI, Francesco. *Memoirs,* 3 vols., Tr. Mary Prichard-Agnetti. London, 1912

D'AUVERGNE, Edmund B. *Napoleon the Third.* London, 1929

FAVRE, Jules. *Discours du Batonnat.* Paris, 1866

FISHER, H. A. L. *Bonapartism.** London, 1908

GANGULEE, N. (ed.). *Giuseppe Mazzini. Selected Writings.* London, 1944

GARRISON, William Lloyd (intro.). *Joseph Mazzini: his Life, Writings, and Political Principles.* New York, 1872

GRIFFITH, Gwilym O. *Mazzini: Prophet of Modern Europe.** London, 1932

HALES, E. E. Y. *Mazzini and the Secret Societies.* London, 1956

—— *Pio Nono.* London, 1954

HERWEGH, Marcel (ed.). *Au Printemps des Dieux. Corr. Inéd. de la Comtesse Marie d'Agoult (Daniel Stern) et Georges Herwegh.* Les Documents Bleus, No. 11. Gallimard, Paris, 1929

—— *Au Soir des Dieux.* Peyronnet, Paris, 1933

JONES, Evan Rowland. *The Life and Speeches of Joseph Cowen, M.P.* London, 1885

KING, Bolton. *Mazzini.* London, 1902

KING, Mrs. Hamilton. *Letters and Recollections of Mazzini.* London, 1912

The Nation. Jessie White (Mario). New York, 15 March 1906, 9 December 1909

RHEINHARDT, E. A. *Napoleon and Eugénie*. Tr. Hannah Waller. London, 1932

SALVEMINI, Gaetano. *Mazzini*. Tr. I. M. Rawson. London, 1956

SENCOURT, Robert. *Napoleon III: the Modern Emperor*. London, 1933

SIMPSON, F. A. *The Rise of Louis Napoleon*.* London, 1909

THOMPSON, J. M. *Louis Napoleon and the Second Empire*.* Oxford, 1954

VENTURI (HAWKES), Emilie Ashurst. *Joseph Mazzini: a Memoir*. London, 1875

WAGNER, Richard. *My Life*, 2 vols. London, 1911

WHITE (MARIO), Jessie Meriton. *The Birth of Modern Italy*. London, 1909

GENERAL HISTORICAL BACKGROUND

ARNAUD, René. *The Second Republic and Napoleon III*. Tr. E. F. Buckley, London, 1930

BENSON, A. C., and ESHER, Viscount (eds.). *The Letters of Queen Victoria*, Vol. III. London, 1907

BOWRING, Sir John. *Autobiographical Recollections*. London, 1877

CADOGAN, Edward. *The Life of Cavour*. New York, 1907

DAVENPORT, Basil. *Great Escapes*. New York, 1952

DE TOCQUEVILLE, Alexis. *The Recollections of Alexis de Tocqueville*. Ed. J. P. Mayer, Tr. A. Teixeira de Mattos. New York, 1949

FABRIZI, Giovanni (Jean). *L'Italie après la Guerre*. Tr. Doisy. Vol. VI. La Question Italienne. Paris, 1859

FAGAN, Louis (ed.). *Letters of Prosper Mérimée to Panizzi*, 2 vols., Tr. H. M. Dunstan. London, 1881

FALCIONELLI, Albert. *Les Sociétés Secretès Italiennes. Les Carbonari, La Camorra, La Mafia*. Paris, 1936

FARINI, Luigi Carlo. *The Roman State from 1815 to 1850*, 4 vols., Tr. W. E. Gladstone. London, 1851–4

FISHER, H. A. L. *A History of Europe*. London, 1936

FROST, Thomas. *The Secret Societies of the European Revolution*, 1771–1876, 2 vols., London, 1876

FULLER (MARCHESA D'OSSOLI), Sarah Margaret. *Memoirs*, 3 vols., London, 1852

History Today. London, Nov. 1951. "The Papal Victory." Elizabeth Wiskemann
Jan. 1953. "The Emperor Entertains: Napoleon III at Compiègne." Christopher Sykes
Apr. 1954. "Louis Napoleon—a Tragedy of Good Intentions." Roger L. Williams
Feb. 1956. "Giuseppe Mazzini, 1805–1872." E. E. Y. Hales

KING, Bolton. *A History of Italian Unity, 1814–1871,** 2 vols., London, 1899

LABADINI, Ausano. *Milano ed alcuni momenti del Risorgimento Italiano.* Milan, 1909

LA GORCE, Pierre de. *Histoire du Second Empire,* Vol. II. Paris, 1894

LUDWIG, Emil. *Napoleon.* Popular Edn. London, 1929

MACKENZIE-GRIEVE, Averil. *Clara Novello, 1818–1908.* London, 1955

MANARO, Howard R. *American Opinion on the Unification of Italy.* New York, 1932

MARTINEAU, Gilbert R. (ed.). *Nagel's Paris.* Les Guides Bleus—English Series. Paris, 1950

MUIRHEAD, L. Russell (ed.). *Northern Italy.* The Blue Guides, 4th Edn. London, 1953

PÉPÉ, Gugliemo, General. *Narrative of Scenes and Events in Italy, from 1847 to 1849,* 2 vols., London, 1850

QUENNELL, Peter (ed.). *Mayhew's London.* London, 1949

SHERRILL, Charles Hitchcock. *A Stained-Glass Tour in Italy.* London, 1913

SPELLANZON, Cesare. *Storia del Risorgimento e dell' Unita d'Italia,** 5 vols. Milan, 1933–

TERENZIANI, Enrico. *I Martiri di Belfiore.* Mantua, 1951

THAYER, William Roscoe. *The Life and Times of Cavour,* 2 vols., Boston, 1911

TREVELYAN, G. M. *Garibaldi's Defence of the Roman Republic,** 2nd edn. London, 1907

—— *Garibaldi and the Thousand.* London, 1909

—— *Manin and the Venetian Revolution of 1848.** London, 1923

YOUNG, G. M. (ed.). *Early Victorian England, 1830–1865,* 2 vols. London, 1934 [illegible] *A History of [illegible]* [illegible]

[illegible]

[illegible] Emil, *Napoleon*, Popular Edn, London 1929.

[illegible]

[illegible]

[illegible], Gilbert [illegible]

[illegible]

[illegible] (ed.), [illegible]

[illegible] London, [illegible]

[illegible] 1847 – 1849, 3 vols., London, [illegible]

[illegible]

[illegible]

[illegible]

[illegible]

[illegible] 1931.

T[illegible], William Roscoe, *The Life and Times of Cavour*, [illegible]

T[illegible], G. M., *Garibaldi's Defence of the Roman Republic*, London 1907.

—— *Garibaldi and the Thousand*, London [illegible]

—— *Garibaldi and the Making of Italy*, London [illegible]

[illegible], G. M. (ed.), *Early Victorian England*, [illegible] London, 1934.

Index